M000028129

❖ ❖ ❖

The Stolen Light of Women
of
Women
A Quest For Spiritual Truth Beyond Religion

C.C. Campbell

Anu Esoteric Press
Boulder, CO

❊ ❊ ❊

Anu Esoteric Press
Boulder, CO

The Stolen Light of Women:
A Quest For Spiritual Truth Beyond Religion
by C.C. Campbell

Copyright © 2014 by C.C. Campbell

All rights reserved.
No part of this book may be reproduced or transmitted in any form or by any means, electronic or mechanical, including photocopying, recording, or by any information storage and retrieval system without the written permission of the publisher, except where permitted by law.

First Edition, November 2014

Cover Image: *The Pleiades* (1885) by Elihu Vedder

Ebook Version
ISBN 13: 978-0-986276-1-01

Print Version
ISBN-13: 978-0-986276-1-18
LCCN: 2014921232

❖   ❖   ❖

This book is dedicated to the two worlds I live in.
To Those on the Other Side who have given me
the keys to knowledge and the wisdom of the Soul.
My soul sings in gratitude.
And to those in this world,
women and men alike (WoMen),
who are ready to reclaim their Light.
My soul wishes you strength for the journey.
May the words in this book bring you answers,
and reveal a path to acceptance, love,
and spiritual truth.

Table of Contents

A Word From the Author

A Word From the Author

This book is a story about faith, but it may be unlike any story you have ever read. There are many books on the market that tell the tale of faith lost and regained, but very few tell the story of faith examined, shattered, and swept away only to reveal something radiant and new awaiting to be discovered. This has never been an easy work, for truly it was never an easy journey. I began my life utterly devoted to my religious beliefs. I sided with those who turned an eye away from the 'things of this world' in order to keep my feet to a straight and narrow path all for the glory of my beloved God.

Then I died...

In dying and being brought back from an out of body experience, a mystical journey began whose twists, turns, and revelations I could not imagine. I felt as though I had reclaimed something that I never knew had been stolen from me. I had found my Light. There were moments of spiritual ecstasy and moments of horrendous despair, bouts of righteous anger and periods of outright denial, but ultimately every high and every low brought me to a place of peace, truth, and Light.

I would do it all again in a heartbeat.

I never wanted nor planned to pen a book, but in my journey so many came forward asking (sometimes pleading) to learn what I had learned that I found I had no choice. And so, with my daughter, I began to tackle the momentous task of winnowing down a lifetime of spiritual and academic learning into a single book. Academic books about the Bible and religion are plentiful, and while I owe a great deal to these works that were the basis of my own research, I began to recognize that the vital information within them rarely reaches regular people. We live in a hectic world and far too many do not have the ability, let alone the time, to tackle reading great academic works. I began to see that the reason so few people had access to the information I was learning was because it was being kept out of reach by the ivory towers of academia. From wording to length, academic works were just simply out of reach for the average reader. On top of that, they were boring! Information is fine, but no one was stopping to explain why it was important or how it applied to the lives of the average person.

That is where I come in.

This book holds much of my own personal story in it, but it also holds a great deal of valuable information. I wanted to help guide the reader through the tangle of historical, political, and religious information by showing you how it impacted my life and changed my views, beliefs, and faith. To be honest, it took ages just to whittle down to what I felt were the most important topics. To keep things simple, I have plucked out the verses from the Bible that are still being used today to cause the most pain and controversy for the gay community, women, and humanity in general. In plain language and with a spiritual eye I examine these verses and reveal their real history and meaning - things your average paster or priest rarely ever bother to address. Why?

Because I want to let you in on a religious secret: Almost every controversial verse in the Bible that is being used against women, and especially against members of the LGBT community, are wrong. I'm not just talking about morally wrong, I mean wrong as in misunderstood, mistranslated, or even forged.

When I was entrenched in my own beliefs, that statement would have made me feel righteous anger and a knee-jerk reaction of denial. If you are as I once was, I beg of you to read for yourself before making such a snap judgement. This book is the work of over a decade of research between my daughter and I, and because I would never ask anyone to take my word simply on trust, I have included at the back of this book an extensive, detailed bibliography and reference section that is broken down chapter by chapter. I implore anyone who reads this book to make use of it. If you don't believe me, or disagree, only good can come from you checking my sources and becoming more educated. You might just learn something you never knew! I certainly will never claim to have all the answers, let alone absolute truth. I also will never preach to you. However, I will do my best to teach you, if you give me that honor by continuing to read this book. Preaching would be telling you how to live your life, but teaching is laying the gift of information at your feet and allowing you to do with it what you will. I can only say that the information in this book changed my life and my Soul for the better, and I sincerely hope it does the same for you.

This book is separated into three easy sections with clearly titled chapters. You are free to read this book in order, but if you see a particular chapter that stands out, I have written so that you will be able to skip ahead and read it as a stand alone.

The first part *The Stolen Light Of WoMen* addresses how this work began. The first three chapters include the majority of my personal story, and in order to understand who I am and why this book was written at all, I encourage you to at least read those chapters before delving ahead.

The chapters that follow focus on the Biblical verses and history that most impacts women. It examines how views about women evolved in Western religious thought and reveals to the reader why the history you have been told is only a tiny fraction of what really happened. Ultimately, it will show you how the mindset of blaming and controlling women began, why, and how it could all have been very different.

The second part *When Love Is Blind* addresses the impact of religion upon the LGBT community. The Bible verses most commonly used against homosexuality by certain religious groups are examined one by one, exposing what the texts truly say and what the true political and religious agendas were behind these viewpoints. The history of homosexuality and even its spirituality are explored to open the minds of readers and empower those who are gay, transgender, or bisexual.

Lastly, the third part *Restoring the Light* takes a deep look at how Western religion evolved, especially Christianity. In showing how the Bible became the text we have today, how Christianity became the dominant religion of the West, the reader will come to understand what was gained, what was lost, and how those who profess to follow the teachings of Christ can help their own faith evolve in our modern world. The chapter on Satan may be worth the price of this book alone. In almost all cases I have chosen to show both the King James Version and the New International Version of the scriptures I reference. While this may seem like overkill, I made this choice because I intimately know that certain religious groups insist upon seeing the KJV as the ultimate authority in Bible translations (in spite of its antiquated language), while a majority of Bible readers have proven the NIV to be the most popular. More than providing diversity, it is helpful to read both translations if only to see how greatly the two often differ on controversial verses and passages.

While this may sound very technical, I promise you that ultimately this is a book about the human Soul. People who felt they were already enlightened often badgered me throughout the writing of this book, asking why I was even bothering to put in so much information instead of just keeping the tone spiritual. Because too many people are walking in darkness, I told them. They think they walk in the light and so they may never bother to look outside of their own religious beliefs. After all, I was one of those people. I could never come to the place I am now without the information within this book. For people who have never been religious, this is a fact they often cannot understand. Some of us need help. Some of us need more than just beautiful words of spirituality. Some of us want proof before we can even think about changing.

If you are that person, or if you are dealing with people in your life who are, this book was written especially for you. For spiritual people seeking a deeper understanding of their world, man or woman, gay or straight, young or old, who wants to be able to educate themselves and others, I pray this book becomes an invaluable tool for inspiration. I have the utmost respect for atheists and agnostics, and to my friends of this persuasion I hope this book may still prove of use as you may find valuable information to help defend your own chosen path from those who refuse to understand.

I wish to make clear that this book is not meant to 'bash' religion. To the mystic, the mysteries of religious beliefs are mysteries of the mind, not of the heart. I believe that all already possess the knowledge and the truth as a gift from the Divine. We come into a world that forces us to seek Truth, for only by looking outside of ourselves do we find the ability to connect to others. Only by looking within ourselves do we find the ability to connect to the Soul. In connecting with the

Soul, we finally connect to the Truth. It is a Truth that must be defined by every individual for themselves, but it is my hope that by sharing what I have learned, what I have seen, what I have heard, and what has been given to me that perhaps I can ignite the spark that will Light each individual's way.

With Light, Peace, and Love to you,
C.C. Campbell
October 31, 2014

Part I: The Stolen Light of WoMen

"The greatest gift to man is woman,
But the greatest gift to woman is herself."
- C.C. Campbell

"Why extremists always focus on women
remains a mystery to me.
But they all seem to.
It doesn't matter what country they're in
or what religion they claim.
They all want to control women."
- Hillary Clinton

"Even though they [women] *grow weary*
and wear themselves out with childbearing, it does not matter;
let them go on bearing children till they die,
that is what they are there for."
- Martin Luther, Founder of the Protestant Reformation

1. Walking In Darkness

This is a message from my Soul to yours. Faith, beliefs, and religion are felt so deeply and purely that it is hard to bring up certain issues without some hint of discomfort. I apologize in advance, but I promise that if you choose to continue on past this point that you will not be disappointed. I do hope that by sharing all that I have learned that people will find the Light by which to better illuminate their path whether it remains religious or simply spiritual. There is no single religion that holds the key to the human Soul. If there was, humanity would not be divided.

As human beings we talk about our souls as though we recognize it as an extension of our human bodies. When death comes knocking at our door, all religions acknowledge that our soul will journey back to where it came from. How many of us truly take into consideration that we are here on this earth for such a short time? Have we taken the time to discover whether our Soul is part of our psyche or has it been overwhelmed by the human Ego? Many will find their answers within their spiritual love for our Creator, but many more will seek answers in the shallow depths of their own Egos, never understanding why the emptiness remains. There are two very different energies that are experienced by the human body. The Ego of man and his religious teachings versus the Soul of spirituality and its unbridled compassion for humanity in a world filled with so many contradictions.

This is where I start my personal story, but ultimately it is a universal story. It is a story about the journey of tearing down the veils of religious ignorance, pain, and sorrow, in order to find the spring of eternal hope whose waters of knowledge feed both the human Soul and the Ego (for one cannot exist without the other).

Every human being carries an Ego. I am not a psychologist, so when I discuss Ego and Soul, I am referring to these two energies on a spiritual level. In using the language of spirituality, the term Ego takes on a much simpler meaning than the one that psychology or psychiatry uses. For me, I define the Ego as the mask of identity that all human beings assume in order to protect themselves in this lifetime. The Ego is shaped by the people around us, especially our parents, and it leads us down paths that the soul may never have intended. This happens because we have allowed ourselves to care so much about what others think of us and in doing so many of us have lost our true identity and our way. We have felt helpless and lost because somewhere deep inside the soul senses the loss of its destiny.

Often these roadblocks are caused by the people we loved and trusted most, people who were well intentioned and felt certain they knew what was best for us like our parents. It is not until later in life that we come to a crossroads and wonder what our lives would have been had we followed what we truly desired. We become so disillusioned, so depressed, so lost that we wonder: What is the purpose of being in this world?

So many of us try to find the answer in a path of faith. For many, religion becomes like the air we breathe, but all too often it becomes something stifling, something that separates us from others and the world around us. Religion has brought humanity to a breaking point. It is no longer deemed worthy of praise simply because it has divided humanity from its true existence in a world filled with the energy of spirituality. Beauty lies in the essence of humanity's Soul connection to its

Mother Earth and the Universe. The time has come for all of us (myself included) to allow our Soul to experience what it was meant to experience in this lifetime. Our Egos have run amok for too long.

I know what I am talking about. I was a pious Christian, and like many well intentioned Christians I believed that I knew everything there was to know (or needed to know) about my beloved Savior. The Bible was my refuge, my rock, my escape from Satan and the horrible evil he had brought into the world. My belief was so strong and unshakeable that any conversation I got into, whether it was with a stranger at the mall or old friends, would eventually become a chance for me to evangelize the Good News and help them accept Jesus into their lives. My husband and daughter got used to this behavior and would discreetly disappear whilst I played religious therapist and missionary. These run-ins would leave me exhausted and while my family was concerned for me, I was more concerned about the souls of the people around me - good people who I was genuinely afraid had not secured their salvation if they did not also accept and love Christ as I did.

I share this with you because I did not come into this research, this work, or this book lightly. To be honest it has been an agonizing and painful path to reality. I had no idea that I had been walking in darkness. I believed that I was walking in the essence of the true light. Can you imagine what that felt like? To go through your whole entire life living and breathing the essence of the word of God, following the footsteps of Jesus, making friends who felt as I did, and then without warning an odyssey began that would teach me what true spirituality was really all about. I spent many sleepless nights feeling the rejection of people who felt that I had fallen from grace; friends who informed me that I was going to be condemned to hell. Little did I know I was already there.

At first it felt as though everything I held so sacred in my heart and soul had been shattered... but as time went on I have discovered that my pain and suffering was due to my Ego that had become broken. Only then did I recognize where my agony truly came from. Anyone who is willing to open their eyes and see, to allow their ears to hear, their minds to open, perhaps the story of my own journey and the information discovered may open a doorway that will light their path. I believe that whether anyone believes in a goddess, a god, a creator, or no deity at all, that each individual must walk down their own path. In doing so they will be free to choose and to help so many others. Manmade religion and its ego kept me in darkness, but the spirituality of my soul gave me the light of salvation.

I personally believe that the final Truth will be revealed when we take our last breath and leave these egos behind along with the chaos of deception that plagues the minds of man. Change must come, but it will not be because the Bible or any other holy book foreshadows the destruction of mankind and the salvation of a chosen few. These were books written by men, for men. They instructed them on how to deal with wars and politics relevant to their culture. They emphasized cultural assumptions about women and their place. These were the customs and beliefs thousands of years ago in the Middle East, not the customs of our modern Western world. Truths that are timeless are just that and they exist in every holy text whether it is the Jewish Torah, Christian Bible, Islamic Koran, Hindu Upanishads, or the Buddhist Dhammapada. All else is up to interpretation because we no longer live in the times that the authors did. How then are we to find our Light and guidance for our souls in this modern here and now?

This is a vital question, especially for women as they begin to realize that the religious mandates of an antiquated past has largely ignored them and their spiritual development (except to tell them what they can and cannot do in society). These are the issues I hope to bring to light; these are the matters of the soul I hope to address. I have fought to strike a balance in this book, to bring you information that can free your minds and spiritual guidance that can bring Light to your soul. Too many spiritual people find themselves bound by the ordinances of the Bible - they fight to love their neighbor even as they are taught to be fearful or discriminate from the pulpit. They are torn between following their hearts, and following what they have been told is God's law. I have witnessed too many families become broken as husbands, wives, or children who seek their own path come into contradiction with the beliefs of their family. I have written this book to hopefully enlighten those who are seeking, and for those who feel they have already found their Light, to educate themselves so that they may educate others who would try to block their path with righteous condemnation. Knowledge is power, but nowhere is that more true than when it comes to the religious beliefs that have shaped our Western world. More than ever we see our peacemakers cut down by those who take religion to its extreme, who see no reason outside of their holy text. Knowledge will be the only thing to change this course. It is this knowledge that I hope to give to you.

If what I have said to you has caught your attention then read on. I hope to grant you the knowledge and the wisdom that I have had the privilege of learning. I hope to empower the women and the men, the LGBT community, and anyone who has found themselves walking in the darkness of the beliefs of others while holding to the hope that somehow, someway they would reach the Light of enlightenment.

I would like to share with you a dream that I had when I first began going down my path. Every night with a heavy heart I went to sleep praying and asking for answers to my questions. I had so many it seemed my mind and heart would rend in two! One night the first of many dreams was given to me. I was reminded of a scripture: 1 Samuel 16:7. I could almost hear the words being read to me loud and clear: "For God sees not as man sees, for man looks at the outward appearance, but God looks at the heart."
As these words echoed, I saw a sea of humanity whilst I stood in the center of a huge stadium. Thousands were shining their light so brightly onto me. I wept with tears of joy to see so many souls come alive with their Light. Each became a beacon of hope, reminding me that the light within all of us will win out even in the darkest of times. I believe I was being told that I am not alone; that many are being shown the path to their Light in this lifetime. This dream is what has encouraged me to write this book. It revealed to me that many will come from all different backgrounds and we will see them as they are, but deep inside their hearts will be filled with so much love. It will reveal the Light that cannot be seen or fathomed by those that walk in darkness. Their energy of hope and joy will be revealed only to those that also walk in the essence and the energy of Light.

When I awoke, I understood that while humanity has set its mind on religion and separates itself through beliefs, it will never see the Light of others simply because they walk in darkness. They do not accept others with their thoughts or beliefs, and I understood then what I was being told: when the heart is open to all, the Soul then reflects its Light. Because I do know that the Ego of man lives by its religious indoctrination, it is difficult for it to see the light of those that walk in the energy of spirituality which has no agenda. It is free to think, move and travel on its own path. It has been the hardest thing I have ever done to reveal the harsh reality of religion and the slow death of mankind's soul, but I know the Light that is within us all will win out.

This was my discovery, this is where I begin. No matter how much it hurt, no matter how many ivory towers of belief had to be destroyed, I could not stop looking, searching, and researching. If you are part of this circle of Light that I saw in my dream and you are a soul that is here to help humanity, then you will bring forth knowledge, understanding, compassion, wisdom, and love. This will be the greatest gift we as human beings can give to one another. This Light brings us peace by understanding that the Ego is part of this world, but the Soul is part of the world we came from. When the Soul and the Ego are brought into balance in this lifetime, we discover that we are truly children of the Light. Because of all that I have learned, I no longer walk in darkness. I have met the Light of my Soul and no longer am I at odds with my Ego. The Ego is meant to be the friend of your Soul, not its enemy. Only the Light can bring us into balance. As women and men regain their Light and shine, no longer will this Light be lost to any human being.

2. Dying To See

This is a story of faith. Not just faith, but blind faith and the journey that gave my Soul back its sight. I never entertained the notion that my religion was flawed. This was inconceivable to me… until my near death experience. I had no idea that I was walking through life with blinders. I believe most of us never realize we are. We walk and see only what is in front of us, never realizing how much we are truly missing. For myself, that meant keeping my feet to the straight and narrow path laid before me by the Bible. Then something happened. Something that made the blinders I had worn so proudly become an exhausting weight. Heavier and heavier they became upon my head and shoulders, yet I was so determined to keep them on and believe that there was only one way to God. With only one way to God, I had to believe that any man who spoke from a pulpit was chosen to speak on God's behalf. Like many, I believed that everything I had been told was the gospel Truth. There was no truth higher than the Truth of God's Word as recorded in the Holy Bible.

I never realized that keeping that belief meant having to turn a blind eye to the world, especially as a woman. Eventually the fear of living without the blinders was eclipsed by the need to truly see. And so the blinders came off. For the first time I could see what had been hidden all around me. It was everything I had been told by clergy that I didn't need to see, things they said didn't matter if you kept your eyes on Christ, the very things I had been taught to fear. But I wasn't afraid. After all that time focused on a stark and narrow path, it was like being surrounded by a vibrant, beautiful, vast garden.

Whether you are a Jew, a Christian, or a Muslim, if you believe that the mark of your faith is to pursue your religion with blind devotion, then you have lost the message of the Creator. Blind faith is just that: a robbing of the divine sight that allows us to see our souls and our world. How fitting that so many creation stories begin in a garden, for it is the vast garden of the Creator that produces humanity in all its forms, cultures, and colors. The divine water feeds every single one of us, even the weeds. If we walk in the light of our Creator, we will see what the divine has wanted us to see. God did not create us with blinders; the blinders are the making of man. I never dared to entertain these thoughts, not until the day I actually met my Soul.

I remembered hearing stories about near death experiences and how these people had seen angels and Jesus. I felt so certain in my heart that this was all just more proof of the validity of my faith. How could the inerrant Word of God not be true when there were thousands of stories of people having visions of being saved by angels, Christ, and God? Every once in awhile I would hear about someone who wasn't a Christian having a mystical encounter - a Buddhist, a Muslim, even an atheist. But I saw it in the shadow that my religion had taught me to see it in: the poor soul had been duped and experienced the trickery of a demon or Satan. It didn't matter if the experience had changed their lives; if it wasn't a Christian experience then it wasn't valid. After all, as a Christian I was taught that Satan had once been an angel of light and so he and his minions were more than capable of fooling us poor humans into false mystical experiences all in order to lead us away from the truth of God's word.

For those who are not religious these words will sound ludicrous, but for those who are or have been religious they are likely nodding their heads in agreement. My point in all of this is to express how drastically my world changed. Some religious people look upon those who have left the faith with pity and console themselves in the knowledge that the person was likely just a 'lukewarm' Christian. They tell themselves that these people never truly knew the intense devotion and love of Christ as they have. I never fell into this category.

For the first fifty years of my life I was as intensely in love with Christ and the Bible as any faithful follower could be. Any conversation I got into whether it was with a friend or a total stranger eventually led to me inquiring about whether or not they had accepted the love of Jesus into their heart. My blinders of faith were on so tightly and securely that I would not tolerate even the sight of other so-called 'holy books' in my home. Why would I ever want to even set eyes on the words of the Buddha, or Mohammed, or Lao Tzu? The words of God and Christ in the Bible were all a Christian needed to know to find salvation. Any other texts were the words of misguided false prophets who may as well have been inspired by Satan. At this point I do feel it is important to define the fact that these were my views as an evangelical Christian. There are many liberal minded Christians who find this mindset as off-putting as the non-religious minded. I wish I could say I had been one of the later, but sadly I was marching proudly down the path of religious fervor. While I cannot say I had hit the fanatic mark, I was happily counting myself among those who would rather martyr myself for my beliefs than ever conceive that anything about my religion was in error. So what changed it all? What made me rip the blinders off? How I wish I could say it was the dawning of common sense, but unfortunately it began on a beautiful Sunday morning when my world came crashing down.

I had been on a roller coaster of ill health for four years following a horrific head injury from a skiing accident. I had never dreamt that fate would use a mountain to get through to me! At least, that's how it seemed as my ski tip caught on a slalom pole in the middle of a race. Sailing through the air, it seemed the mountain was careening towards me and not the other way around. My world became so silent and only the sick crunching of the vertebrae in my neck let me know I was still alive. What had been a bright, sunny day became darkness. It would take years to realize how fitting that moment of literal blindness was. My vision did recover. I was shaky, but slowly light came back into my sight and the vision returned. The day my vision left and was restored was the same day my life changed forever.

At the time the mountain town where we lived did not have advanced medical facilities. I stayed up all night, aware I had a concussion. Though my body was in so much pain I could barely walk, I never dreamt I had suffered a head injury. In that day, I had the mindset of an athlete. I powered through the pain and convinced myself I was fine. I fought to stay awake, telling myself that I would get through this as I had gotten through numerous prior injuries. I had no idea the Other Side wasn't done with me yet.

As if They felt I had not gotten the message clearly, a week later I lost my balance walking into the post office, slipped on ice and hit the back of my head on concrete. The impact focused on the occipital area of my brain and again I found my vision blacked out, only to slowly return again as strangers helped me to my feet. This time, my memory and my speech became affected. My photographic memory was gone, and I fought with every breath to speak as I once had. The trauma of not one, but two head injuries set my poor body into a state of red alert. My pituitary gland (located in the brain) went haywire, and with it the entire system of thyroid, thymus, and adrenal glands.

When I finally went to see a doctor, the head injuries were shrugged off, but only seconds later they witnessed my heart rate become erratic, my breathing becoming labored, beads of sweat began to pour down as my face became flushed with heat, and the doctors finally had to acknowledge this was not all 'in my head'. When they were done with all the blood tests, they could see my thyroid had gone hyper, and without any warning they called in a specialist. Without time to think, research, or even ask if it was the best course of action, I was given a nuclear oblation. I tried to ask if it was necessary, if it was the proper dosage. The response of the technician covered from head to toe in a full protective suit while holding a concrete cup of radioactive 'medicine' was: "Don't worry." How the hell was I not supposed to worry when he looked like he'd retrieved my 'medicine' from Chernobyl?

Shrugging off the jokes about whether or not I would glow in the dark for awhile, I was sent back home. The treatment was declared a success as my thyroid levels went back to normal. That lasted for all of a week. My vitals began to drop. My poor husband tried to hurry what was a two hour drive from our mountain home to the city hospitals. When I arrived, I was stabilized, poked and prodded and examined. My thyroid was dead. That crucial lynchpin gland that controls so much of body function and acts as a gateway with all the other glands, had effectively flatlined. Normal thyroid function is at 1.0 to 5.0, but I was registered at 199. I had been given too much nuclear medicine and the doctors knew it. My only saving grace was that I had been an athlete in prime condition as the doctors acknowledged that anyone else's heart rate would have not just slowed, but stopped. I was treated immediately with T3 and T4 hormones that were so necessary to keep up the circadian rhythm of the heart and even breathing. With my thyroid still in my body, yet atrophied, the rest of the endocrine system - the vital group of glands that controlled so many hormones and even the sympathetic nervous system functions of heartbeat and breathing - went haywire.

Doctors who had little knowledge of these glands began to misdiagnose me with one mysterious autoimmune disease after another. For a woman who had been an athlete, whose independence and activity had been my entire world, it felt as though my body had betrayed me. Weak, shaking, weight fluctuating, heart rate often erratic, even my body temperature could not stabilize as I found myself shivering cold in the heat of summer or sweating buckets in the middle of winter. Everything I had worked so hard for was gone and living took a backseat to simply surviving. I was put on medication to try to make up for the vital hormones my thyroid no longer produced. What I didn't know was even that was an act of 'guestimating' by the doctors and their error was priming me for a physical cataclysm.

The moment came one bright and sunny morning in the middle of breakfast with my husband and young daughter. I remember staring out the window, the morning news droning in the background, and thinking about how incredibly beautiful the sky was, the miraculous wonder of God's creation. From nowhere a great surge emanated up from my lower back, washing over my head, and then through my whole body. My heartbeat became erratic and the fluttering that followed made me realize that something was terribly wrong. It became immensely hard to breathe. I knew I was not long for this world. I became vaguely aware of my husband and daughter calling out to me, their voices filled with panic, and yet something incredible happened at that very moment.

There was a sense of sweetness. I could feel I was no longer with my body. From outside of myself, I saw a body. With utter detachment it took several moments to even recognize that I was somehow looking at my own physical shell. A sensation of euphoria overtook my being and I was not afraid.

As a Christian I had no fear of death. I knew I was saved by my faith and when I died I would go to heaven. As much as I loved my husband and daughter, I trusted God that my family would be okay. As I felt myself slipping away, I wondered what it would be like to finally meet my Savior face to face. As a Christian this is what you expect. I was a Christian, very much in love with my heavenly Creator, but this is not what happened...

My experience did not give me the vision of light at the end of the tunnel. It did not show me heaven. There were no shining angels in waiting or the kind visage of my beloved Savior. It was just a feeling of being detached from my body and knowing that I was no longer in pain. It was completely euphoric. This was just a very small part of what I would later learn is called an out of body experience. In those moments of total release from my physical body, I saw and experienced something that had absolutely nothing to do with anything I had ever been taught in my religion. Unprepared, I was overwhelmed by wonder. I never had words then for what happened, but I do now, and they can only be shared at the end of this book.

When my little infinity was over, all I can say is that it was a thousand times more painful to come back into my physical body than it had been to leave it. While recovering in the hospital, I was hooked up to a myriad of monitors as they tried to keep my heart stabilized. When I asked what had happened I was told I had suffered adrenal failure. The doctor informed me that most people do not survive this experience. The thyroid medication I had been placed on had not included the vital T3 hormone which the adrenal glands needed to control fight and flight reactions. Running on empty, the adrenals had given one final massive flush of adrenaline and cortisol throughout my body. Overwhelmed, the heart, lungs, and sympathetic nervous system functions had simply crashed. My existence at that point was a miracle and the doctor told me how lucky I was. Ever a good religious woman, I reminded the doctor that luck had nothing to do with it - I was blessed!

After my ordeal I had time to think that night in the hospital about all that had occurred. I had survived something very few ever do. As I lay there, my daughter had left me with a small stuffed brown rabbit with floppy ears for comfort. Stroking its ears, I wondered: Was I not a good enough Christian? Why hadn't I seen Jesus or the angels come to guide me to heaven? I remembered stories of people who had experienced hellish visions of the Devil and demons, but that had not happened either. The echo of the bliss and serenity I had experienced outside of my body was still with me.

That night was a tenuous one and a constant fight on the part of the hospital staff to keep my vitals stable. Eventually, I was finally cleared to be placed in a recovery room. Somewhere in the earliest of morning hours the Voice came. My eyes scanned the room, certain I must have heard a nurse or someone in the corridor, but I was completely alone. Yet alone was not how I felt. Puzzled, I wondered why I could not see this Presence that seemed to hold my hand. There was no face, no body, no great beacon of light like I had expected to see from angels or even Christ. Neither male nor female, the Voice spoke, delivering a message that became seared into my very being and would haunt me in the days and years to come.

The Presence was faceless, without body, yet its warmth and its Voice lingered with me through the darkness and into the light of morning.

Later in my recovery, I tried to push the Voice from my mind. Fearing that 'crazy' would be added to the growing list of ailments on my medical report, I told no one what I had felt, seen, or heard. The only person I felt I could trust was my daughter, and even then I made her promise not to share it with anyone. I was troubled that my spiritual experience had in no way mirrored the experiences of other Christians I had heard or read about. In so many ways what I had felt transcended religion, but I hadn't grown nearly enough yet in my Soul to comprehend that. I was actually afraid that just maybe I was being tricked by one of Satan's minions, for I had been taught that any experience that didn't come from God could only have its source in the side of evil.

Instead I focused on a mystery my mind could handle. I was hungry to understand why I had not recognized my own body during my out of body experience. Retrieving the Gideon Bible out of my hospital drawer, I flipped to a passage in the New Testament that I knew well. The moment of Jesus' Resurrection in the Book of John chapter 20.

Mary Magdalene and the other women have just come to Jesus' tomb when they discover that the stone has been rolled away. The other women flee, but Magdalene remains and begins to weep. Jesus appears from the tomb, asking why she is crying. She tells him that someone has removed the body of her lord and master. When Jesus reveals himself, she is shocked and goes to embrace him, but Jesus pulls back and warns her that she cannot touch him because he has not yet ascended to his Father in heaven.

I remember the intense feeling of revelation I had rereading this passage. For years I had puzzled on it and wondered why Magdalene didn't recognize Christ. Now I knew. The soul does not look like the body. I could not recognize my physical form any more than Magdalene could recognize Jesus in his pure soul form. Perhaps to others this will seem like a small thing, but for me it was a turning point. It was the first time I began to sense that there was something greater and deeper waiting to be discovered beneath the veneer of religion. There were secrets to the words in the Bible that I had never seen before, secrets waiting to be found out, greater revelations needing to be uncovered. My curiosity was aroused and my thirst for knowledge unquenchable. That night I read my Bible, seeing deeper meanings in things I had not seen before. It occurred to me that I had always depended upon clergy to explain the meanings of the Bible instead of thinking for myself. Deep down I think I was trying to fight another nagging feeling. It was the feeling that everything was destined to change and that the revelations were not going to stop at the Bible.

I knew I had been brought back for a greater purpose, but while many Christians would feel they had come back to preach or evangelize with greater zeal, deep down I knew that was not going to be my path. Something had changed in me. Something I could not name or describe. I wondered at that moment if Satan was putting me in this state of confusion. My religious knee-jerk reaction was that the thought of questioning the Bible in any way was so taboo that it must be the Devil influencing my thoughts. But how could that be? For the first time in my life was I seeing what I was always supposed to see? But what was I supposed to be seeing?

The Voice I tried to forget came again that night as I slept:
It is not time for you yet.
You are to teach.
Teach them how to love unconditionally.
You are here to bring change.

Before I could teach, I would have to learn. Before I
could bring change, my entire worldview would have to
change. I did not know then what They were going to teach
me. I did not know They were going to open doors I had never
known were there. I had been blind for so long that it was
going to take time. The doors that were going to open were
doors of greater knowledge that would lead to spirituality.
That word has been thrown around so casually by religion,
that I honestly had considered myself to be spiritual as a
Christian. My experience that night in the hospital had shown
me that there was so much more to the realm of our Creator.
In receiving this message, I began to ponder about the reality
of the unseen place where the soul exists before we are born
and after we die. Deep down I realized I actually knew next to
nothing about the God I worshipped. And so I was on a
mission.

3. The Forbidden Truth

The message that came during my death experience haunted me for years. For quite awhile I managed to remain on my religious path without too much discomfort. I had always loved studying the Scriptures and learning about its history… as long as what I learned didn't contradict what the Bible actually said. But just like the story of Jesus and Mary Magdalene, I wanted to understand the Bible to a greater depth. I wanted to know all about the history from the times when the Bible was written. While I was homeschooling my daughter, she began to notice the change that had come over me. She noticed that I was studying the Bible voraciously. Wanting to know what I was doing, I explained to her that mommy needed to learn more about God. I had no idea then that what I really meant was that I needed to know more about the god that man had written about.

Because I had managed to instill in her the same fervent faith, she joined me in all the things that I was learning. Though I tried to push her towards other extracurricular activities and circles, she so often would snuggle up beside me with one of the books and say: "I'm meant to do whatever you do, Mommy." I did not know that her comment would come to haunt me decades later. At the time I really did think that this was cute (she was eight after all) and that she'd grow out of it eventually. That didn't happen. My daughter made herself my constant companion in this quest. Every step, every turn, every crossroad we took together no matter how many times I told her that she needed to go and find her own path in life. In future books I will discuss what I learned about souls and how it illuminated our understanding of each other's purpose in this life, but for now it is enough to say that we are the best of friends. In teaching my daughter I began to see things I had not seen before in my own religious education.

I remember one evening sitting with my young daughter on the sofa watching the news. There had been a horrible natural disaster in Pakistan and many children and adults had perished. Her eyes welled with tears and she looked up at me gravely and asked, "They're in heaven now, right, Mom?" "Of course," I told her.

As I held her it dawned on me that the majority of the people were not Christians and had likely been Muslims or even Hindus. All my life my religion had taught me that a person can only go to heaven when they die if they have accepted Jesus Christ as their lord and savior. I suddenly had to ask myself, what about the good people of other faiths or no faith at all?

Recently I was on a social networking site and someone posted a beautiful image of the sunrise with the quote: 'I am saved by Christ's grace and not by my own works'. Years ago I would have read those words and felt a swelling of pride. Instead an immense sadness came over my heart, especially as I read the comments that followed. Hundreds of people had responded, all expressing rousing choruses of 'amen'. They left messages of gratitude for the post, recognizing that as 'sinners' they could never hope to achieve heaven without the grace of Jesus' sacrifice on the cross. The great problem with this view is that these same people also fervently believe that if you **don't** accept Christ that you can never hope to enter into the kingdom of God, aka heaven, when you die. For a majority of Christians this is a solid fact of their faith.

But what does this really say about religion?

Please allow me to paint a picture for you: A man lives his life doing horrible things. He molests a child. He has beaten his wife. He has cheated his customers. By society's standards he is an awful, cruel person who hasn't done a single good thing in his life. This man discovers he has terminal cancer. Suddenly he is afraid and he turns to religion. He goes to church. He weeps for all his bad deeds and accepts Jesus Christ into his heart and so is forgiven for his sins. He has received the grace of God. A few days later he dies. According to the tenants of Christianity, this man will be welcomed into heaven.

Now, at the same time another man comes down with terminal cancer. This man is a Hindu from India. He knows about Christ from missionaries, but he insists on keeping his Hindu faith. This man showered love and devotion upon his wife and children. He was honest in his business and gave away great portions of his wealth to help the poor. He has lived his life with more love and generosity in the world than most others. When he dies, he is remembered for his legacy of kindness. According to traditional Christian doctrine, this man will go to hell for refusing to accept Christ.

No matter how wonderful a person is, no matter how much good they do on this earth, if they reject Jesus Christ as their lord and savior, I was taught that upon death they suffer the everlasting torments of the Christian hell. Some Christian sects insist that someday in the future there will be a resurrection of all who have ever died. Whenever this happens, Christ will give everyone a final chance to accept him. Even if I had believed this, it didn't change the harsh reality that someone like that kind Hindu man would still be stuck suffering the tortures of hell for quite some time. Never did it occur to me to ask if this seemed right. Even in the most liberal of Christian churches, the fact that the religion is

founded upon this tenant that Christ died for our sins and that
by accepting him we are saved is basically unchangeable. This
is what makes Christianity the religion it is! If you do not hold
to this, then Christ's teachings may as well be the same as the
Buddha's: no longer a true religion but more a philosophical
choice for how you live your life. If you live by this belief,
most ardent Christians will feel you are not a believer at all. I
was a believer. I knew I had to accept that Christ was the only
way to salvation... and yet I slowly realized I did not accept it.
It was the first time I had to acknowledge that my own
personal belief was contradicting the Bible.

Time and time again I would open my Bible and see the
verse of Samuel 16:7. Samuel, a prophet, has gone out to
choose a king for Israel. This king will be chosen by God to
replace the corrupt king whom the people chose. Samuel
comes to the home of Jesse who has many sons. They are fine,
tall, strapping men, but this is not who God chooses. God
chooses the youngest son; a mere boy who tends flocks of
sheep becomes his chosen king of Israel. Both Samuel and
David's own father are surprised, but God reminds him that:
'*man sees what is before his eyes, but God sees what is in the
heart.*'

Though I believed in Christ and felt I was saved, I
realized that I did not believe that meant Christians had an
exclusive right to heaven. If God knew every person in their
mother's womb according to Jeremiah 1:5, and knew every
hair on your head as Matthew 10:30 insists, then he knew who
was truly good and deserving, regardless of whether they
accepted his son as their lord and savior. I thought that this
was an innocent assumption, but as I soon discovered, I was
actually challenging the very core of my religion. Now the

whole house of cards began to tumble down. What else about my religious beliefs had I not bothered to look at closely enough?

Religion was like the air I breathed and had been since my childhood. I grew up in the influence and mentality of the 1950s and '60s. It was a time when, as a woman, it was best to be seen and not heard. The superiority of men was without question and sexism was simply normal. I was raised by a young mother who had very little education and lived in poverty. To add to this stifling environment, my family was extremely religious and immersed in a culture that believed the only true gift of women was to give birth, raise children, and be subservient to their husbands. Marriage and motherhood were the only acceptable roles. Sons were sources of pride and daughters were in training to continue this morose drudgery into the next generation.

To make matters worse, my mother joined a sect of Christianity that many today consider a cult - an irony, since Christianity itself began as a cult during the Roman Empire. We were soon memorizing whole tracts of the Bible and having it drilled into our young minds that we were amongst the chosen faithful while the rest of the sinful world belonged to Satan. Those who were not like us, even other Christians, were not saved and were damned to hell. We went through rigorous training in order to evangelize from door to door, but socializing with anyone outside of the church was nearly forbidden for fears that we would be led astray. To be honest it is a miracle that I ever developed the intense love for God and Jesus that I did.

Even as a child I saw so much hypocrisy around me. I saw men who had gone out on their wives, who abused their children, who did awful things behind closed doors. I knew because this was the plight of my own home. Sexual abuse was rampant, and any child who dared speak up to Church Elders saw their abuser given a slap on the wrist, forgiven, and brought back into the fold. The abuse never stopped, and the idea of reporting to any other authority like the police would mean excommunication not just from the religion, but your own family. Throughout my youth I blamed myself and saw myself as disgustingly sinful because God never saw fit to save me from my abusers. As a female - no matter how young - I was taught that I had called it onto myself. Men were never to blame, but I was. God had made man in his image, and 1 Timothy had concreted the mandate that men had been given divine authority over women. Wives that dared to dissent were reminded that God himself decreed that their husbands were the head of them. My own mother never had the strength to question anything; the moment my abusers begged forgiveness and blamed Satan for their crimes they were welcomed back with open arms.

As twisted as this sounds, in my young, impressionable mind, the only way I reconciled what I lived through with the teachings of a loving God, was that God showed his love for me by keeping me alive. I had nowhere to go. No one protected me. My only refuge for a long time was my indoctrination. How I ever held onto the belief in a loving Creator, I don't know. Perhaps it was because even in the worst times, I did feel that Presence of love and peace. This book is not about my sexual, mental, or physical abuse, but it is important to say that in my teenage years the situation of my home life had become horrific. I finally found the courage to leave not only my home, but the religious sect that had only served as a safeguard for my abusers and so many others.

As a young woman I made the decision that I was going to try and seek out the path of God. My quest took me to the doorstep of mainstream religions, to church after church, denomination after denomination. My faith in God and his son Jesus remained strong, but I was more confused than ever. I was starting to ask myself: If we are all Christians and read from the inerrant word of God, why is the Church splintered into so many different denominations? I met wonderful people wherever I decided to worship, but there was always something amiss. Every pastor, minister, and reverend used their pulpit to explain what the Bible was really saying, yet they all differed from each other. While their explanations made sense to them, ultimately it seemed they were spinning the words to suit their own agendas or beliefs.

Scriptures were used to prove that women were created to be subservient to men, while others were used to prove that women were equal in the eyes of God. Scriptures by the Apostle Paul said that women were forbidden to preach or even speak in Church, yet other scriptures proved that Jesus relied on women's financial support and had no problem with them evangelizing. Scriptures were often used to condemn homosexual people to hell, but others could point to a Scripture about God's love and insist that people who believed in Christ were saved no matter what their sin. I saw people chained by their beliefs, and I saw people freed by their beliefs. I saw people who cowered before an almighty, judgmental God and I saw people embracing everyone in the name of an all-loving Creator. As strange as it may seem, deep down I always felt strongly that I knew who God was, and I could not bring myself to believe that he had ever meant for so much division in his name.

My daughter was in her senior year of high school when we began to earnestly study Judaism so that we could have a deeper understanding of the religious tradition that had produced the oldest texts of the Bible. She had her sights set on becoming a Biblical archaeologist with a focus on the Old Testament, so we found ourselves drawn into the study of Israel and its people. By this time I was still a hardcore Christian, but I had embraced the *Kumbaya* mentality that the God of the Jews, Christians, and Muslims was one and the same. In my eyes we were all children of the Almighty. For a religious person, I felt I was pretty open minded. Granted, I was still very uncomfortable with homosexuality, but I never felt that God would send a perfectly good person to hell just because they were misguided in their desires. I believed strongly in the equality of women, for Jesus himself had been financially supported by women. I did not judge anyone for their crimes, sins, lifestyle, or even for belonging to a different religion, because I felt that God would be the one to deal with each individual soul based upon their own merits. I suppose you could call us fairly liberal Christians at this point. I had spent years now studying the ins and outs of my own religion, but for the first time my eyes started to open to the beliefs of a different faith.

I remember how I was looked upon with thinly veiled disdain by pastors and church leaders when I told them of my studies. I used to believe that the days of the Church disapproving of learning and research were left behind back in the Dark Ages, but sadly it is a contempt that is alive and well in the Western religions. Do not get me wrong, not all religions disprove of education, but usually it is only when that education fits their belief system. No one had any issues as long as I read books by authors who were Christians,

scientists who were Christians, historians who were
Christians, programs created and made by Christians. I think
you get the point. Anything done by non-Christians were only
shown as examples of the misguided delusions of the secular
world around us that had rejected the truth of God's Word.
Daring to step outside of my faith was taboo to all but the
most liberal of my Christian friends.
Didn't I understand the dangers of being swayed from my
faith?
Didn't I know that outside of our faith were all sorts of clever
lies and illusions made by the Devil to lead believers astray?
If you are noticing a pattern of blaming Satan, all will be
revealed towards the end of this book in Chapter 21 *Satan, the
Devil, and God: A Human Trinity.* I was warned that if I
insisted on pursuing this path, then I had to make certain to
guard my belief and remember that God's Word was the Truth
above all truths. Maybe I could have done that if it weren't for
the echo of the Voice that kept coming back in my dreams.

My dreams were the one place I could not push away
and ignore what had happened in the hospital all those years
ago. The same Voice was making itself known to me and
reminding me. I kept having dreams about being in places of
the past that I knew nothing about. Sometimes I would see
whole throngs of people coming towards me, reaching out to
me, looking to me, and always that Voice telling me that I was
to teach. The most poignant dream was one in which I found
myself in a beautiful wooden building akin to a church, with
hundreds of people waiting for me to speak from the pulpit. At
least I thought it was a pulpit. I stood before a wide lectern
with a narrow base and books were piled on each side of the
stand as if to act as a balance. On one side I could see the
Bible, the Torah, and the Koran. On the other were books

whose titles I could not make out clearly. Unbeknownst to me, the years would reveal the names of those books.

I went to reach for the Bible and wanted to search for the verse from Samuel about how God focuses on the heart of a person... but when I opened the pages, every single line on every single page had been blacked out. I began to panic in the dream until a wise old man resembling the beloved Billy Graham came to my side and comforted me. I had always loved Billy Graham and his presence calmed me immediately in the dream. He said to me that I shouldn't worry because it had happened to him as well. At the time I didn't know what any of it meant. It was only a dream, like so many others that I tried to push away. The Church had always frowned upon any kind of divination, including messages in dreams or by any other means. Divine messages were reserved only for the holy men of the Bible like Joseph and Daniel. It would be almost a decade before I would learn the true meaning of this dream. Its revelation will come at the end.

As my daughter and I became more involved with Judaism and made wonderful friends in the Jewish community, I started to be plagued by the nagging insistence of my hardcore Christian friends. No matter what I believed, I could not get away from the fact that my religion insisted on the doctrine that without Christ a person was not saved. I was reminded by ministers and pastors that this was true even of the Jewish community and they had plenty of Bible verses behind them to prove it.

Sleep no longer came easy to me. On many occasions I would fall asleep exhausted from crying out to God, asking for the truth: Was it only through His Son that humanity could be with Him in heaven when they died? The thought of thousands of human beings never being able to experience the God of the heavens that I believed in was unbearable for me. This had gone on for many nights when I suddenly found myself woken in the early hours one morning. The Voice was echoing in my head like a drumbeat:

Look at the Gospel of John.
Get your Bible.
Look at the book of John.

The clock struck 3 AM as I went into my study and pulled out my well-worn Bible. As if guided by the hand of whomever had awoken me, it fell open to the Gospel of John 4:22. My eyes instantly latched to the words printed in red. For those outside of the Christian faith, it is tradition in versions of the Bible such as the King James to emphasize the words of Christ by printing them in red. As a Christian I believed that these words were Christ's own and had been meticulously recorded by his beloved disciple John. The text drew me to a well known moment in Jesus' ministry when he spoke with a Samaritan woman at a well. It all seemed so fitting, since I saw the Bible as being the well from which I quenched my thirst for knowledge.

From my studies I knew that the reason this particular conversation was so important was because the Samaritans were outcasts according to the Jewish laws Jesus had grown up with. Jews and Samaritans were forbidden from intermarriage and there were often violent conflicts between the two. Even though they were ethnic cousins to the Jews, they were despised by their brethren.

Long before the birth of Christ, Israel had been separated into two kingdoms - Israel to the north, and Judah to the south. Around 722 BC the Assyrian empire sacked Israel and dispersed its peoples to the winds. Somehow a sizable group of Israelites managed to stay in the area of Samaria.

A couple of centuries later the southern kingdom of Judah was exiled to Babylon and their temple destroyed. Generations later the Persian king Cyrus the Great opened the door for Jews to return to their homeland. Only the most pious Jews took him up on it while thousands who had discovered a good and comfortable life amidst the Persian empire remained in Babylon.

The Jews who returned to rebuild the temple discovered that their Samaritan brothers held beliefs that differed from their own. The Samaritans were branded as half-breeds and pagans because they had intermarried with other peoples from the empire. In Jewish eyes the Samaritans practiced a corrupt version of the faith, but the Samaritans felt that it was the Jews from Babylon who had returned with a bastardized religion. Samaritans accepted only the five books of Moses and insisted that the holy place of God was Mount Gerizim. Their Jewish cousins insisted the holy place was Jerusalem and brought along not only the Torah, but all the other books of the Old Testament. The two groups built their walls, each feeling the other was the heretical sect. Eventually intermarriage and even communication was forbidden between the two.

While Rome largely did not care about this division, in Jesus' time the conflict was still alive and frequently resulted in bloody confrontations between Samaritans and Jews. For Jesus to use a parable about a 'Good Samaritan' and even deign to speak to the Samaritan woman at the well shows how great his mission was to reach out to all people. I had read this passage hundreds of times before, but somehow my eyes became opened to see that which is glossed over and ignored in Jesus' words as recounted in John 4:22: *'For you worship that which you do not know, but we worship what we do know, for salvation is of the Jews.'*

A bucket of ice water might as well have been poured over my head! At the time I still naively believed that the words of the Gospels were written by Jesus' disciples and that any quotes of Christ had been recorded perfectly. As such, this verse stopped me in my tracks. Regardless of whatever else Jesus might have said, at that moment in history sitting at the well with the Samaritan woman, Jesus had just confirmed that the Jews were already saved. Supposedly these are Jesus' own words! He is God made flesh, the Father incarnate, would this not be the ultimate moment for Jesus to clarify all the theological muck and say: 'For salvation is through me, Jesus Christ, the Son of God'? No matter what other arguments Jesus may have had with his own people, two things he makes clear: 'we worship what we do know' (Jesus is including himself with all the rest of his Jewish brethren), and 'salvation is of the Jews', meaning that the Jews have always been saved regardless of him and his eventual death and resurrection.

In that moment my world cracked wide open. I cried uncontrollably. I took one of my pillows to muffle the sound of the painful agony I was experiencing lest I wake up my husband. There it was, written as clear as could be, my beloved Jesus being quoted by his disciple that salvation was of the Jews. I would wipe the tears from my eyes and read it again, rub my eyes and read it again, that's how difficult it was to accept what I was reading. Finally I ended up on the floor on my knees. A strange and sudden comfort came over me, as though the same Presence that had told me to find the verse was trying to bring me consolation in that dark moment. I became aware that I wasn't alone even though there was nobody in the room with me. It was another mystery, this Presence, this sense of Others, that I would not understand for some time to come.

After the shock wore off, still in the early predawn hours, I went to my daughter's bedroom and knocked on her door with a sense of desperation. As she turned on the light, I took the Bible, sat beside her bed and read the scripture that I had been awoken to read. Seeing my distress, she wiped the sleep from her eyes, but I was greeted with a blank look. I read with emphasis once, twice, three times. Understanding began to creep into her eyes. She took the Bible from my hands and read for herself. A look of denial began to cloud her face. A pang of sorrow struck me to know I had once refused to see what was right before my eyes. Watching her, I had to ask: Was this truly how blindly I had read this book my entire life?

Look at the words he uses, I insisted: 'for salvation is of the Jews'. Suddenly, in having to spell it out for her, I was forced to speak aloud the terrible truth that was bringing my religion crashing down. The foundation of my faith was that Christ was my Savior. He was the incarnation of the almighty, all-knowing God, and we are saved by his death and resurrection and nothing else. Yet here were Jesus' own words contradicting that sacred doctrine.

The Church had taught me to see the Gospels as direct recollections of Jesus' every word and action by his disciples. The Bible was supposed to be the Word inspired by God and without error, but in that moment I dared to question everything. If Jesus was supposedly aware that John was recording his every word for posterity, how could he not say to the Samaritan woman that salvation was through him, the Son God? How could he not say that salvation would come through his death on the cross? In my faith, Jesus and God were the same being. God, knowing the entire future of mankind, knowing all the horrific evils to come, the bloody battles that would occur for thousands of years over his Word, how could God as Jesus not put a stop to it all then and there by saying: "Salvation is through me, the Son of God, and by my sacrifice which is to come." In one verse, Jesus as God could have put a stop to so much of the religious turmoil that would plague humanity for the next two thousand years, so why hadn't he?

Suddenly the foundation I had stood on for over five decades, a foundation of belief that had seen me through all the trials and tribulations of my life began to crumble. Every brick, every bit of stone that had made up the whole bedrock of my life began to break apart as the answer became sickeningly apparent: these were not the words of God, but of a good man who was on a quest to make a difference. And a man, like any other, is imperfect. Even if the author was John the disciple, he too would have been an imperfect man. Reason dictated that imperfect men were incapable of writing a perfect book. The dangerous instinct that had been nagging at me suddenly exploded in dawning realization that the book I had built my whole existence on was as imperfect as any other book written by human authors. Through years of study that came later, I would learn that no two Bibles hand written throughout time are alike. They are full of the errors made by one copyist after another, after another, after another for hundreds, if not thousands of years. How can anyone insist a document is 'inerrant' when its entire history is full of error, from its inception to its translations? After all, is not an all knowing and almighty God capable of ensuring that his 'Word' survives in a suitable state of unsullied perfection? My own words came crashing back to me from an incident that had occurred years before. In the midst of chatting, a well meaning Baptist woman had been aghast to discover that I was once Catholic. She insisted that according

to her minister the Catholics were 'going to hell in a hand basket'. I had regarded her for a moment before asking: "Do you believe the Bible is the inerrant Word of God?"
"Of course!" she replied.
"And you believe it is perfect because God chose every man who wrote it, guiding them by the Holy Spirit?"
"Absolutely!"
I sipped my coffee and chose my words carefully, "The New Testament was written in Greek-"
"I know that!" she interjected.
" - but then they were translated to Latin. Eventually it would be translated again, but guess who translated the Latin?"
She remained silent as I continued, "Catholic monks and scribes did. They often took vows of silence and could not inquire about certain verses or the meaning of words. You insist that every man who took part in writing or translating the Bible was chosen by the Holy Spirit of God. How can the Catholics be damned to hell when God himself chose them to translate his holy Word?"
I never did get much of an intelligible response after that, but incidentally she was far less judgmental on the issue of Catholics. I know my simple observation had caused a tiny revolution in her thinking. I wish my own revolution had been as gentle, but instead I felt like my beliefs were being pried from my death grip and incinerated before my eyes.

Ironically the words of Jesus came to me in that bitter moment: A house divided cannot stand. My inner house, my own soul, was more than divided. It had come crashing down and was being washed away by a tsunami of tearful emotions. I cannot express the period of mourning I entered, but make no mistake that I grieved the death of my religious beliefs as purely as if it had been my own mother. In this wake, in this moment of inner destruction, I could not envision who I would become. I could not imagine the rebirth that awaited. This is where my whole life journey changed.

While the out of body experience had been the starting point of my journey, it was this moment more than any other that set me upon my path in this life. The words of Jesus had never been truer when he had said: 'I am the Way, I am the Truth, I am the Light'.
It was through him that I began this journey of self-discovery and the quest for truth and Light. I have never lost my love for the man who became known as Jesus Christ, and the reality that he had an incredible heart that longed for a true spiritual change in the world is as strong as ever, but I will enter into the discussion of the true soul of Jesus later in Chapter 21 *Satan, the Devil, and God: A Human Trinity.* What mattered most was that for the first time in my entire life I found myself questioning just who Jesus truly was.

I brought the issue of Jesus and the Samaritan woman to several clergy, but received no true answers. I was unable to find a single Christian historian or theologian who had dared to tackle these questions. Without any other option, I did what was so forbidden to my fellow believers. I began to listen to religious scholars who had no religious agenda whatsoever. For the first time I set my own religious beliefs aside.

It was hard. Every time I heard something that contradicted the Bible I had to resist the preconditioned urge to walk away or launch into an evangelical defense. I set aside faith and began to use the reason that I believed God gave each and every human being. I had been completely unaware of how much darkness I was in. My soul had not come to the Light yet. When you are a person of faith, your entire world rests upon it. No matter what else in your life crashes around you, it is the bedrock that keeps you hopeful, sustained, and sane. Without it, the world does become bleak.

Without it, you begin to wonder what on earth it has all been for. You think of all the lives given up in the name of God because of religious wars and the breath is knocked out of you by its pointlessness.

You feel lied to.

You feel betrayed.

You wake up.

Suddenly, you feel alive to the world for the first time.

My childlike reverence for the Bible fell away as I began to see my holy text for what it was: a book. A book like any other written by many, many men, over thousands and thousands of years. A book that was far from perfect. A book that contained lots of inaccuracies, contradictions, prejudices, and commandments that could never be the work of a perfect, almighty God, but was becoming more and more clearly the work of imperfect men with loaded religious and political agendas. Translated and mistranslated, torn apart and sewn together, the Bible ceased to be the inerrant Word of God and instead became a patchwork of human myths, histories, political battles, with only the occasional glimpse of spiritual truth. I was beginning to see the God that had been created in the image of man.

From that day on it was as though a great chain of events had been set in motion. A series of dreams led me to divinely placed people and events, each one causing me to ask questions I had never dreamed of asking and look into things I would never have dared before examine about my faith and religion. This is where my mystical life began. In solitude, praying, and meditating, I found answers through the beautiful messages that would come in dreamlike states. Through it all there were so many immense discoveries that shook my beliefs to their core, leveling everything I had ever thought I knew. In its wake came a miracle of rebirth, knowledge, and understanding.

A strange thing happens when you suddenly find that the safe and sturdy walls of everything you once believed have fallen down. As the dust settles, you are forced into a new world you never knew existed. It was a world that was always there the whole time, but I never knew it because I was so insulated in my own small religious cocoon. I had no idea then how drastically my views of the world and faith would change, especially when it came to women.

A lot of people who find themselves disillusioned with organized religion feel so alienated and disgusted that they end up becoming complete atheists. It was a sight I frequently witnessed in college as students discovered the truth of how the Biblical books were written, by whom, and for what political agendas of the ancient world. I came to have a tremendous respect for atheists. I cannot speak for all, but those I met were amongst the few living their life with compassion and morality out of love for their fellow humans.

They needed no gods or religious mandates to understand that being a good human being was what mattered. They needed no indoctrination or belief system to explain why compassion was important. Because they approached the world with unbiased eyes they were able to ask the most fearless questions about the universe. I had always feared atheism because it seemed hopeless and dark, but I discovered people who found the greatest spiritual connection to the living world around them because they were the ones exploring the scientific marvels of our universe. A life without an afterlife was no less significant to them; in fact, it made life and its complexity all that much more important.

I witnessed human beings who, whether atheist, agnostic, or simply spiritually ambivalent had committed themselves to helping humanity through science, humanitarian works, or charities not because it was a religious mandate, but because they knew it was the right thing to do. These same people were often the most accepting of the differences of the world, blind to race, gender, or religion... at least until the religious deemed it their right to condemn or interfere with their lives. For the first time I understood their hostility as 'well intentioned' religious people showed themselves to be judgmental and outright controlling. More and more I found myself separated from the mindset that had ruled my life for well over fifty years, but while I respected those who chose to see a world with no divine intervention whatsoever, I could not join them fully.

Because of my death experience and hundreds of other mystical experiences I had encountered over the decades, I could not bring myself to believe that nothing Divine (such as a Creator) existed in this life. In this respect I had to personally disagree with my atheist friends. Unlike my old Christian friends, at least this viewpoint did not make me a pariah. As I released all my old beliefs and preconceptions, I held deeply to the only thing I had left: an unshakeable trust in the existence of the Soul and the belief that there was Something much greater at work in this world that no human being could ever fully fathom.

From the connection I have felt to the esoteric world, I know without a shadow of a doubt that there is a power greater than all of us at work in the universe. Most see this power as God. Others see it as a Goddess. Some believe it is the work of spirits or even aliens. After studying all of the major world religions, I can honestly say that there is no right or wrong answer. Everyone must feel a sense of comfort and connection to what they believe is in control of this universe. The difference is, do they then insist on using that belief to try to control others? This is the great battle between true spirituality and religion.

I have experienced so much in this life that I would be remiss to believe that there is nothing beyond our physical world. Even at my lowest points I never saw myself as going through a crisis of faith; instead a part of me recognized that I was having to undergo a *revolution* of faith. Deep down I knew that the Force that had guided me, loved me, protected me, watched over me, and ultimately spoke to me during my death experience was still the same. It was my human understanding (my Ego) of who it was that needed to be torn down completely. As my mind opened, I had to acknowledge that the God I had known from the Bible was simply too human and too small. As I began the emotionally exhausting and sometimes downright depressing process of dismantling my old religious belief, I found myself having to think in a totally new way. In time my daughter and I would explore all the major world religions. We would make friends from all ethnic and religious backgrounds. Eventually I made the decision to earn a Doctor of Philosophy in Religious Studies degree and use my knowledge of all faiths to give spiritual guidance. By no means did earning my PhD make me some kind of authority in my field and I am fond of telling people who want to call me 'doctor' that I feel my credentials stand for 'P.ush H.ere D.ummy'! Though it's true that I have studied for many years and will do so for as much time as I have in this world, when we take our last breath, whatever awaits on that Other Side is not going to say to me or anyone else with a title that we deserve to go to the front of the line! What is of this world belongs to this world and once you leave it, it will certainly not be accompanying you to wherever our Souls go on their Journey. Where once I strove to save the world through a knowledge of Jesus, I now work to help people become enlightened through an understanding of their own beliefs, the beliefs of their neighbors, and of their own Souls.

Though I recognize that the deeply religious loathe to hear anything contradictory about their own faith, that even the mere mention of something inaccurate about the Bible is enough to launch a holy war, I want to make clear that this book is about bringing humanity back to the essence and the beauty that lies in the soul of whatever spiritual teaching you follow. It is vital to seek the truth and eliminate the manmade dogma and politics from your faith. Doing so can only serve to return you to the path of a Creator who made the masculine and feminine in equality and who has given beauty and truth to all cultures and peoples.

It was made clear to me that I am not here to preach, but to teach. When you preach you are telling someone what to do, but when you teach you simply give people information. From that information each person is responsible for what they then do with the information. If it causes them to go on their own journeys of discovery, may it be so. If it causes them to cling to their religion more fervently, may it be so. My only mission is to be a source of information, a bridge for those who wish to cross the divide from their Egos to their Souls. Those who do will have the beautiful revelation of what awaits them and the energy that is created by spirituality… but only if they so desire.

The path I have traveled is my own, but in the process so many crossed my path who wanted to know what I had found that I had no choice but to share the information. At first I shied away because I felt that this was my journey and they would find their own paths by themselves just as I had done.

But I could not outrun the fate that the Voice had spoken all those years ago. I found myself with people hungry for information, and so I had no choice but to teach. After all, this was what They told me I would do. As I shared information their questions flowed forth like water from a ruptured dam. They entrusted me with their own doubts, curiosities, and deep desires to know the truth, as well as their admittance that no matter how often they went to church or tried to be religious that they just did not feel connected spiritually at all. They felt empty. They would say to me that they felt a connection to God, but no connection to their religion. What I kept finding was not men and women who lacked faith, but instead lacked understanding.

You see, the job of religion is to create a pathway that can connect people to the divine and for many people it does, but for equally many the very dogma and trappings of religion turn them away. They come asking hard questions and feel that they get so few answers from their religious leaders and groups. They are told constantly that they must rely on faith alone and if God does not provide the answers then they must simply trust. Many find contentment in never contemplating the harder questions, but for those who recognize that God gave humanity a mind to reason and to seek, this response will never be able to satisfy their souls. Amongst the many grappling with these questions, the majority who felt that they were coming away from their religions with empty hands and spiritually deprived souls were overwhelmingly women.

Because I was born in the 1950s I have been part of a generation that has seen immense change occur in America concerning the role of women. One of the great waves of change was the women's liberation movement. When I was a teenager it seemed as though women had suddenly awoken from a deep slumber to the realization that maybe, just maybe, they should start to question why the only acceptable roles given to them by society was homemaker and mother.

In the world of academics this meant women scholars began investigating aspects of medicine, history, archaeology, and religion that the majority of male academics had never even considered bothering to study. What role had women had in prehistory? How was a woman's body and hormones affected by medicine differently from a man? But perhaps most importantly, why had the whole subject of women been so completely overlooked and pushed aside by the majority of society, academics, and clergy?

Somehow the answers that were available kept coming back to a mindset shaped by the Biblical excuse of Eve's mistake in Genesis. Biblical proof cited that the male gender was favored by God not only by creation but again in the New Testament by Paul's enforcement that wives were at the bottom of a divine pecking order with their husbands having authority over them. These answers were unsatisfactory a thousand years ago and they still are today.

At first this book was going to be solely about women; a response to all the wonderful women I have known who have so earnestly sought answers. But as I kept writing, as I kept linking up all the important things I had found, I realized that women were the core of the matter, but it was bigger than that. Women were the connecting filament between all the things that have been hidden and masked in religion, issues like the truth about homosexuality, women's issues, and even Satan (all of which are discussed thoroughly in this book). While women are largely ignored or pushed into secondary roles in organized religion, in the mystical sects of religion women tend to feature prominently and are recognized as the ones who have been blessed to bring the Light into this world. This is not an honor reserved for select holy women, but all women. The more I studied the more I discovered why women were such a sticky subject for the writers of the Bible. I began to see how an effort to elevate one gender over the other had damaged the psyche of women and men, sabotaging our relationships to each other and even to our own planet. I began to see how the repression of women resulted in the oppression of more than just gender or sexuality: it was the oppression of the Soul itself. It is time to see the Light that is every man and woman's birthright. It is time to release the Soul to experience its rebirth.

4. A Woman's 'Place'

Finding my Light as a woman showed me the path I needed to take. In doing so, it gave me the knowledge and the courage to keep going no matter how hard the journey became. I have never once considered going back. The path I was on before was filled with so much darkness and confusion. I frequently needed to remind myself how far I had come. I will always hear the voices of pastors, preachers, and priests reciting verses that have kept women 'in their place' for over two thousand years:

"Let the woman learn in silence with all subjection. But I suffer not a woman to teach, nor to usurp authority over the man, but to be in silence. For Adam was first formed, then Eve. And Adam was not deceived, but the woman being deceived was in the transgression. Not withstanding she shall be saved in childbearing..." 1 Timothy 2:11-15, KJV

"A woman should learn in quietness and full submission. I do not permit a woman to teach or to assume authority over a man; she must be quiet. For Adam was formed first, then Eve. And Adam was not the one deceived; it was the woman who was deceived and became a sinner. But women will be saved through childbearing..." 1 Timothy 2:11-15, NIV

And especially:

"Wives, submit yourselves unto your own husbands, as unto the Lord. For the husband is the head of the wife, even as Christ is the head of the Church and he is Savior of the body. Therefore as the church is subject unto Christ, so let the wives

be to their own husbands in everything." Ephesians 5:22-24, KJV

"Wives, submit yourselves to your own husbands as you do to the Lord. For the husband is the head of the wife as Christ is the head of the church, his body, of which he is the Savior. Now as the church submits to Christ, so also wives should submit to their husbands in everything.' Ephesians 5:22-24, NIV

Because the King James Version of the Bible is the most popular amongst most fundamentalist groups of Christianity, I will use it for my main quotes, but I have chosen to also include its counterpart in the New International Version (NIV) Bible because of its popularity. It is useful to be able to see how one version of the Bible may interpret certain phrases or wording differently. Ironically most Biblical scholars now agree that these words were never written by the Apostle Paul and were actually late add-ons made by leaders of the early Church, a problem I will address fully in Chapter 18 *A Christian Revolution?*. I recognize that there are many liberal churches and Christians who no longer take these verses literally. Unfortunately, for the many who feel that every single word of the Bible is inerrant and must be followed to the letter, these damning verses are still being used to try and keep women in a status of subservience to men. The coup-de-gras of Biblical reasoning against women is where God himself declares:

*"Unto the woman He said, I will greatly multiply thy sorrow and thy conception; in sorrow thou shalt bring forth children; and thy desire shall be to thy husband and he shall rule over thee."*Genesis 3:16, KJV

"To the woman he said, "I will make your pains in childbearing very severe; with painful labor you will give birth to children. Your desire will be for your husband, and he will rule over you." Genesis 3:16, NIV

It is no joke that these verses constituted the backbone of theological arguments for thousands of years in favor of keeping women in a role that was little more than that of a slave. In my youth, these verses were still being used to assert the superior role of men. Men were simply held to a different standard; a standard we were told God himself had endorsed. Education, that simple but powerful tool, was frowned upon, especially for girls. In my religious household it was felt that a girl had no reason to think about college. All that mattered was that she would know how to keep house and tend to her husband and children. I was reminded that Eve had brought the entire world into misery and sin all because she had wanted knowledge. It saddens me to think that the knowledge she really wanted according to Genesis 3:5 was knowledge of what was good and what was evil… but we will return to Eve very soon.

I still see these ideas pervading our society like a cancerous plague and it all comes back to the Biblical mentality. These verses have set a tone for how the majority of men throughout Western history looked upon women and controlled their lives.

If you truly think that what I am saying belongs to the past and not our modern time, consider the words of the founder of Seattle, Washington's Mars Hill mega-church Mark Driscoll: *"Women will be saved by going back to that role that God has chosen for them. Ladies, if the hair on the back of your neck stands up, it is because you are fighting your role in the scripture."*

This pastor is listed as one of the twenty-five most influential pastors of the past twenty-five years (according to his website). Thousands of people listen - and agree - with this man's interpretation of scripture. He is perpetuating a mindset that has plagued humanity for thousands of years and is a near echo of the Protestant Reformer John Calvin (AD 1509-1564) who said over five hundred years ago that a woman, "*Who had perversely exceeded her proper bounds, is forced back to her own position.*"

So many religious believers forget that the mindsets of the Church Fathers who were pivotal in shaping Christian doctrine were so blatantly anti-woman (aka misogynist). Protestant founders who are still celebrated as great men of God include Martin Luther (AD 1483-1546) who made his position on women clear: "*The word and works of God is quite clear, that women were made either to be wives or prostitutes.*" Even while Luther would fight for men to have the right to read the Bible in their own language, he felt that: "*No gown worse becomes a woman than the desire to be wise.*"

Saint Augustine (AD 354-430), considered a cornerstone of the early church, asserted man's superiority by reminding women that they were, "*Not the image of God, but as far as man is concerned, he is by himself the image of God.*" I would like to note the irony that Augustine is completely ignoring Genesis 1:27 which implies that male and female are both made in God's image: "*So God created man in his own image, in the image of God he created him; **male and female he created them.**" (emphasis added)

The New International Versions of the Bible recognizes that the translation allows for some ambiguity in gender and translates it as: "*So God created* **mankind** *in his own image, in the image of God he created them, male and female he created them.*" (emphasis added)

It recognizes that it was not a singular 'man', but the idea of 'mankind' which included both men and women. The King James, translated at a time when male superiority was at its height, chose to infer that it was only man who was made in the image of God. Clement of Alexandria (AD 150-215) was happy to remind women that, "*the very consciousness of their own nature must evoke feelings of shame.*"

Tertullian, who came before Augustine, was so influential in building the early Church that he became known as the father of Latin Christianity and the founder of Western theology. Born in northern Africa, Tertullian lived his life in the midst of the Roman Empire in Carthage (now known as the modern African nation of Tunisia) from AD 160-225. Because of his influence, Tertullian enforced the most damaging theological mindset that could ever befall women. The Ego of this man set the stage for the oppression of women in the Church and the inhumane treatment of the female sex for the next two thousand years. Highly regarded and respected as a Father of the Church, his statements on women would become the holy laws by which the Church stripped women of all rights and hopes for their future.

It is Tertullian who hits the real core of the issue of the Bible's condemnation of women when he quotes Genesis 3:22: "*In pain shall you bring forth children, woman, and you shall turn to your husband and he shall rule over you.* **And do you not know that you are Eve? God's sentence hangs still** *over all your sex and His punishment weighs down upon you. You are the devil's gateway; you are she who first violated the forbidden tree and broke the law of God.* It was you who coaxed your way around him whom the devil had not the force to attack. With what ease you shattered the image of God: Man! Because of the death you merited, even the Son of God had to die... **Woman, you are the gate to hell.**" (emphasis added)

That last line in particular has been debated by many church historians, but ultimately Tertullian's meaning is quite clear when he clearly states that women are the 'devil's gateway'. If you think that this was the height of this church father's misogyny, I welcome you to go search out some of his other works.

Tell me how hard it is to overcome the Biblical idea of women's inferiority when it has stretched since before the first century all the way across two thousand years to our time? For nations, cultures, or denominations that still insist upon a literal interpretation of the Bible, these verses condemn women to be servants of man with no rights over their own bodies, property, education, or even their own souls. At certain points of history it even would become justification for the torture and slaughter of thousands of women and the men who dared to defend them.

Influential men like Tertullian and Augustine claimed their views on women were justified by the Bible, and to this day many blame verses attributed to the Apostle Paul as the reason such beliefs became a standard of the Church... but this is not true. As I would learn, the real source of these men's misogyny lay in a completely different source than simply the words of the Apostle Paul, but that is for Chapter 18 *A Christian Revolution?*. Looking beyond the New

Testament, there still remains the problem of Genesis and the undeniable fact that the character of Eve shoulders the burden for mankind's fall from grace. Like most other believers, I accepted the story without question and was never aware of the layers of meaning that were hidden beneath the surface of the first few chapters of the Bible's first book.

I never was aware of these issues, not in the normal sense, for I was caught up in the translation as man has preached it. It was a time when I was wearing my religious blinders. I did not question them or if they were wrong. The moment I began to investigate the Bible, I began to see the plight of women. For all of the insistence that woman is subservient and somehow less than man, I had to ask: Why would God give the greatest gift of creation, the gift of producing life and birth, to women if He really felt we were inferior (or 'the gate to hell' as Tertullian insisted)? These men felt that their opinions were as good as gospel because they believed themselves chosen by God to interpret the Bible on His behalf. They placed themselves so high that their 'divine opinions' became Church doctrine.

Anyone who insists upon the Bible's inerrancy also insists that the men who founded the Church were chosen by God, so are we to still accept these opinions? Why did God not give the gift of procreation to man to carry the child? If man is the ultimate image of God, and God can give life and creation, why are human men so deficient in this area, unable to produce life by themselves? Apparently these are not questions that so called 'holy fathers' of the Church such as Tertullian or Augustine could bear to fathom, but should we be surprised when they glorified a God that they were bit by bit shaping into their image? More and more with every morsel of information I devoured, I began to see how God was being shaped by men and not the other way around. Following this path, I soon began to learn about the true Light of women, and how Western religion has robbed an entire gender of their birthright all because it blamed one single woman from the very beginning: Eve. In rediscovering Eve, I had no idea I would find two other powerful images of women that had been exiled from the story of Creation...

5. Eve

According to Genesis, in the beginning there was a garden named Eden, and in the garden were the first man and woman ever created. Adam and Eve lived in the bliss of innocence, like children they had the whole of God's creation as their playground. There was no pain, hate, hunger, or sadness. Knowledge of these things did not even exist. There was only the beauty of Creation, the joy of each other, and the love of the God who visited them. Into this perfect world came only one law:

"And the Lord God commanded the man, saying, "Of every tree of the garden thou mayest freely eat, but of the Tree of the Knowledge of Good and Evil, thou shalt not eat of it, for in the day that thou eatest thereof thou shalt surely die." Genesis 2:16-17, KJV
"And the Lord God commanded the man, "You are free to eat from any tree in the garden; but you must not eat from the tree of the knowledge of good and evil, for when you eat from it you will certainly die." Genesis 2:16-17, NIV

You see, God never gave this commandment specifically to woman, because woman had not been created yet. It was after this command that God recognized that his male human had no partner, and so, as a divine afterthought, God anesthetized Adam and created a helpmate from Adam's rib. Upon awakening, Adam names her: *"woman, because she was taken out of Man."* Genesis 2:21-23, KJV

We are not told how long Adam and Eve live in child-like bliss, but all too soon it seems Eve has a clandestine meeting in the garden:

"*Now the serpent was more subtle than any beast of the field which the Lord God had made. And he said unto the woman, "Yea, hath God said, Ye shall not eat of every tree of the garden?" And the woman said unto the serpent, "We may eat of the fruit of the trees of the garden; but of the fruit of the tree which is in the midst of the garden, God hath said, Ye shall not eat of it, neither shall ye touch it, lest ye die." And the serpent said unto the woman, "Ye shall not surely die. For God doth know that in the day ye eat thereof, then your eyes shall be opened, and ye shall be as gods, knowing good and evil." And when the woman saw that the tree was good for food, and that it was pleasant to the eyes, and a tree to be desired to make one wise, she took the fruit thereof, and did eat, and gave also unto her husband with her, and he did eat. And the eyes of them both were opened...*" Genesis 3:1-7, KJV

"*Now the serpent was more crafty than any of the wild animals the Lord God had made. He said to the woman, "Did God really say, 'You must not eat from any tree in the garden?' The woman said to the serpent, "We may eat fruit from the trees in the garden, but God did say, 'You must not eat fruit from the tree that is in the middle of the garden, and you must not touch it, or you will die.'" "You will certainly not die," the serpent said to the woman, "For God knows that when you eat from it your eyes will be opened, and you be like God, knowing good and evil." When the woman saw that the fruit of the tree was good for food and pleasing to the eye, and also desirable for gaining wisdom, she took some and ate it. She also gave some to her husband, who was with her, and he ate it. Then the eyes of both of them were opened...*" Genesis 3:1-7, NIV

Every time I heard this part of the story I would feel that dramatic sense of dread and sadness. How awful that Eve and Adam had disobeyed God! All I was ever taught to focus on was the message that the first woman had betrayed God's trust and then coerced Adam to follow right along. For this ultimate disobedience all of mankind paid the price by being thrust into an imperfect world full of evil, danger, and pain. It took years of study to see the layers of this story and their true implications. Perhaps the most shocking was the realization that even though the serpent is demonized as a villain, the serpent technically never lies. Christianity would later equate the serpent with Satan, but Judaism never taught this connection. Nowhere in Genesis is it inferred that the serpent is somehow Satan or a demon in disguise (more on this subject in Chapter 21 *Satan, the Devil, and God: A Human Trinity*). For all the connotations of trickery and deception that would become associated with the serpent, let us take a moment to consider that the serpent actually tells the truth!

God made Adam and Eve believe that to even touch the fruit of the Tree of Knowledge would kill them. The serpent insists that this is not true. God is essentially hiding the truth that to eat the fruit will actually bring knowledge of good and evil and make them 'like gods'. I remember being taught that even greater than the sin of Eve's disobedience was that she dared to desire to 'be like God'. Is there a strange double meaning here? After all, Adam is made in the image of God and the highest pinnacle of God's creation. Is Eve somehow aware that she has been put into a secondary role, a role that she is unsatisfied with?

The meaning of words are everything when it comes to unlocking the secrets of any holy text, and in this case there was a big surprise hiding in the serpent's words to Eve. For as long as I could remember, this moment was used to show that Eve's greatest sin was that she dared to desire to 'be like god'. What a blasphemous thought, to even dare to assume that you could somehow make yourself as powerful and omnipotent as the one and only God! But what if that is not what is really being implied? The Hebrew language is complex, and words often serve several purposes and meanings. The word used in Genesis 3:5 is entry number 430 in the *New Strong's Exhaustive Concordance of the Bible* for Elohim: "gods in the ordinary sense... occasionally applied by way of deference to magistrates."

In this case, the same word translated as 'god', is also the same word that was used to imply someone of great authority and power like 'magistrate' or ruler. How does the meaning change if the serpent's intention is to say to Eve: "You shall not die. For God knows that in the day you eat of the tree, then your eyes shall be opened, and you shall be as **magistrates**, knowing good and evil."

Notice that the author of this chapter of Genesis would have known what he meant by the word 'magistrate'. Eve is not seeking to be a 'god', but she may be seeking to be an equal 'magistrate' or co-ruler with Adam. She eats of the fruit because it means that she will become wise, capable of discerning between good and evil. Giving the fruit to her husband implies something even more radical: she and Adam could become equal rulers of God's new world. More importantly, it would not be 'God' who gave Adam knowledge, but his female counterpart. With the understanding of good and evil, a person becomes capable of making their own decisions and governing their own lives. This is the essence of free will. Though many religious people insist that Adam and Eve had free will, how much did they truly have if they were denied such knowledge in the first place? If this theory is followed through, it could be said that free will was not given by God, but was given by Eve who was the first to act on her own desires and not a divine mandate.

Eve seeking equal rulership with her husband may seem a strange thing to people who have read the Bible their whole lives like I did, but when you begin to learn about the history of the ancient world, you discover that it was not uncommon at all for women to rule as queens, priestesses, and magistrates. For a monotheistic religion trying to separate itself from their neighbors, the idea of women having any kind of political or religious power was strictly forbidden. Eve was more than a story about how a single woman ruined paradise. For the people who read the Bible in their own time and language it would have taught another tale: Women have no place in any level of authority.

I would like to point out that up to this point in the Genesis story, Eve technically has no name other than the designation of 'woman'. When she is made from Adam's rib, he simply calls her 'woman'. When the serpent addresses her it is simply as 'woman'. When God finally speaks to her, he does not call her by a name as he does Adam. It is not until after God has placed the curse upon them all the way in verse 20 that Adam finally gives his wife a proper name. There are two possibilities here. The first is that woman is being denigrated the same way a person might have a dog and not bother to give it a proper name ("Here, dog, here, girl!"), and the second is that by not addressing Eve with a given name the

teller of the story is intending to address **all women** who
would listen or read the tale. Even when God calls out to find
the disobedient pair, he calls for Adam alone. It seems an
immense irony that when God inquires of the man (made in
His image) what has happened, Adam's first response is not
one of wisdom, but of blame: *"The woman whom thou gavest
to be with me, she gave me of the tree, and I did eat."*

Once upon a time I believed that the reason Adam ate
the fruit along with Eve was because he loved her so much
that he did not want to risk God taking her away from him.
Now, reading the story with fresh eyes, I could see that love
was not the issue here. The first man was showing that his first
instinct was for self-preservation in passing the blame to both
God and the woman. It made me wonder which side of the
fruit he ate, the Good side or the Evil side? The Genesis story
seems to infer that Adam was there with Eve when she first
ate. Adam could have refused and stood strong for them both,
but instead it would seem Adam was every bit as curious as
she and as willing. Instead of owning up to this, he is
defensive, blaming the woman, and even God for being the
one to give her to him. Eve fares little better, admitting that
she ate because she was 'beguiled' by the serpent.

In this divine blame game, God turns his curse upon the
serpent first, condemning it to slither on the ground eating
dust all the days of its life. Are we seeing a pattern here? One
snake tempts Adam and Eve, and all snakes become cursed.
One woman disobeys and all women for all of history are
cursed. Is this truly a just God who condemns the millions yet
to be born because of the mistakes of the parents?
Interestingly, the 'fall' of Adam and Eve is used in
Christianity as the source of 'original sin' and is the reason
why every human being born supposedly needs salvation. Yet
this doctrine does not exist in Judaism which is the religion

who had this story first! Though so many in Christianity accept the idea of 'original sin' without question, in the end it is a justification that blames everyone for the mistake of a few.

Consider that for hundreds of years in the Middle Ages the Roman Catholic Church blamed all Jews everywhere for the death of Christ, even though the Jews living at that time had nothing to do with any of their ancestors a thousand years before! Today this mentality is condemned as backwards and ignorant, and yet the concept of 'original sin' which condemns all humanity for Adam and Eve is seen as valid. This is what happens when you live in the religious mindset instead of one that is full of spirituality and reason. I would later learn that the serpent in the story has no connection to the modern idea of Satan, however it is connected with a far different and much more deeply hidden figure of the Bible which I will reveal soon.

Next on the list of divine punishment is Eve, who, for the sin of desiring knowledge, is cursed to bear the pains of childbirth and be under the dominion of her husband in the verse I quoted at the start of this chapter. How strange it became to me as I began to ponder why would God punish woman with a painful birth? What did that really have to do with her seeking knowledge? The answers to that would come only when I began to discover a hidden female figure in the Old Testament (see Chapter 8 *Asherah*), but let us continue with the divine punishments. Turning to Adam, God curses him to a miserable life of toil and struggle, but not before He heaps some more guilt onto Eve by starting with: *"Because you listened to the voice of your wife..."* Genesis 3:17, KJV

God could have called Adam out on trying to hide from him. He could have brought him to task for his attitude in trying to blame God and Eve instead of taking responsibility for his own freewill. God places more importance on chastising Adam for listening to his wife. On an interesting note, the word 'wife' is a choice made by English translators. The word used in Genesis 3:17 is number 806 in the *Strong's Concordance* and reveals that the Hebrew word actually means 'woman'. It is ambiguous and simply refers to a mortal woman, so translators have chosen to use the word 'wife' because it fits into their personal interpretation of the text, not because there was any kind of institution of 'marriage' between Adam and Eve.

Notice that God never says to Eve: 'Because you listened to the serpent'. Why? For thousands of years of human history this moment when Eve listens to the serpent will become the excuse to see women as disobedient, gullible, weak, and inherently less capable of reasoning than men. And yet, the fact that Eve convinces Adam to eat from the Tree of Knowledge of Good and Evil shows that Eve already possessed far more power and self-certainty than she is given credit for.

This is where we see the beginning of men being warned not to listen to women and indoctrinated to view women as untrustworthy and dangerous. It becomes the strangest of double standards. On the one hand woman is made to look like the weakest and most rebellious of creatures, but on the other hand men begin to view her as being subtle and cunning as the serpent! If this were not enough of a smear campaign on the female gender, God's additional curse that all women should suffer immense pain during childbirth had an even worse impact.

For hundreds of years in Europe any kind of pain relief was denied to women during childbirth because the Church insisted that to circumvent God's curse by making birth easier on a woman was to flout His divine judgement. This mindset actually remained popular until 1853 when Queen Victoria silenced the clergy of the Church of England by undergoing her own labor with the aid of anesthesia. Even if this is not the fate that the authors of Genesis originally intended, this is how dangerous the power of men in religious authority have given these words and their interpretation of them. We see this even to our modern day in the relentless battle that women face in nations controlled by fanatical religious clerics who insist that a woman is the property of her father and husband with no right to her own free will or her own body. Even when husbands do seek to take the side of their wives and help their daughters have a better life, they also face the condemnation of the religious authority and are made to fear the backlash of 'God' in the form of physical punishment by the men in religious power. Biblical verses such as these have become like a loaded gun. They are not dangerous in and of itself, but in the hands of men who seek control through dictatorship and violence it becomes a weapon of horrific destruction.

There was a time when I took this story for face value. I understood it the way that men had interpreted it from their pulpits for ages: Human beings are sinful and that sin originates from the moment that Eve listens to the serpent and eats from the Tree of Knowledge of Good and Evil. No more Eden and no more paradise. Humanity for all of time was barred from paradise all because of this one decision. By the time I returned to this part of the Bible after I had some years of study and knowledge under my own belt, I was able to read Genesis with fresh and eyes and new understanding.

Many religious men throughout history have chosen to make this story into a religiously sanctioned reason for treating women as little more than property. It is as if Eve became a scapegoat for all things wrong and the inherent dangers women could bring into male dominated worlds. For thousands of years women were denied any real position of authority or any kind of independence and it all harkens back to these few verses in Genesis. Why was this imagery of a man and a woman, a snake and a tree of knowledge, so very important to these writers?

When I lived my life with the blinders of faith, I assumed that the Holy Land was some kind of beacon of monotheism. In my religious fantasy, I never once thought about the fact that the people of the Bible lived, traded, warred, and encountered other nations and peoples more frequently than most. If you look at a map, the area of the Middle East that we know as the Holy Land was right in the middle of incredibly vital trade routes. Large numbers of people traveled through this region on their way back and forth to rich empires like Egypt, Greece, Babylon, and even further out towards India and the Asian countries.

I always thought of the people of the Bible as being so isolated, but the truth is that just as goods like cloth and gold were traded, so too were ideas, ideologies, and stories. Imagine the days so very long ago before electricity, before there were even written books, imagine the tradesmen housing their foreign guests and listening to stories of their land by the fire. Stories became so important to share, and the greatest stories were not just the ones dealing with real life, but the stories of their religious beliefs, mythologies, and journeys through life. The Hebrew religion did not develop in a vacuum. That is to say that the texts and stories of the Bible did not just suddenly appear out of thin air. They were written by men who lived in a diverse part of the world where many traders and journeyers went back and forth carrying well known stories from neighboring lands. Imagine my utter shock to discover that many of these neighboring lands also had stories about a tree, a serpent, and a divine woman...

6. The Serpent

Adam named Eve 'The Mother of all Living' and it is a big clue to the fact that Eve holds a much bigger identity than just a mortal woman. Her original Hebraic name of Chava means 'life', but in the ancient world, the title 'Mother of All Living' was carried by divine female figures: goddesses. Particularly the goddesses Isis and Ishtar, both of whom were held in very high regard in the ancient world. They were beloved and their worship was found throughout the region stretching from Egypt, the Middle East, and all the way to modern day Iraq. Both of these figures are goddesses of creation, pregnancy, childbirth, the beauty of life, the act of love, they guarded the processes of death and the promised rebirth into eternal life.

Isis belonged to the Egyptian religion, while Ishtar belonged to the Babylonians, but the adoration of these two divinities was widespread throughout the Middle East. Both cultures believed in sacred trees that held knowledge **and** immortality, a divine tree upon which the entire world is set. This idea of a Sacred Tree is held by numerous cultures who predate Judaism, from the Aborigines of Australia and the Vedic religions of India, into more recent ancient history with the Vikings of northern Scandinavia. Trees are symbols of regeneration and immortality because they undergo a death and rebirth every year in shedding their leaves, becoming dormant, and returning to verdant life.

Like the Tree, snakes were a symbol that held immense respect and recognition in ancient cultures. A well-known symbol in Egypt, even worn on the headdresses of royalty, snakes denoted wisdom and eternal life. In Sumeria and later

Babylon the snake was a sign of priestesses and women who represented the deity. In ancient Crete, a small Mediterranean island whose culture was filled with art and advancements like indoor plumbing, images of their priestesses holding snakes in their hands is prevalent. If this is beginning to sound familiar to you, it should, because in the ancient world there was a consistent and intimate connection between women and serpents.

As I said before, the Hebrew stories were not created out of thin air; the writers of the Bible were well acquainted with the beliefs of their neighbors. The story of Eve and the serpent at the Tree of Knowledge is well connected to these older religious stories, but it is the first time the result of the woman and serpent is one of a curse instead of a blessing on humanity. To this day the snake's association with the powers of life and death is still recognized in our modern medical symbol of two snakes entwined on a rod called a caduceus. So powerful was this association that in spite of God commanding his people to never make graven images, it is through the image of a bronze snake on Moses' staff that God heals his own people from snake bites:

"And the Lord said unto Moses, Make thee a fiery serpent, and set it upon a pole: and it shall come to pass, that every one that is bitten, when he looketh upon it, shall live. And Moses made a serpent of brass, and put it upon a pole, and it came to pass, that if a serpent had bitten any man, when he beheld the serpent of brass, he lived." Numbers 21:8-9, KJV

"The Lord said to Moses, "Make a snake and put it up on a pole; anyone who is bitten can look at it and live." So

*Moses made a bronze snake and put it up on a pole. Then
when anyone was bitten by a snake and looked at the bronze
snake, they lived.*" Numbers 21:8-9, NIV

These are the moments in the Old Testament where I
truly began to question this 'God'. Why would a loving God
send a bunch of snakes to inflict his own people that he
cherished so much, resulting in a great number of deaths, only
to change his mind and give Moses the power to heal them
through the image of a snake? How contradictory is this 'God',
when He has commanded his people to not put any kind of
faith in manmade images, yet instead of just reaching out his
hand to heal his people, he has Moses make them look upon a
manmade metal serpent? The very same creature that God
himself deemed to curse since the very beginning in Eden. Is it
just me or is the god of the ancient Israelites coming across as
a bit bi-polar?

For a creature that is now feared for its bite, why does
the snake have this reputation for healing and rebirth? In spite
of some breeds of snake being highly venomous, many are
also harmless and non-aggressive. They serve an important
function in nature by keeping rodent populations down, or
even smaller species like garden snakes who eat flies and
insects. Like the cat, this quality of the serpent is a healing
quality in that it eats creatures that have been responsible for
bouts of plague and illness. The one thing all snakes have in
common is that they shed their skin in order to grow; in a way
going through periods of 'rebirth'. A woman's constant
shedding and renewing of the womb via the menstrual cycle
mirrored this serpentine ability, for often menstrual blood
carried similar healing powers and taboos and I believe there
is a link between the two. Snakes may have become a
feminine symbol because of the determination and

protectiveness of mother snakes to their eggs and offspring.

Born of eggs (like birds), many species of snake are capable of not only moving on land but also in water, an ability that the ancients equated with being able to travel across the boundaries of life and death which is attested to in many Egyptian and Indian iconography. Anthropologists have found that these beliefs about the serpent continue even in indigenous cultures like the Native Americans and tribes in South America and Indonesia. The undulating, spiraling motion of the snake can be hypnotic, a method for going into trance and experiencing altered states of awareness. These images have existed for tens of thousands of years in the spiral forms found on paleolithic rock art all the way to the concept of the spiral labyrinth and even themes in modern art and jewelry. We still see this acknowledged and even celebrated in certain sects of Christianity who willingly handle snakes as part of their religious experience. For all of these reasons and more the serpent was not only regarded but respected as a symbol of power, secrets, and especially the knowledge of death and rebirth.

Because it was woman who also carried the secrets of conception and birth, it was frequently women who handled many aspects of death, sitting and caring for the ill and dying and helping them as they transitioned from the world of the living into that of the dead. For instance, the goddess Ishtar was said to have entered into the world of the dead, passing through seven gates, at each gate having to remove an article of clothing - much like the snake shedding its skin - until at the very last she was completely naked. After spending three days and nights in the dark of the underworld, Ishtar is finally reborn in all her splendor (just as Jesus and numerous other deities do). For this reason she was seen as a guide for those in the process of leaving behind their mortal bodies to enter into this world. I wish to remind you that in our time we see these stories as mere 'myths', but during the times of the Bible, these stories were the foundation for the religions that surrounded the Holy Land.

These images of a goddess and the snake guarding the Tree of Knowledge and Life while her male companion stood beside her were well known in the ancient Middle East and certainly to the ancient Hebrews who lived in an area that was the crossroads between empires such as the Egyptians and Babylonians. Knowing this, it is easy for Biblical historians and scholars to see that the writers of Genesis were using motifs and themes that had been familiar for thousands of years in the area. The difference is that the meanings became completely recast and twisted.

The Hebrews were trying to establish a monotheistic belief, a religion of only one all-powerful and all-knowing God. To do this, they had to axe any belief or mention of a divine female counterpart - something done with great success to Yahweh's divine wife Asherah (Chapter 8 *Asherah*). All other gods and goddesses and spiritual stories were threats. Instead of knowledge and eternal life through rebirth being a gift of a feminine and masculine divinity, they instead became forbidden objects. Even the images of a woman and a serpent, the very symbols of birth and everlasting life through rebirth, became twisted. The Light of this allegory became lost when it was turned into propaganda about woman's weak will and the serpent's deviousness. Why?

Because under the Hebraic belief system all power, all knowledge, all life must fall under only God's control. To have it accessible any other way would undermine this idea of God and reduce his power, making him like any other man-made deity. In a way their fears were well founded, for the Hebrew God did begin as any other deity.

Yahweh was a war god known to certain tribes in the southern Middle East for centuries before the rise of what we think of as the Hebrew people. Scholars now believe that Yahweh was part of a pantheon of deities that included El, Baal, and Asherah, which is why these names are so prevalent in the Old Testament. At some point the followers of Yahweh experienced a schism and broke away, which explains why there are so many incidents of Yahweh's prophets and priests fighting against followers of Baal and Asherah. Yahweh still retains these qualities in the numerous Biblical passages glorifying war and unflinchingly commanding the Hebrews to violently slaughter innocent women and children:

"*Now go and smite Amalek, and utterly destroy all that they have, and spare them not: but slay both man and woman, infant and suckling, ox and sheep, camel and ass.*" 1 Samuel 15:3, KJV

Before I began to understand and learn any of this, I was as blind to the inconsistencies of Genesis as any other religious person. I did not realize that these were stories that were being related by the Hebrews for the Hebrews! Everything written in the Old Testament serves the purpose of Hebraic politics, hopes, fears, and propaganda to further their own people. It was never originally intended to become the holy text of non-Jews! This is why there is such chaos and commotion when Christianity picks up during the Roman Empire, because the Jews recognized that these texts belonged to their culture and was never intended to hold power or sway over the gentiles. To this day Judaism does not actively seek converts and those who wish to join the Jewish faith often must prove themselves. This is how strongly Judaism recognizes that their belief is intended for their own culture and theirs alone.

One aspect I certainly had never noticed is that, for all of
the blame laid on the serpent, the serpent is actually the
innocent character in this story. God warns Adam not to eat
the fruit of the tree of knowledge, saying that if Adam does so,
he will surely die. The meaning and intent is that to eat of the
tree will cause immediate death. God never tells Adam what
else will happen if the fruit is eaten. The serpent, in speaking
to Eve, tells her that she and Adam will not die, but instead
will have their eyes opened and 'become like God' but the
actual translation should be 'become like gods'. In the previous
chapter, I showed that the word being used may even mean
'magistrates' or 'rulers'. The reason for so much confusion is
that the way the Hebrew text is written leaves a lot of room for
uncertainty. The Hebrew texts do not contain vowels and
punctuation did not exist in the ancient world. Because of this,
translators are often left to pick and choose what is
emphasized and what is not based only on their own
preferences. Nothing smashed my perception of the Bible's
'inerrancy' like discovering just how much difficulty
translators have had in discerning what certain words or
passages really mean. One would think God would have given
them visions to make it all clear, but alas that never happened.
So instead we are left with ambiguity and more questions than
answers. Still, what matters to this interpretation is that, true to
the serpent's word, neither of them dies.

Some in the religious area argue that God did not mean
that Adam and Eve would die instantly, only that because of
eating from the tree that death would come into the world for
the first time. The problem with this interpretation is that after
God curses the pair, he then speaks to someone else (whose
identity will be addressed later), saying that it is imperative

that man not be allowed to eat of the Tree of Life, lest he live forever…

"And the Lord God said, Behold the man is become as one of us, to know good and evil and now, lest he put forth his hand and take also of the tree of life and eat and live forever…" Genesis 3:22, KJV

"And the Lord God said, 'The man has now become like one of us, knowing good and evil. He must not be allowed to reach out his hand and take also from the tree of life and eat and live forever." Genesis 3:22, NIV

Adam and Eve had not gotten the chance to eat of the Tree of Life; since that is what grants immortality, it meant that death was already built into the human condition. One also has to wonder, why does God even need a Tree of Life to imbue immortality? Why are these forbidden trees even in the vicinity of Adam and Eve if it is so vital that humanity not have access to them? Was he already playing the part of a trickster, challenging them from the very beginning? When I thought about this, it made me feel as though God was treating humanity as little more than a species for observation in a test tube. How can we be taught moral values by a God that deceives his own creation through his contradictory way of thinking?

This is what I've had to deal with in my heart. This is why I have understood who God really is… at least the god of man. Some will say that we should not question God, but I beg to differ when God so blatantly behaves in the manner of an imperfect human being and not something worthy of worship. To make matters even more interesting, there is a big elephant in this religious room that is rarely discussed and often pushed aside by Jewish and Christian translations alike. One of the words for 'God' that is used frequently in Genesis is 'Elohim'. Elohim in Hebrew is **plural**. So, technically, the word that should be used in Genesis is 'Gods'. This discrepancy has never adequately been explained by either Jewish or Christian theologians. It has been the will of human translators over the centuries to translate Elohim as 'God', rather than 'Gods'. This will only make sense once I address the figure known as Asherah.

Part of this mystery can be explained, but only with knowledge gleaned not from the Bible, but from the very earth of the land we've come to know as Israel. Archaeologists excavating in Israel have uncovered a great deal of evidence from the early kingdoms of Israel and Judah indicating that religious history was nowhere near as simple as the Bible tries to paint it. For spans of centuries they have uncovered a persistent presence of clay figurines of women, most of which are on display at their universities and museums. These clay figures are usually pillar shaped, with a head and face, and small arms that support large breasts. They are believed to represent a goddess named Asherah, and despite a constant religious mandate that there was only one single God, she seems to have had a continuous presence in Hebrew life. To scholars' great surprise, these 'graven' images were even found in areas lived in by the families of Levitical priests - the very last places anyone expected to find an image forbidden by God. Before we discuss who this vital feminine deity was, allow me to continue with this issue of Genesis. As if everything I have shown here did not sow plenty of doubt in my mind, I soon found that there was a twist to Eve's story. There was an Eve before Eve, a woman whose story had not only been concealed but turned into a cautionary work of sex and horror!

Nothing prepared me for meeting Lillith.

7. Lillith

Lillith: Sexual deviant, demon, saboteur, the very first feminist, and the original 'Eve' that no one was supposed to know about. Those in ancient days who recognized that the story of Adam and Eve was written purely as an allegory had no problem removing Lillith from the Garden of Eden. Her tale was too dangerous for men, and too inspirational for women. In the very beginning when Hebrew nomads began to tell the story of Adam and Eve, it held the purpose of showing women what their 'natural' role was in society. Ultimately, it emphasized that women were never supposed to think of themselves as attaining any role that was equal to men. In our modern day we take for granted a society in which women have a voice, but even only a hundred years ago women had no roles in most modern governments and were fighting for every little bit of equality they could get. How much worse for women in a time when the population was illiterate and every word that came out of a religious leader was taken to be the ultimate judgement?

Lillith's story appears nowhere in the Bible, so it's no surprise that most religious people have never heard of her. Some sects of Judaism know of her, but in their eyes she remains only as a shadow of her former self: a demon. This is what was made of a woman who was supposed to have been the first ever created. A woman made in the image of God just as Adam had been, created from the same earth as man. Unlike Eve, made out of Adam from his own rib, Lillith was created separately and equally. But Lillith's story could never have a happy ending in a society where men needed to keep women in their place domestically and even sexually.

Nomadic societies like the early Hebrews rely on family groups staying together and a continuous replenishing both of the animals that are their livelihood and the people who make up their population. Just as female livestock were vital, so were their women. Death from childbirth was common and most women did not live past their teens. But was that desert life something that women would have always chosen for themselves? Did some look with envy upon the cultures of Egypt or Babylon where women could move freely, dress how they pleased, love whoever they wanted, get divorced, and even hold their own power through wealth and religion? These 'foreign' women that the Bible warns its men about held statuses of independence that nomadic Hebrew women could not even dream of. Women have never been stupid. Those who would have witnessed the happier conditions of their neighboring societies must have wanted some of the same freedoms. What better way to keep your wives and daughters close to the tents than to instill in them the recognition that women who reach too far are made to suffer divine wrath?

In every generation there have been women who have tried to speak out against oppression, women who have sought to attain so much more than the roles dictated to them. This must have been true of women in Biblical times or else the constant barrage of rules confining what they could and could not do would not have been so important. For these women, Lillith became the warning to any woman who dared to demand more of life and man.

So where is Lillith's story? I certainly never heard of her when I read the Bible. Lillith did not become known to me until I began to discover that there are hundreds of books in existence that never became part of the Bible because they were too controversial. Lillith's story is one of these books. To understand why other books matter, you have to understand a little history about how the Bible came into being. For so many who believe that the Bible is the inerrant word of God, the belief is that the Bible is the same today as it was hundreds, even thousands of years ago. From the number of books included to the order in which they are arranged, I really used to think that the Bible had always looked that way. What a rude awakening I received! Far from singular and perfect, the Bible is a patchwork of history, the work of many authors whose identities and names are lost to the sands of time.

Many of the texts can be dated to particular times in history based upon evidence not only from carbon dating but literary and language analysis. Scholars compare the writings to other works written in roughly the same time periods. They are armed with a historical understanding of what was going on at the time politically and religiously. They shed light on the authors' motivations for interpreting a story a certain way or emphasizing a particular issue over another. Before we continue, I want to share a little knowledge about how scholars have been able to recognize the work of different authors in the Bible, for instance the fact that the book of Genesis has at least two different authors separated by time and culture.

The belief that Moses authored the first five books of the Bible (known in Judaism as the Torah) is a religious fallacy. Those with religious blinders will insist that each word is attributed to the man who supposedly led the Hebrews out of the land of Egypt, but there simply is little to no historical or archaeological evidence for this belief. Not that this ever bothered me when I had my blinders on. Through sheer blind faith I really felt it was just that archaeologists hadn't found the evidence yet, but someday they would. Now I understand why that view wasn't just naive, it was completely ignorant. Ignorance is not bliss. What is known is that the people who would become Israelites began as a nomadic tribe of the desert.

Unfortunately what scholars know has had little impact on the beliefs of religious people whether they are Jewish, Christian, or Muslim. This is not because the information is not available, but because religious clergy simply do not want to hear it. After all, it is in the best interest of those in religious power to keep a status quo. Their religious systems give them political clout and allows for great sums of wealth to flow in all by the influence of 'God'. Biblical scholars feel certain that there are four authors at work in the Torah and that the books were never a single unit, but the work of multiple generations and centuries of Israelite culture that were finally edited as a whole and stitched together sometime after the end of the Babylonian exile around 332 BC.

When it comes to the Creation story in Genesis, scholars believe that the two Creation stories were written at different times in Israel's history and by two very different writers. The first Creation story (Genesis 1) belongs to an author who wrote somewhere around 597-586 BC, around the time of Israel's exile into the metropolitan kingdom of Babylon (modern day Iraq). Much of the wording actually mirrors creation stories of the spiritual traditions of both Babylon and Egypt - two well established kingdoms whose cultures and stories were well known throughout the area, including what we know as the Middle East. The second Creation story (Genesis 2-3) was written by an author living in the northern kingdom of Israel around 799-700 BC and so is believed to be the older of the two stories. God behaving in such a human manner (much like the gods of Sumeria, Egypt, etc.), shows that Hebrew belief was still evolving, still developing especially in its concept of a single god.

Even the imagery of a man and woman standing before a mystical fruit bearing tree with a serpent entwined around it was not unique to the Genesis story - as I have already addressed, it was a scene familiar to thousands in the ancient Middle Eastern world because it was depicted on coins and seals that survive to this day in museums. In particular, a cylinder seal dated to between 2330-2150 BC with 'Sacred Tree, Horned Goddess, Serpent, and Priest'. Images can easily be found by putting these items into an internet search. The great difference, of course, is that while the Hebrew tradition painted it as the scene of humanity's 'Fall', the rest of the ancient world viewed it as a sign of the gift of wisdom and knowledge from the Divine pair of feminine and masculine.

For over two millenniums the Bible was not the single bound book we have today. The Old Testament was not even a single volume, but instead a loose collection of stories, histories, and laws. When Jewish leaders finally set down to canonize (legitimize) the books of the Bible, it involved a long process of looking over dozens and dozens of texts and putting it to a vote on what should be allowed into the Bible and what should not be allowed. Notice that in spite of certain religions claiming the Bible is the inerrant word of God, they never bother to really mention this aspect of the Bible's history. They ignore the fact that the Bible came down to the decisions of a governing body of religious men to pick and choose at their discretion what was and was not worthy to be in the Bible. For instance, though the Book of Esther is beloved in the Old Testament, it was nearly put on the chopping block and left out of the Bible. In the records of these religious councils it is apparent that these delegations of religious men frequently disagreed with each other and sometimes even came to stalemates on deciding if a book was to be accepted or tossed aside. So much for being a work of the Holy Spirit! The Tanakh (the Old Testament) portion of the Bible was canonized over a long period from 200 BC to around AD 200, while the Christian Bible took shape over an even longer period with the first 27 books of the New Testament being chosen by St. Athanasius in AD 367, and officially closed and agreed upon in AD 1442. Dozens of books were declared 'heretical' and left out of the Bible - not because God declared it so, but because human men with religious power took a vote and made it so based on their own interpretations and preferences.

I think it is fair to ask that if the Bible is truly the holy word of God and that God himself chose holy men to complete this task, then why do we have councils of men who barely could agree with each other? If the process was supposed to be holy and perfect, why so much disagreement and argument? Are we really still expected to believe that the Bible is a book of perfection when even the books contained within it were never chosen 'perfectly' let alone written perfectly? So many books and stories were left out of the Bible that they began to form their own collection known as the Apocrypha, as well as mystical texts deemed too 'heretical' for consideration that continued to be written for centuries after the Bible had been canonized.

One of the stories that was thrown aside was a long standing myth about Adam's first wife. The story of Lillith survives in a medieval Jewish text called *The Alphabet of Ben Sirah*. Though the book dates from sometime before the year AD 1000, the character of Lillith had been around since at least 2000 BC, and was well known to Babylonian, Assyrian,

Israelite, and Egyptian cultures. She is referenced once in the book of Isaiah 34.

Just as scholars have noticed that there are two Creation stories in Genesis, some religious leaders noticed it too and actually expanded upon it. In this retelling of the Creation, God did create Adam, but he also created a woman:

"So God created man in his own image, in the image of God created he him; male and female created he them."
Genesis 1:27, KJV
"So God created mankind in his own image, in the image of God he berated them; male and female he created them."
Genesis 1:27, NIV

Acknowledging that this meant God may have made a woman before taking Eve from Adam's rib, the authors of this work named her Lillith. They believed that the first Genesis story implied that she was created at the exact same time and the exact same way that Adam was, essentially making her equal to Adam. Because of this knowledge, Lillith has an instant attitude problem… at least in the eyes of her male authors and readers. She will not obey Adam and does as she pleases. In her eyes, Adam is full of pride and she resents his attempts to make her submit. Lillith is more than happy to remind him that because they were both created from the earth they are essentially equal and he has no right to claim dominion over her. I would like to point out that Lillith does not try to control Adam and only resents his attempts at controlling her. The final straw comes when Lillith insists that she does not enjoy having to be on the bottom sexually and refuses to lay beneath Adam, insisting instead on being on top.

When Adam and God try to force her into submission, she does the unthinkable by uttering the sacred name of God which gives her the power to flee Eden. Vanishing into the wilderness, she apparently finds sexual satisfaction with demons. Lillith becomes a demonic entity herself, the true 'Mother' of demons! In the wake of Lillith's desertion, God then creates Eve out of Adam's rib, sending a clear message that this time the woman is simply a part of man and not equal to him in creation. After Adam and Eve are expelled from Eden, Lillith becomes a curse to humanity. She is faulted with targeting pregnant women to miscarry and is blamed for coming to men in their dreams, seducing them, and causing 'nocturnal emissions' (aka 'wet dreams').

How telling that the first woman created in equality is reduced to a monster responsible for killing unborn babies and stealing men's semen in their sleep in order to create more nightmarish demons to plague humanity. Some Jewish traditions will even insist that it was Lillith who took the form of a serpent to cause Adam and Eve's downfall. It seems men of all time periods have acknowledged that 'hell has no fury like a woman scorned'! It is obvious that the writers of these texts recognized that women were capable of having immense power and influence. They used Lillith as a tool to instill fear of women who insisted on equality or thought for themselves.

Interestingly, just like the Tree of Knowledge and the serpent were part of the spiritual traditions of Sumeria and Babylon, so was Lillith. To the Babylonians, Lillith was a divine being in her own right, associated with death and the darkness of the night in the form of owls and lions. Lillith's name means 'night owl'. In Babylonian myths she is a figure you never want to run into in the dark, wild deserts. The manner in which the Jews adopted her as a figure of their own, making her into a wife for Adam, is a good example of how cultures frequently swapped stories and mystical characters.

Judaism absorbed and adapted many elements of Sumerian, Babylonian, and Egyptian religion into their own religious and mystical traditions. Lillith became a popular legend in Jewish circles for many centuries, and her story only emphasized points that had been made with Eve: Women who think they are equal to men are dangerous; they have no place in a society controlled by men both politically and religiously.

It's fascinating how the issue of sex is paramount in Lillith's story. It is bad enough that Lillith had a will of her own because she was capable of denying Adam, but the biggest battle ground was the issue of sexual submission. From these early beginnings we begin to see these themes that a woman who dares to assert any kind of control over her own body and desires is not only dangerous, but bound to end up a sexual deviant, whoring with demons and seducing the dreams of righteous men.

If I thought that Lillith was going to be the great surprise of the Old Testament, I had no concept that an even greater female figure loomed. So great was this feminine force that she could not be relegated as some 'demon' the way that Lillith was. She was no mere seducer or deviant. She was Holy Mother, the Creatrix, and the divine half of Yahweh. She had been skillfully hidden by scribes for thousands of years until the hard work of Biblical historians and archaeologists would raise her back to life. I was about to discover the Wife of God.

8. Asherah

What a beautiful and pleasant surprise that God the Father had indeed had a consort: Goddess the Mother, his Wife, and our Divine Mother in heaven. I had no idea that Yahweh had a wife named Asherah! For all the years of my religious life, I had only ever been preached to about my Father in heaven. Even in the midst of my religious mindset, I had to ask myself why was there no heavenly Mother? For Catholic Christians the belief remained that Mary, the virgin mother of Christ, was in a way divine and had earned the title 'Blessed Mary, Mother of God'. And yet Catholics were always reminded that their worship must ultimately be directed to God the Father in whom all power lies. Mary may have been good enough to carry the child of God, but she was apparently not divine enough to be his consort. I will return to the crucial figure of Mary when I look at the treatment of women in Chapter 19 *Eve and Mary: The Sinner and the Redeemed.*

In the Old Testament God rules alone in heaven, a King with no Queen, a divine Father who had shut out the Mother. I believed that this was the way things had always been since the beginning of the Bible and that this had been the belief of the Israelites. I would soon discover that early Israelite culture and religion may have been every bit as diverse as early Christianity and that their monotheism may never have been so black and white.

Though ancient Israel is credited with a staunch belief in a single God, monotheism does not seem to be a belief that always sat well with the people of Israel. Again and again the words of Hebrew prophets such as Isaiah, Jeremiah, and

Ezekiel are constantly berating and cajoling the people of ancient Israel to let go of the worship of 'idols' and return to the strict adherence of following Yahweh alone. One of the most persistent 'idols' in these texts is Asherah. Asherah is mentioned more than forty times throughout nine different books of the Old Testament.

For many years Biblical scholars were left scratching their heads about who or what 'asherah' was. In some places it seems as though Asherah is a foreign deity and might even be male, in other parts of the text asherah seems to refer to some kind of wooden idol. Commands against anything having to do with her worship can be found in the Torah book of Deuteronomy:

"Destroy completely all the places on the high mountains, on the hills, and under every spreading tree, where the nations you are dispossessing worship their gods. Break down their altars, smash their sacred stones, and burn their Asherah poles in the fire; cut down the idols of their gods and wipe out their names from those places." Deuteronomy 12:2-3, NIV (the KJV translation chose to completely remove the reference to asherah).

Was Asherah a person or a thing? The confusion of Asherah's identity would not be clarified until the science of archaeology began to reveal one of the most stunning and hidden figures of ancient Israel.

While the Bible may try to say that Israel believed in only one God, the archaeological evidence began to say that God had a matching Goddess and that the Biblical texts were purposely trying to hide and confuse her identity. Many scholars began to suspect that Asherah was related to the Mother goddesses Ishtar and Astarte whose worship was prevalent amongst Israel's neighbors. They suspected that Asherah was being worshipped alongside Yahweh even as late as the time of Jeremiah in the seventh century BC when the prophet refers to her by the common title of 'Queen of Heaven':

"But since we left off to burn incense to the Queen of Heaven, and to pour out drink offerings unto her, we have wanted all things, and have been consumed by the sword and by the famine. And when we burned incense to the Queen of Heaven, and poured out drink offerings unto her, did we make her cakes to worship her, and pour our drink offerings unto her, without our men?" Jeremiah 44:18, KJV

"But ever since we stopped burning incense to the Queen of Heaven and pouring out drink offerings to her, we have had nothing and have been perishing by sword and famine." The women added, *"When we burned incense to the Queen of Heaven and poured out drink offerings to her, did not our husbands know that we were making cakes impressed with her image and pouring out drink offerings to her?"* Jeremiah 44:18, NIV

For many years Biblical scholars simply did not know for certain whether or not their suspicions were right until an archaeological find in 1975 in Kuntillet Ajrud in the Sinai Peninsula. There ceramic jars were found with strange symbols of humans and animals alongside Hebrew inscriptions. One of the inscriptions includes a blessing for the owner: "May you be blessed by Yahweh and his Asherah." As the years went on and more archaeological sites were dug, hundreds of artifacts began to appear that by all means should never have come into existence in a land where the people followed only one almighty Father.

Clay statuettes of women began to appear in the hundreds and more references to Asherah were found. It became quickly apparent that Asherah was a goddess and one of her most important symbols were trees.

From references in the Bible it would seem that her worship often took place outdoors beneath whole groves of verdant trees. She even had associations with serpents, leading many scholars to question whether or not the story of Eve, the serpent, and the Tree of Knowledge may have been a leftover from far older beliefs of the Israelites. If Asherah is a goddess with ties to the serpent, then it is arguable that Lillith, who was also a candidate to have been the serpent in the garden, was also seen in a goddess role. If this is the case, then Lillith's demotion to being made from the muck of the earth alongside Adam as a human being may have been a purposeful twist in the story to demote her from the goddess status she once held. Though Asherah's worship seems to be prevalent amongst laypeople in ancient Israel, for some reason Asherah became enough of a threat to the Levitical priesthood that by the time they address her in the Bible they make her out to be little more than a foreign idol and just another pagan fertility goddess. This knowledge is even more shocking considering that her statues were found not just in the homes of everyday Israelites, but in sacred areas and temples devoted to Yahweh.

Why was Asherah's worship allowed at all in a nation who claimed to follow only a single God? The answer lies perhaps in the fact that the reigning Levitical priesthood was trying to enforce a religion that was unique. So much so that it went completely against the grain of human experience and spiritual common sense. Let us begin with this insistence upon the masculinity of God. Because there was only one God, some have insisted that God had no gender at all, and yet the God of Israel could not help but be completely masculine. Yahweh was a war god and the words used to refer to him are always distinctly masculine. Even in the story of Creation in Genesis, the laws of nature are turned upside down when God chooses to create man first and then the woman out of the man. Since the dawn of human experience birth was a gift to women. Whether human or animal, new life must always be gestated, birthed, and nurtured by the body of the female. The masculine also has his part in nature and because of this nearly every single culture and empire that surrounded ancient Israel believed that the Divine always came in pairs of masculine and feminine: a God and a Goddess, a Father and a Mother. There were great implications in this idea when it came to human sexuality, but I will address that in the next section *When Love Is Blind.*

In our modern world we still recognize the wonder and the dangers of conceiving a child and giving birth. Today the world is overpopulated, but in the ancient world giving birth and raising children was crucial to the survival of whole cultures and nations. Without the benefit of modern medicine, it was not uncommon for whole peoples to be wiped out by plague, famine, or war. Because of this, God's commandment in Genesis 1:27-28 to 'be fruitful and multiply' was taken so literally that nearly all of the sexual laws in the Bible revolve around ensuring that women continue to give birth to ensure the survival of God's 'chosen people' the Israelites. This mandate is not just to fill census records, but because without a thriving population there can be no viable army to protect, defend, and continue this way of life. Given the high death rates, when a nation needs to survive, the fertility of women become the doorways and only insurance for an ethnic religious group like the Israelites to survive. But in a nation where birth was the greatest importance a women had, who could women look towards for comfort and spiritual reassurance in the midst of pregnancy and motherhood? Certainly not an almighty Father God of war.

Though Yahweh commands his people to be fruitful and multiply, he offers little support when it comes to the actual moments of birth or the trials and travails women must face. After all, this is the same God who made childbirth painful as a curse upon all women for all time. Just as human women have looked towards their mother figures for comfort and support during pregnancy, so too women of the ancient world looked towards a Divine Mother for guidance and strength. Who better to worship and find reassurance in than Asherah, Queen of Heaven, Mother of All Living who birthed all life and who knew intimately the pains, worries, hopes, and sorrows of women?

Some Biblical scholars hypothesize that the reason Asherah's worship continued for so long in ancient Israel is because the ruling Levitical class chose to look the other way. I highly recommend the work of William G. Dever and his wonderful book *Did God Have A Wife?* for anyone who wishes to study this topic further. He takes a long and in-depth look at all the archaeological evidence for Asherah and comes to the conclusion that there may have been a disconnect between the high born Levitical priesthood and the common folk of ancient Israel. Because of this, the strict monotheistic religion being practiced in the Old Testament may not actually be a fair representation of what the common everyday men and women of the Holy Land were actually practicing. Because of cleanliness laws, men had little to do with overseeing the health of pregnant women or helping at all in the birthing process. These things were women's true domain and because of this when the women chose to have a clay idol of Asherah, it is likely that men simply ignored it as being part of 'women's religion'.

No matter how much this issue may have been whitewashed in the Old Testament, there is precedent for women in the Bible looking towards their own goddess. In Genesis the patriarch Jacob falls in love with Rachel, but is tricked into marrying her older sister Leah and must work for their father seven more years in order to marry Rachel. I would like to note that Jacob is Rachel and Leah's first cousin on his mother's side. Eventually he packs up both wives to return to the land of his grandfather Abraham. Rachel does something that seems strange to Bible readers; she steals her father's household 'idols' and takes them with her. This means that Jacob's uncle Laban is worshipping idols. This is further proof that early Hebraic belief was not fully monotheistic and divisions of belief already existed.

In the midst of their journey Leah and Rachel's father Laban rides out and accuses Jacob of the theft; Jacob informs him that he is free to search the camp. Unbeknownst to him that his beloved wife is the culprit, Jacob curses the thief with death. When Laban comes to Rachel's tent, she hides them beneath her cushions and claims she cannot rise because she is menstruating. Laban leaves, but Rachel has no idea that her own husband has cursed her. Ironically, though many interpret her as saying she was menstruating, we are then told she was pregnant and during the journey gives birth to her second son Benjamin. The birth is so traumatic that she dies and is buried.

Why did the 'idols' mean something to Rachel? I personally believe one possibility is that Rachel suffered infertility in a culture where the ability to produce sons was a woman's greatest worth. By the time Rachel finally conceives a son for Jacob, her sister had already given birth to six sons and one daughter. Since it is obvious that Yahweh had no interest in helping her conceive, it is possible that Rachel turned to goddesses such as Asherah who would understand her plight. That she is pregnant with her son Benjamin when she takes the idols may show that she felt it was Asherah who had helped her successfully birth Joseph and who she hoped would help see this difficult pregnancy to term. Jacob having no clue that Rachel took the idols may prove that Israelite women often had their own beliefs and their own religious customs that men simply ignored and had no part of. Given that women in these cultures were rarely able to read or write, it is unsurprising that no records remain of the thoughts, feelings, and personal beliefs of these ancient matriarchs.

Discovering Asherah, the consort of Yahweh, I had to wonder, why did Israel's ruling priestly class feel the need to eviscerate her from the Bible? Perhaps for the same reason that God would choose to 'curse' a woman with childbirth. In cursing Eve, the God of Genesis places three specific burdens on the shoulders of all women:

"To the woman he said, "I will make your pains in childbearing very severe; with painful labor you will give birth to children. Your desire will be for your husband, and he will rule over you." Genesis 3:16, NIV

It is my hope that by now you have gained enough understanding to see that the Bible reveals the workings and politics of the men who wrote it instead of the spirituality of an all loving God. Now that you understand that the Genesis story was written as a way for early Israelites to separate themselves and put their own twist on the familiar religious stories of their neighbors, you can begin to see why this particular 'curse' speaks volumes about the way in which the patriarchal religion of the Bible sought to control women. Up until now I have resisted using the term 'patriarchal'. It means a religious or political structure that is created solely by men and serves to keep men in positions of authority and control at the expense and exclusion of women.

In the ancient world, even as other empires began to denigrate women and restrict their rights and powers, the one domain that was seen to be a woman's greatest gift was the gift of life and birth. God curses Eve (and all women after her) to experience the excruciating pain of childbirth, to be a slave to her 'desire' for her husband, and to recognize that she is under her husband's 'dominion'. Even in our modern world we do not have to go very far to witness what this kind of life looks like for women. It is a life in which a woman has no say whatsoever when it comes to her own body. It is a life where a woman is married off at the behest of her father and the right to use her body is solely at her husband's discretion. She does not have the right to say 'no'. She has no right to birth control. She has no right to terminate an unwanted pregnancy even if she is in ill health or is physically exhausted from the strain of multiple pregnancies one after the other. She is taught that any sexual feeling is meant to be geared towards her husband. There is no room for the knowledge that she can satisfy her own sexual desires. While there are many women to this day who find their greatest joy and purpose in motherhood, what becomes of the women who long for something else? Even in our modern world of emancipated women, women who choose to never have children are often looked upon as strange and treated differently. There is good reason why many ancient women did not live past their twenties and it is because of the fact that their role in life was reduced to being the possession of their husband for the purpose of making children to continue his family line.

I remember when my daughter and I first began researching this area, we kept hearing the word 'fertility' an awful lot. After awhile it seemed as though the ancient world was obsessed with it and perhaps nowhere more so than in the Old Testament. We take so much for granted in our modern world. We are so used to seeing the multitudes of people that inhabit this earth that we forget that without the miracle of conception and birth the entire system would come to a halt. Life depends upon life. If herds of animals were not fertile, ancient people would have run out of food and goods like leather and wool for clothing. If crops were not fertile then a whole nation could be wiped out by famine, and if women were not producing large families than the next time an invading army came into town their entire culture and way of life would become extinct! This was the reality of the ancient world and it is still the reality of our modern world.

So why, at a time when the rest of the ancient world was glorifying the act of sexual love and birth, does the patriarchal God of Genesis seek to place a curse upon it? In one fell swoop the writers of Genesis stole the authority of a power and process that had elevated women for thousands of years. In spiritually removing the divine matriarch Asherah they stole the divine Light that has existed in women since the beginning of time. They took away the whole concept that women had an equal say and stake in rulership. The God of the Bible becomes the sole ruler of a religious nation ruled by the words and laws of men and men alone. This is the essence of patriarchy, where women were given no say in how they lived their lives or even in pursuing what spoke to their souls.

Without Asherah, there was no room for human matriarchy, no room for a system in which women can assert the right to govern themselves. In our modern day the theft continues as we look at a Western world shaped solely by the minds of men.

Without the matriarchal Goddess Asherah to balance the divine, women lost their Light.

9. Stolen Identity

For so many years I felt that it was ridiculous to view the Bible as being 'anti-woman' or misogynistic. After all, how could God be either of those things? The truth is that the Creator of humanity isn't, but the god of the Bible as created by man is. The men in political and religious power at the time these books were written certainly were and it was because of their culture and their personal beliefs that the God of the Bible acts the same way. The Levitical priesthood had nothing to lose and everything to gain by enforcing a religious code that stripped women of their status and their rights. In lands like Egypt and Babylon, women could own their own property, divorce their husbands, they had access to birth control, methods of abortion, held positions of authority in their communities and were sometimes magistrates (remember that word from Eve) and rulers in their own right.

We might think of birth control as a modern invention, but the ancient world had a vast knowledge of herbs that our modern world has lost. Women had access to quite a variety of plants and herbal concoctions that served as contraceptives, as well as methods to ensure that there was adequate time between the birth of children to give a woman's body time to rest and recover. Ancient women had an intimate knowledge of the process of conception that women would not regain until the time of modern medicine. As the Biblical mindset took hold many of these methods became forbidden and their knowledge was lost until they became rediscovered by historians. For more on this amazing subject, I recommend *Eve's Herbs* by John M. Riddle. It would even appear that what we think of as 'late term' abortion was rare in the ancient world because most ancient women were able to terminate a pregnancy early on before the flutterings of life began in their womb. Women during the time of the Roman empire apparently had access to an herb that was so effective in preventing conception that it was harvested to extinction. Even pomegranates, a fruit plentiful in the Middle East, had chemical properties that could knock a woman's fertility cycle off course. Again I refer to the important book *Eve's Herbs* for anyone seeking more information even on the history of natural contraception (or to see if common foods or herbs may be preventing conception for women seeking to get pregnant).

Some women could even choose to never marry by entering into a temple devoted to a particular deity as a priestess. As a priestess, some engaged in the acts of sacred lovemaking, never facing the stigma of being the mother of 'illegitimate' children. Such examples of female independence were great threats to the strict religion of ancient Israel and so the lessons of Eve in Genesis served as a warning to any Israelite woman who might start getting ideas. If Genesis did not put women in their place, the rest of the Levitical laws found in the Torah leave little room for doubt.

Before I continue, it is worth learning something about this time of history. During the time of Abraham and his sons Isaac and Jacob, there were no such thing as 'Israelites' and they were considered a loose nomadic tribe. It is not until the story told in the book of Exodus which records how Moses brought the people out of Egypt and into the land of Canaan that the idea of an Israelite identity is formed. Significantly, Israelites are defined by which tribe (or son of Jacob) they descend from. Moses and his brother Aaron, who become the first Levitical priests, are from the tribe of Levi. It is the Levitical priesthood that ordains itself (albeit they claim God has told them they are ordained) as the law makers and law keepers of ancient Israel.

While all the other tribes take portions of land, the Levites instead keep bases in each tribe. They do not have to work the land or toil themselves, instead it is up to the people to bring 'offerings' of flour, oil, and livestock to them. These 'offerings' to the Lord are really the livelihood of the Levitical priesthood and their families. Animals slaughtered as offerings to God, were in fact cooked and eaten by the priesthood while the leftovers were burnt as the offering. This may seem strange, but remember that Levitical priests were married and would have had many children to support and feed. Imagine the stench of the blood and cooking meat that was a constant basis of the Levitical centers - no wonder they had to burn so much incense! Why would God need to have burnt offerings, unless this came from a different need and had been scavenged off of other religious beliefs? Does this really sound like the commandments of an almighty God, or is it the religious and political control of a group of men who set themselves up to be the ultimate power in early Israel?

It is the laws that these Levitical priests created that became the most detrimental and cruel to women. For the Levites the greatest importance was to have sons who could inherit their father's wealth and property. In the eyes of the Levitical priesthood, the only way to establish their family lines was to control the fertility of their women by ensuring that women did not even dare to think about having sex outside of marriage. Because of this we begin to see an immense emphasis on a bride's physical virginity and warnings against marrying foreign women or allowing women to have any contact with non-Israelites. Interestingly, 'adultery' in the ancient world is almost purely a woman's problem. Married men who go out on their wives are never punished as adulterers. It is only if men dare to sleep with a woman who is already married that they have then trespassed against another man and become subject to punishment. Single women are fair game, and especially slaves and foreigners. Ultimately it was only the virginity of their own daughters that became paramount.

Before I began studying ancient history, I really thought that this obsession with a woman staying pure until marriage was something that all ancient cultures shared. I was very wrong. It is true that there were certain spiritual sects in the ancient world where if a woman wanted to be a priestess she might take a vow of chastity. If she broke that vow she would be severely punished or even killed, but even this only applied to certain cultures and deities like the Roman priestesses of the goddess Vesta.

Overall, the ancient Middle East did not show much of a concern over the state of a woman's virginity. In ancient Egypt and Sumeria there were severe laws to punish rapists, but there were no laws punishing women who had premarital sex.

I realize that through religion I was taught that all the other cultures and people who lived around the tribes of Israel during the time of the Bible were nothing but violent, over-sexed pagans. The truth is that Israel's neighbors were no more or less violent than the Hebrews themselves, something which is attested by the hundreds of Bible passages glorying in war and the slaughter of any men, women, and children who are not part of the tribe. It is true that some cultures had human sacrifice, but it's not as constant or prolific as the Bible makes it sound. As for over-sexed, the only reason the Bible views these peoples this way is because the Biblical laws about sex are so incredibly repressive. Cultures outside of Israel viewed sex as something that was not only for the creation of life, but for the sake of pleasurable communion between men and women… and men with men, women with women, but I'll get to that in the next part.

In many cases these ancient societies had a much healthier view about sex than even our own modern day society. From herbal contraception to abortion, ancient women had a deep understanding of their bodies and the mysteries of conception and birth. Thousands of years of these women's knowledge would become lost after the Roman Empire because of the Church declaring such knowledge a criminal offense. The point is that just about anywhere else in the ancient world, women were not persecuted if they had premarital sex and they usually had some form of contraceptive method at their disposal… so why would this be denied to women in the Bible?

To begin with, we really do not know what women in Biblical times did or how they felt about any of this. Because the Bible was written by men, we read only the thoughts and concerns of men. What the women thought of these laws, how they felt about them, or how seriously they even took them is all a mystery. Denied their voices in history, we are denied any knowledge of the hearts, minds, and souls of the women of the Bible. What we can see from the laws is what issues were of the most concern for the men who ran Israel both religiously and politically. When I first came across all these issues, the point kept getting made that these laws were meant to control women through their fertility. The very thought was ridiculous to me! But then I kept investigating and discovered to my total disgust that, yes, they really were.

Before the days of paternity and genetic testing, there was a recognition in the ancient world that a man could not always be sure that the children born in his house were truly his. The identity of the mother was never an issue because the child was born straight from her body, but what about the father? In the Hebrew society of the Bible, all land, all property, all wealth had to pass down to the firstborn son. The greatest concern of an Israelite man was being able to know that the children he worked and cared for were indeed his own blood. In other cultures like the Egyptians, Sumerians, or Babylonians this was not a great concern because women inherited their own property and wealth. Women could pass their inheritance on to their children regardless of the father's identity. In all these other cultures, a woman's sexuality was praised and allowed to be expressed, but in Hebraic culture, woman became the sexual property of her husband. She was available only for his pleasure, to bear his children, and any expression outside of this came with dire consequences. This dangerous concept became inherited by both Christianity and Islam, as both of these religions have based their foundations upon the Old Testament.

This is the kind of society that is obsessed with a woman's virginity, because the man's paranoia is eased only by knowing that he is the first and last man she will ever sleep with. He feels confidence only if she has not had any kind of sexual awakening prior to him. With this notion women are bred from the beginning to understand that their role in sex is only to be receptive to their husbands and bear his children. Remember, this was the lesson of Lillith: A woman who understands and owns her own sexuality is one who will rebel and cause a man nothing but grief.

The incredibly sad thing is that this is a mindset that I still see being perpetuated even by the younger generation! The advent of 'purity balls' are nothing but a continuation of this demented mindset as these young women pledge their virgin status to their fathers until they are married. In our society the notion continues that to be a virgin is to be a 'good girl'. I have even heard mothers still instructing their sons that it's fine if they have sex with a woman, but to always remember that these are not the girls they should marry because they are 'loose'. How can anyone think this mentality is long gone when even now some healthcare systems will cover a drug so that a man can achieve an erection for sex, yet will not cover a woman's birth control? How can we still be having discussions about a woman's right to choose as men in political and religious authority declare that the life of a child unborn is more important than the life of an adult woman? Apparently these religious men have no idea that Judaism does allow abortion and states that the life of a mother outweighs the life of a fetus. This may be so because many mystical sects of religion teach that the Soul does not enter a child until the moment of birth, not the moment of conception. The truth is, we still live in a culture in which men suffer no condemnation by society for sleeping with numerous women, while women who do the same still get stereotyped as 'sluts', 'whores', and 'bad girls'.

The day I actually found out what the word 'virgin' meant was like discovering a new identity. My first clue that something was odd came when I started looking into other gods and goddesses. Over and over again I came across goddesses who bore the title of 'virgin'… and yet these were goddesses whose stories included the fact that they had sex! The concept of 'virgin' was very different in the ancient world and had no connection to the idea of sexual purity in the Bible. To be a 'virgin' did not mean that the woman was sexually inexperienced. It meant that she was a woman who was not owned by any man. To be a 'virgin' was to be a woman who had chosen of her own freewill to not enter into marriage or any relationship that put her in the position of being ruled by a husband. A woman could have never had sex or had sex a hundred times and as long as she was independent of the control of a man she lived in a state of 'virginity'. So, technically, any unmarried or divorced single woman today can honestly say that she is a 'virgin'!

These 'virgin' goddesses were symbols of womanhood, examples of what is possible when a woman was allowed to have power, her own will, and make her own choices about her body. Notice that under Biblical law, virginity became a literal commodity. It was something that was owned from birth by her father before becoming the divine right of her husband. It was never something that belonged to her. It was not hers to give to the man she chooses, but was something that her husband bought by paying her father as he would for any other animal meant for breeding.

Here are some examples of the ways women were treated as property and subjected to crueler and more repressive laws than Biblical men:

"Speak unto the children of Israel, saying, If a woman have conceived a child then she shall be unclean seven days; according to the days of the separation for her infirmity shall she be unclean... But if she bear a maid child, then she shall be unclean two weeks, as in her separation: and she shall continue in the blood of her purifying threescore and six days." Leviticus 12:2,5, KJV

"Say to the Israelites: 'A woman who becomes pregnant and gives birth to a son will be ceremonially unclean for seven days, just as she is unclean during her monthly period... If she gives birth to a daughter, for two weeks the woman will be unclean, as during her period. Then she must wait sixty-six days to be purified from her bleeding." Leviticus 12:2,5, NIV

It is significant that a woman is 'unclean' for twice as long after birthing a daughter as opposed to a son and is a sign of the preferential placement for sons over daughters.

"And the daughter of any priest, if she profane herself by playing the whore, she profaneth her father: she shall be burnt with fire." Leviticus 21:9, KJV

"If a priest's daughter defiles herself by becoming a prostitute, she disgraces her father; she must be burned in the fire." Leviticus 21:9, NIV

Because the Levitical priests were the true religious and political power in Israel, any form of subversion in their own household could not be tolerated. I see many fanatical Christians holding up signs condemning homosexuals, and yet how interesting that they turn a blind eye to a verse like this! I can honestly say I knew a couple of homophobic pastors in my more religious days who had teenage daughters who went 'astray' sexually with multiple partners, and yet they never advocated burning their daughters at the stake for their 'whoring' (according to Levitical laws).

"If a man finds a damsel that is a virgin, which is not betrothed, and lay hold on her, and lie with her, and they be found; then the man that lay with her shall give unto the damsel's father fifty shekels of silver and she shall be his wife; because he hath humbled her, he may not put her away all his days." Deuteronomy 22:28-29, KJV

"If a man happens to meet a virgin who is not pledged to be married and rapes her and they are discovered, he shall pay the girl's father fifty shekels of silver. He must marry the

girl, for he has violated her. He can never divorce her as long as he lives." Deuteronomy 22:28-29, NIV

Intriguingly, the verse that comes before this one states that if a virgin is raped, but is betrothed (engaged) to be married, then the rapist must be put to death. And yet, if she is not engaged, she has automatically been forced into marriage to a man who violently attacked her against her will. If any verse emphasizes that women are seen as property in the Old Testament this is the prime example. You see, if the virgin is engaged, she is already making the transition from under her father's control to her husband's household. If she is raped, her rapist has technically damaged the 'property' of the future husband so there is no financial way to make up for it and he is put to death. Yet, if she is not engaged and is violently attacked, this poor young woman loses any right to a better marriage. As long as the rapist pays off her father, she is utterly his. Women, like horses, cattle, sheep, any living animal, were a commodity; a worker and a breeder whose virginity was priceless not because it made her 'pure', but because it ensured her husband that any children from her womb would be his and his alone.

"When men strive together one with another, and the wife of the one draweth near for to deliver her husband out of the hand of him that smiteth him, and putteth forth her hand, and taketh him by the secrets: Then thou shalt cut off her hand, thine eye shall not pity her." Deuteronomy 25:11-12, KJV

"If two men are fighting and the wife of one of them comes to rescue her husband from his assailant, and she reaches out and seizes him by his private parts, you shall cut off her hand. Show her no pity." Deuteronomy 25:11-12, KJV

This fascinating law reveals a lot about the emphasis on masculinity in Hebrew culture. There are many disturbing laws and verses in the Torah, but the fact that the writer feels the need to include the phrase: 'Show her no pity' is revealing. Notice, there is no law against a wife defending her husband, only against her touching/yanking/pulling/desecrating the genitals of the attacker (a viable option for any woman trying to defend herself or her husband). To command others to 'show her no pity' means that even in ancient Israel the automatic response would be to show her compassion. After all, this woman was just defending her husband from great bodily harm. In a way she is also defending herself as the death of her husband would result in catastrophe for her since she cannot inherit his property. We see this kind of message again thousands of years later during the worst of the witch hunts in Medieval Europe, where manuals instructing torture repeatedly warn men to 'show no pity' and to even avoid eye contact with the victim lest they feel pity or compassion.

To further prove that ancient Hebraic religion was immensely concerned with literal masculinity and ensuring that children were born to the man who owned his wife and concubines:

"He that is wounded in the stones, or hath his privy member cut off, shall not enter into the congregation of the Lord. A bastard shall not enter into the congregation of the Lord; even to his tenth generation shall he not enter into the congregation of the Lord." Deuteronomy 23:1-2, KJV
"No one who has been emasculated by crushing or cutting may enter the assembly of the Lord. No one born of a forbidden marriage nor any of his descendants may enter the

assembly of the Lord, even down to the tenth generation."
Deuteronomy 23:1-2, NIV

If we are taught that God is loving, that God embraces all who come to Him, why on earth would He command that men who have had the misfortune of having their genital area mutilated or injured (for whatever reason) should be shunned from the group? And what loving God shuns children, regardless of whether their origins are legitimate or not? This cannot be the Creator of humanity, but a god who is the creation of man seen through the eyes of man for the glory of man.

These cannot possibly be the orders of a perfect and loving God, but they are clearly the laws and orders of men who have made god in their image and not the other way around. These were human men living in a particular time and culture who are trying to keep their society a certain way. But perhaps the worst story of the Old Testament which emphasizes the absolute lack of any kind of concern for women is:

"Behold, here is my daughter a maiden, and his concubine; them I will bring out now, and humble ye them, and do with them what seemeth good unto you: but unto this man do not so vile a thing. But the men would not hearken to him: so the man took his concubine, and brought her forth unto them; and they knew her, and abused her all the night until the morning: and when the day began to spring, they let her go. Then came the woman in the dawning of the day, and fell down at the door of the man's house where her lord was, till it was light. And her lord rose up in the morning, and opened the doors of the house, and went out to go his way:

*and behold, the woman his concubine was fallen down at the
door of the house, and her hands were upon the threshold.
And he said unto her, Up, and let us be going. But none
answered. Then the man took her up upon an ass, and the man
rose up, and gat him unto his place. And when he was come
into his house, he took a knife, and laid hold his concubine,
and divided her, together with her bones, into twelve pieces,
and sent her into all the coasts of Israel."* Judges 19: 24-29,
KJV

*"Look, here is my virgin daughter, and his concubine. I
will bring them out to you now, and you can use them and do
to them whatever you wish. But to this man, don't do such a
disgraceful thing." But the men would not listen to him. So the
man took his concubine and sent her outside to them, and they
raped her and abused her throughout the night, and at dawn
they let her go. At daybreak the woman went back to the house
where her master was staying, fell down at the door and lay
there until daylight. When her master got up in the morning
and opened the door of the house and stepped out to continue
on his way, there lay his concubine, fallen in the doorway of
the house, with her hands on the threshold. He said to her,
"Get up; let's go." But there was no answer. Then the man
put her on his donkey and set out for home. When he reached
home, he took a knife and cut up his concubine, limb by limb,
into twelve parts and sent them into all the areas of Israel."*
Judges 19:24-29, NIV

From the start of this tale, we see how little value
women really had as anything but property. Notice that the
keeper of the house whom the Levite man is staying with
would rather have his virgin daughter raped and abused than
to allow the same abuse to come upon the male guest of his
home. We also see how completely worthless a woman was

deemed; because the Levite's woman is a concubine and not
the main wife of his household, her body holds next to no
value. There is not a second thought to shoving her out into
the night to be used by these sadistic men. Notice that the
Levite even sleeps through her rape and torture! There is no
mention that he at least stayed awake with concern over what
was happening to her. To add even more insult, when he sees
her laying there on the ground, there is no shred of
compassion for what she has endured. "Get up, we're leaving."
is his only recorded response. Is she already dead? In Jewish
law, a body must be buried as soon as possible after death, so
the fact that he tosses her over his donkey and rides home with
her could suggest she was barely alive and died on the journey
back.

How much more disgrace is there that he then
undertakes to dismember her body instead of giving her a
proper burial with the rites due to her as a member of his
household? Of course the reason is given that he sends the
parts to the different tribes in order to rally them to return to
this town and defeat the cruel men, but still, for a religion that
has so many laws against dealing in blood and how a body
must be taken care of in death, this Levite has transgressed
them. Yet it is all excused because of his position and the sake
of rallying the tribes (apparently a well written letter to each
tribe was not enough).

What irony that the men of Israel rise up to smite these
wicked men… and yet never is there an ounce of
condemnation for the Levite who literally threw this woman to
the wolves and did nothing for her in life nor in death. How
strange that these are the actions of a man who is part of the
priestly tribe, the very same men who claim to hold
themselves to a higher standard and represented the same God
who supposedly holds life as being sacred, and yet this Levite

shows how little respect he had for the life of a concubine.

When this story would come up, the excuse was frequently given that we had to read the story according to the context of its history. The actions of this story were excused because this was something that was acceptable back in this Levite's day and age...

This is the whole point I am trying to make!

Why do religious people read the Bible and accept that certain verses only pertained to the time and era in which they were written, and yet other verses and stories such as Eve's disobedience are still read as though it were meant to be valid in our time? It is not only hypocritical, it is a mindset that has been extremely damaging to women throughout Western history! In this day and age we still see men in religious positions insist on treating women the same way they were treated two thousand years ago.

We see this in an economic system such as the United States' that still insists on paying a woman less for doing the same job as a man and cannot give her any real justification for why. The reason why, by the way, is because when women first entered the workplace during the Industrial Revolution, it was agreed upon by corporations and companies that paying women less was a win-win. On the one hand if a woman was desperate to work they got labor at a cheaper price, and on the other hand it would serve as a deterrent to keep women in the home as housewives. No one addresses this as being the historical reason for unequal pay for women in our modern world and it hearkens back to the Biblical mindset that a woman is worth less than a man.

We certainly see it when a woman is forced to carry a child she does not want, may not have the ability to care for mentally, emotionally, or financially, she may have even become impregnated through rape, all because a group of men in political or religious control feel that her life is worthless in comparison to an unborn fetus. The ludicrous position of this mindset is made more apparent when considering that the God of the Bible shows no concern for the life of unborn children when the Biblical hero Joshua is commanded to slaughter women (pregnant or not) and innocent children all for the sake of claiming the Holy Land. How can male leaders insist they are following a Biblical moral compass by insisting women must carry unwanted children because all life is precious, yet ignore that the same God in his warmongering had no issue with the death of thousands of innocents across the land of Canaan. Nor, for that matter, when God supposedly annihilated humanity with a catastrophic flood, seeing as how pregnant women and small children inevitably drowned during that Biblical event.

Is this the mindset of our modern age, or are we still seeing how much sway the mindset of a small group of men living in a desert thousands of years ago holds over our Western society? It is at this point, that I must state that I will always be grateful for the men that understand that they are not part of this mindset and have chosen to free themselves. They have become champions for equality and a woman's right to choose her own fate. These men, in listening to their own Souls, have managed to awaken from the sleep of mindless dogma and risen to the challenge of not only defending the rights of all human beings, but of trying to change the world for the better.

When do we as women come to the threshold of knowledge and recognize that we lost control of our bodies long ago to the politics and dogma of men in a religion that could not comprehend that women had a right to think and choose for themselves? After all, man throughout history has seen himself as having that privilege because he has been told he is created in the image of God. Thanks to this god complex mankind decided that he held the right to make decisions for womankind who was created second and lesser than man. This is the danger of taking so much of the Bible literally. There is evidence that even the people of ancient Israel may not have taken things as literally since we have seen that they frequently incorporated the divine feminine in the form of Asherah (to the chagrin of religious fanatics like Jeremiah, Isaiah, and Ezekiel).

Scholars know that ancient Judaism was already experiencing deep divisions of belief within their own people. By the time of Christ, Judaism was becoming split between those who sought to follow zealous religious laws (like the school of Shammai) and those who were open to embracing the ways of non-Jews and more philosophical interpretations of their religion (like the school of Hillel, both of which were influential in shaping Jesus' outlook, but that is information for another time and perhaps a whole other book). So many of these Biblical stories were meant to be read allegorically, but they were also stories akin to a cultural diary giving accounts according to the author's point of view. Often the Biblical texts were meant to be instructive lessons to Israelites and reinforce a Hebraic culture in which women were taught to believe that they were the property of their husbands. That is not our world anymore and only through the recognition of these truths can the Light of women shine when we insist that this mindset has no place in our modern world.

Perhaps the best example is the constant political and theological push and pull happening in the modern state of Israel. Though a Jewish nation created by the very men and women who understand and know the issues of their ancient religion better than anyone, there is a great divide between those who insist upon following the Bible strictly and those who acknowledge the Bible as part of their culture, but refuse to let it dictate who they are as a modern society. They have never asked the rest of the world to convert to their beliefs, and many pay proper honor to the beliefs of the past, but they do not let it dictate how they are evolving as human beings who are now part of an international community. No matter what the political turmoil of Israel with its neighbors, it certainly can never be accused of launching holy wars to convert others to their belief system. Even when it comes to politics, like any other nation, we see great schisms between those who seek peace and those who seek war. How ironic that we still see such a disgraceful thing as anti-Semitism when of all the people in the world, it is the Jews who have never actively pursued nor violently proselytized the rest of the world. Ironically, it is not even the fault of Judaism that the Western world has clung to outdated religious notions, but instead the blame lies at the feet of the Roman Empire (an issue to be dealt with in Chapter 18 *A Christian Revolution?*).

I soon discovered that the oppression of women and the control of their sexuality had a greater impact on the history of humanity when it came to love, compassion, understanding, and the expression of the human soul. This is the reality of what we have to deal with at this time, in this century, in this era more than ever as we face issues of discrimination against women and those who are not heterosexual.

.

Part II: When Love Is Blind

"The mirror of life shows you woman or man,
but in the heart of the Soul you are neither.
This is why Love is blind."
- C.C. Campbell

"A man should remain man
and yet should become woman;
similarly a woman should remain woman
and yet become man."
- Mahatma Gandhi

10. The Rebellion of Compassion

I have always heard time and again that the eyes are the mirrors of the soul. I never truly quite comprehended what that really meant. It sounded good to me, very mysterious and mystical, but the truth is that it is not mysterious. Mystical maybe, but only to those who really have come to understand the true meaning of the soul. The Soul is the gift that we inherited the day we were born, the day when we took our first breath in this magnificent universe. The energy that came in with our breath was the beginning of the Soul uniting with the flesh of mankind, the genesis to the introduction of the human Ego. The human Ego would introduce itself to humanity with its own birthright, recognizing that it would become a challenge to itself and to others in the process of its own development through the eyes of man.

In the beginning the birth of humanity on this planet experienced challenges, trying to learn its own behavior and the behavior of others, having to interact with the souls of animals, eventually becoming an energy that has survived on the life force of all living things. At some point the Ego of man was challenged and through the challenge of space and time man began to acknowledge the immortality of the Soul and started to accept the mortality of the human Ego. This paradigm of knowledge was the birth of spirituality and, eventually, religion. The heart of it all was a recognition that reality is a compilation of life and death. It is, in a way, but not the kind of death that is seen to be so final. This is the death of the Ego that lacks the understanding of the true immortal nature of the human Soul.

In this chapter where Love is truly blind, I intend to show that the human Soul has no gender, but the Ego, being part of the human mind, will represent its gender through the physical appearance of each individual. The Ego becomes enslaved to the mentality into which it is born, shaped by the approval and disapproval of its parents, its community, and its religion. It is the Ego which tries to force the Soul to conform to the image of the body, all because the opinions of others have told it what is right and what is wrong. In doing this, not only is the Soul silenced, but the true essence and possibilities of Love for humanity are hidden and denied.

Many prefer to turn a blind eye to this issue, but as we see our world evolve, the issues of homosexuality, transgender individuals, and gender equality cannot be ignored or repressed. I have come to recognize that ignorance is not bliss. Ignorance has given birth to destruction. I see a person that is ignorant about the topics of Love as someone that refuses to see, hear, or understand. Within their Ego they feel they have all the knowledge they need according to what they read in their holy texts, not according to what they truly sense and feel beyond the human Ego.

As long as man sees the human body for what it represents, it will not allow itself to see the genderless Soul that has fallen in love with the genderless Soul of another human being. You have been told that if you are going to feel any kind of physical or romantic attraction it must be to the opposite gender. The Ego has almost never been told that it is okay to feel attraction to either gender. The human body is a vessel, but the Soul is what keeps the vessel alive. When two human beings fall in love through the eyes of the soul, they begin to live. The human vessel will fulfill the act of lovemaking at its fullest and only then can love release its energy back into the Universe where it was meant to manifest itself into compassion and understanding. They experience love at its richest, as the most fulfilling energy that anyone can experience.

When individuals fall in love only through the sight of the human Ego, it cannot last. It will destroy itself and the other individual simply because it is existing only on the level of the energy of man. When love is experienced at the deepest energy of the human Soul, it will live on beyond this world. It will exceed the expectations of the human Ego. The Ego can never have the monopoly on love. Love is the life, the energy of the human Soul. Through it the Soul sheds a Light that overwhelms the darkest thoughts of the human Ego. If the Soul can open the eyes of the Ego to the beauty of two human beings that surrender themselves to one another unconditionally, never seeing the person in the physical sense, but seeing the beauty, the wonder of the other through the mirrors of the eyes of the Soul, then the Soul will be free to live and love.

Many of you may remember the news about a young man in the state of Wyoming who was tied to a split rail fence and brutally murdered for committing no offense other than being attracted to other men. They say his face was covered in blood save for where his last tears were shed. To this day his mother and father work tirelessly to give a voice to gay youth who face violent abuse all for being who they were born to be. Another story that came to light was about a woman who chose to wear men's clothes and be called by a man's name. She was sadistically raped and beaten by men who became filled with fear and hatred all because their masculinity was threatened. More recently soldiers, someone's son or daughter, was brought home to be laid to rest and the mourners were met with a small crowd of fanatical American Christians.

This maniacal sect does not care whether a soldier is gay or straight, they believe every death is God's punishment to America for being a nation that allows homosexuality. These people picket the funerals of soldiers, spewing poisonous words on homemade signs that read: "God Hates Fags and America! Leviticus 18:22!"
Ironically this soldier laid down his or her life so that these very people would have the freedom to express themselves in any manner they wished, yet Leviticus 18:22 means more to them than Jesus' words in John 15:13: "*Greater love hath no man than this, that a man lay down his life for his friends.*"

We are supposed to be living in a time and a nation with greater tolerance and understanding than ever before, and yet we still see so much division and so much fear based hate on the issue of gender. Would it surprise you to know that there were many, many places and points in history where these issues did not exist? Many who oppose gay marriage, homosexuality, or transgender people will make the argument that these are all 'modern inventions', examples of 'sexual perversion' that are somehow unique to our time and culture. They claim it is a result of living in a 'godless' nation that has allowed far too much sexual freedom and become too secular. In spite of the fact that many churches, synagogues, and even liberal mosques are becoming open and accepting of gay members, there are still numerous groups who will raise their Bible and use it as the justification for their own homophobia.
        What none of these people understand is that homosexuality and, yes, even 'transgender' men and women, have existed since the dawn of time. For much of recorded history the existence of such people was a normal part of life and even celebrated. No one was a pariah or condemned to hell. Even the Biblical verses used to condemn homosexuality

are loaded with deeper meaning and have been the object of blatant mistranslation to suit the needs of certain religious leaders throughout history. Ignorance and blindness seems to follow human beings who allow themselves to be used as pawns by leaders who have their own agenda about how humanity should act and worship. Just as the previous chapters showed that there was a very human and political reason behind the oppression of women in the Bible, I will show that the same is true when it comes to the oppression and even violent hatred of homosexuality, bisexuality, and transgenderism. Believe it or not, there has been great advantage for certain groups in insisting on making others believe that God hates people who choose to love their own gender.

I have struggled for many years with trying to understand why humanity has always found ways to treat one another so cruelly over their differences. Even the way we look, the color of our skin, the way we speak, and our different cultural traditions all become fair game for someone looking for a reason to treat others cruelly, to judge, isolate, repress, and sometimes even to kill. Thankfully there will always be human beings whose Souls are awakened with enough Light, love, and compassion to refuse to accept the cruelty of those who insist their religious beliefs give them the right to become persecutors. What is right in these people's eyes is usually something that has been dictated from a pulpit by a man or woman claiming righteousness from a book they believe to be the inerrant word of God.

I truly believe that in the hearts of many who are sincerely filled with the love of God that something deep within them tells them that there is something inherently wrong with this viewpoint. If what they read in their holy books makes them question their belief, that should give them pause to explore and question further why the text says what it does and how it even came to say it. The problem is that despite Christ's insistence in Matthew 7:7-8 to "Ask and it will be given to you; seek and you will find; knock and the door will be opened to you.", the truth is that these kinds of questions are not encouraged in most churches. In fact they are quickly stamped out when whoever is in charge chooses to gloss over a problematic text with their interpretation. In doing so the individual who dared to ask often finds themselves agreeing only because they feel that they lack the education in the Bible whereas their minister/pastor/priest has (supposedly) studied these texts. This brings up the next big problem in that the majority of clergy lack the knowledge of the **history** and cultural backgrounds of the Bible and the true sources who wrote the texts.

When I was a devout Christian with my blinders firmly in place, I saw only what I wanted to see and heard only what I wanted to hear. I felt strongly that I did not need to question the men and women who had studied the Bible and felt as I did. To do so, it seemed, would show a lack of faith. For me loyalty has meant everything, and the greatest mark of my loyalty to God was accepting every word of His holy book without question. And so I did not question God's condemnation of homosexuality, not when it seemed to be spelled out so clearly in Leviticus:

"Thou shalt not lie with mankind, as with womankind: it is abomination." Leviticus 18:22, KJV
"Do not have sexual relations with a man as one does with a woman; that is detestable." Leviticus 18:22, NIV

As a devout Christian, that was that; I believed God didn't want anyone being gay. And yes, in spite of this, as I watched other so-called Christians condemning and vilifying gay men and women, I found a horrible tug of war going on within myself. I did not agree, but I kept quiet out of loyalty to my faith.

Looking back, I never felt any real judgement or dislike of gay people, let alone righteous hate. I was incredibly torn between my instinct of love and compassion for human beings regardless of sexual orientation, race, gender, or belief, and the desire to follow the righteous indignation that many ministers were so fervently trying to instill. Even when a minister wasn't outright homophobic, I still encountered the watered down version of 'love the sinner, but hate the sin'. In this case, love the person who is gay but hate their 'gayness'. In church a gay person was a pariah, to be loved at a distance and prayed for until they could experience God's salvation and suddenly, miraculously become heterosexual in compliance with God's commands in the Bible. I could not escape what the Bible said, but I also could not believe that a loving God would hate or condemn gay people just for being gay and staying gay. Again and again I found myself returning to a verse in Jeremiah :

"The word of the Lord came to me, saying, 'Before I formed you in the womb I knew you...'" Jeremiah 1:4-5, KJV

While this verse is often used against abortion, I saw a deeper meaning. I pondered, if God truly knows a soul before it is born, then God knows that a man or woman will be gay from the moment they are conceived. If He truly hates homosexuality, then why would He even allow that person to be born? But, as I have said, I ignored those lingering doubts in the name of faith, figuring that it was God's place to judge and not mine. I did not condemn homosexuality… but neither did I ever support it or stand up for those who were, and in that respect I may as well have been holding one of those poisonous picket signs.

I still remember where I was in 1998 when American news released the gruesome story of the Matthew Shepherd murder. Sorrow washed over me for his family and I felt a strange, sharp pain that seemed to scream at me: *Can't you see how wrong this is? Can't you see that as long as there are human beings on this earth insisting that gay people are an abomination and you do not question it that you might as well be an accomplice to this hate?*
The answer was no, I could not see. I had turned a blind eye. Again and again stories would come to my attention of a gay man or woman being physically harmed or harassed and while I hurt for them in my heart, on the outside I simply turned my back from the reality. No matter how much I wanted to ignore it, it seemed fate kept bringing the issue to my awareness.

There was a gentle, beautiful young man named Chris, barely out of his teens whose parents were Christians and lived in an area that was heavily influenced by evangelical religion. Fate put his parents, himself, and I in close contact for a weekend. I found myself confronted with the tortured mental conflict that he and his parents were undergoing. Not only did he face fear and condemnation for being gay, but his parents were facing the horrible pressure of their neighbors, church, and community to either shun him for choosing 'sin' or find a way to force him back into 'righteous' heterosexuality. Because of my background, I remember speaking extensively with them as a family and, even in my own religious state, commending them for giving their son the support and encouragement he so rightly deserved. I don't think I had ever felt so conflicted in my life either, as I wondered again, how could my instinct about God's love for this young man, regardless of his sexuality, go so against what was being expounded in many evangelical pulpits from the Bible?

Not long after I would also experience interacting with the young son of a woman whom I became good friends with. She had two wonderful boys, but from an incredibly young age one of them behaved in a manner that society would call 'feminine' (and, indeed, he finally came out in his college years). Though he did not try to wear girl's clothes or make-up, everything about his mannerisms, from the gait of his walk to his gestures and expressions screamed feminine. Yet he did not grow up in a household where this was encouraged and his father and older brother were as stereotypically masculine as they came! In that moment, watching this incredibly sweet, smart, and compassionate little boy, I had to be hit with a hard reality. This child was not choosing this, as I had heard so many clergy insist. What I was seeing was completely normal and natural for this child, and if God knew every hair on his head, how could the same God condemn him in the same breath?

Either the God of the Bible was fickle and cruel, or there was something far, far deeper in those texts. And then it dawned on me: What was I afraid of? Why didn't I, an educated person, look deeper into this once and for all? The question led me to a disturbing answer. I realized that I did not dare to tell anyone of my own faith about what I believed in my heart to be so wrong. I was afraid of being told that I was not a good Christian, that I could not be loving the same God that they professed to love. I was truly afraid of being pushed away, rejected, and ostracized. What if someone thought that I was standing up for gay people because I was secretly gay myself! This is how fear makes you feel helpless in the face of injustice. How it can make you feel so small. How it keeps you in line. Fear had a hold on me.

My soul was crying out for human beings who did not deserve to be treated so cruelly and I recognized that the internal conflict I was experiencing on the issue was absolutely nothing compared to what society and religion were doing to anyone who was gay, bisexual, or transgender. How many young people were committing suicide because they felt so hopeless and unloved all because they were not heterosexual? And even worse, the stigma attached to men and women who deep down inside recognized that they needed to be the opposite gender! I will have a lot more to say about transgender, but for now my focus is on homosexuality because of the emphasis the Bible seems to place upon it.

When I look back over the years to all the things that have changed since my near death experiences and awakenings, I embarked on educating myself in everything I could about the history, politics, philosophy, and theology of religion. Nowhere has my understanding and opinion altered so drastically than in the case of homosexuality. In the early time of my spiritual journey, I was led to reexamine the book of Leviticus, where the Biblical 'gay bashing' truly begins. I was guided to look closely at the laws against homosexuality. I began to realize the path I was being led down had come because of my sincere desire to make a difference in humanity against the ugliness that hatred and ignorance can produce. I was shown and told things that I was not aware of until the awakening led me to such a hunger for truth. It was not the truth that Christianity endorsed, but nevertheless real Truth in terms of what society should be able to see without the prejudice of religion.

As serious study and research verified what I was being shown, I realized this information needed desperately to be shared. Because I came out of such an ingrained Biblical mindset, I knew firsthand that the only thing others in my situation would listen to was the Bible itself. This is perhaps the greatest mistake being made by those who are trying to start a dialogue between the LGBT community and staunch religious people. For these people who were as I once was, it is not enough to say that Jesus commanded us to love one another and because of this there is no place for judgement or condemnation. A religious minded person will instantly pull out the very scripture or verses I am about to discuss and use them as proof that they feel that God Himself is commanding them to feel the way they do. But if you understand these verses, not just what they say, but how to read between the lines with the history and context hidden behind them, then you will find not only enlightenment for the religious person, but the empowerment to face religious individuals with the truth (and mistranslations) of their own book… which, sadly, is the only truth they may ever open their eyes or ears to.

So let us begin with the beginning.

11. Leviticus and the Origins of Hate

The first five books of the Bible - Genesis, Exodus, Leviticus, Deuteronomy, and Numbers - are the foundation stones of Judaism, as well as Christianity, and, by proxy, Islam. The concerns of Genesis include the Creation story (which I went over extensively in the last section) and the foundation of the patriarch Abraham as the originator and father of the Jewish people. Exodus continues the story with Moses leading the Israelite nations out of Egypt and into the Promised Land. The next book, Leviticus, is so named because it is the book of laws set forth by Israel's governing priesthood: the Levites. While the Ten Commandments had been set forth in Exodus, Leviticus is a massive body of do's and don't's supposedly handed down by God to the Levites detailing every aspect of life from religious rituals to dietary customs, lifestyle, marriage, and especially sex. It is here that we run into the first staunch prohibitions about homosexuality in the Bible:

"Thou shalt not lie with mankind as with womankind: it is an abomination." Leviticus 18:22, KJV

On the surface this looks like a very straight forward condemnation of homosexuality, but it is not. To begin with, something is glaringly absent and it is only thanks to divine guidance that I ever even noticed it. When I realized what I was looking at, I felt such a painful tug at my heart. My own tears blinded me for a short moment, as if to remind me that I had read this verse before and yet been so blind to something so crucial. As I read aloud, the truth lay literally between the lines in the next verse:

> "*Neither shalt thou lie with any beast to defile thyself therewith; neither shall any woman stand before a beast to lie down thereto: it is confusion.*" Leviticus 18:23, KJV
> "*Do not have sexual relations with an animal and defile yourself with it. A woman must not present herself to an animal to have sexual relations with it; that is a perversion.*" Leviticus 18:23, NIV

For as long as I could remember, any clergy interpreting Leviticus 18:22 would say that the word 'man' and 'mankind' was meant to be interpreted as including both genders. In other words, condemning both homosexuality and lesbianism equally. This is blatantly wrong! The proof is evident when the rest of chapter 18 is read. With eyes wide open, the reader will clearly see that in numerous places care is taken to include both genders, like in the verse I just quoted. In Leviticus 18:23, which forbids bestiality, care is taken to address **both** men and women. Had the author (supposedly Moses) meant to forbid men and women from homosexual sex, he could have done so. Notice that nowhere is it mentioned that woman lying with woman is an abomination to God. Nowhere in the verses before nor after Leviticus 18:22 does the writer bother to forbid homosexual acts between two women. Technically, Leviticus forbids gay men, but not gay women (lesbians).

There is not a single law forbidding lesbianism in the whole of the Torah and this fact has created a strange problem in Orthodox Judaism (the current sect which tries to obey every Torah law to its letter). While homosexuality is forbidden between men, rabbis generally turn a blind eye to when it occurs between women. In fact there is a greater stigma on a woman in Orthodox Jewish culture if she does not marry and have children than if she is a lesbian. Being a lesbian does not matter to them religiously as long as she still gets married and has children! Perhaps the most disturbing rationale with some (though not all) Orthodox sects is to see the homosexual impulse (be it in man or woman) as neither wrong nor sinful in and of itself. In their eyes, it is only the act of sex between two men that is 'an abomination'. In other words, God will not condemn a person for being gay, as long as they never actually have gay sex. Talk about being in the crosshairs! A poor gay person is basically being told that it's okay to be gay, they just can never actually find love or sexual release with the person they fall in love with. Instead, God wants them to languish mentally and emotionally and live their life as a lie as long it means getting married and having children according to the religious law. How is this mindset not expected to drive a gay person to depression and even suicide? Is this really fair to them or to the poor man or woman expected to be their spouse?

I have heard this justification from other religious sects and am always left shaking my head at it. This means that hypothetically two men who love one another, live together, and build their lives together would not be an 'abomination' so long as they do not have sex together. There are heterosexual couples who live together who do not share sexual relations and yet their marriage is referred to as a holy union. If sex is not allowed and two men live and love each other just like heterosexual couples do, cannot their union also be deemed 'holy' as well? I have also come to understand that for those who are born homosexual, it would be little better than a living hell to 'have gay inclinations' and yet be asked to repress them so that they never actually act upon them. That is not healthy for the mind or the soul, and it is certainly just as damaging for any man or woman the gay person is expected to marry and live their forced, normal 'hetero' lives with! Let's set that conundrum aside for a moment as we investigate things a little further.

Next, we must look at the wording that is used. Written by Israelite people, these books were originally written in Hebrew. The Bibles we read today have come a very long way and have gone through thousands of years of translations. Walk into the Bible section of any bookstore and a single glance will reveal how many different translations are available, and that is just in English! In the process of translation from one language to another, much is lost and even confused. English and Hebrew are vastly different languages and Hebrew tends to have many more layers of nuance and meaning in a single word than English does. It also does not help that the people who wrote and originally read these texts lived in a world over three thousand years removed from our own. The people of the Bible were of a vastly different mindset and came from a cultural world completely foreign to us. Consider that even in this day and age Middle Eastern culture is still seen as totally alien to the Western world, now imagine trying to understand the culture of the same area over three thousands years ago!

Homosexuality is a fantastic example for this. The very idea of homosexuality as we understand it today is actually not in the least bit what is being referred to in the Bible. Today we have an understanding of homosexuality as encompassing a lot more than just sex between two men or two women. In our modern understanding, homosexuality also implies that two men or two women wish to live their lives together. They fall in love with each other, care for one another, and even commit to one another as life partners with the desire to someday marry and even raise children together. In today's world, to be homosexual is part of a person's very identity the same way that race and even religion are. This is not the concept that existed in the Biblical world. I will return to this point a little further on, but try to keep it in mind as we look at the words chosen in this verse.

The Hebrew word used in Leviticus 18:22 when describing male on male sex as an abomination is 'toevah'. It is a word that implies something that is unclean and taboo in a religious sense, but does not mean something that is morally wrong or evil. Had the author wished to declare male homosexuality as something evil and morally heinous, he would have chosen to use the Hebrew word 'zimmah'. The difference in meaning between these two words is stark. One word means something that is considered unseemly for religious reasons, while the other means something that is evil and forbidden for all humanity.

So, in Leviticus 18:22, we have a verse that condemns only gay men, but not gay women, and leaves one to question whether or not it is truly a 'sin' because the Levitical priesthood is not calling it an atrocity or horrendous act. While no actual punishment is incited in this verse, we find another mention in the subsequent chapter of Leviticus 20:

"If a man also lies with mankind, as he lieth with woman, both of them have committed an abomination: they shall surely be put to death; their blood shall be upon them." Leviticus 20:13, KJV

"If a man lies with a man as one lies with a woman, both of them have done what is detestable. They must be put to death; their blood will be on their own heads." Leviticus 20:13, NIV

Sadly, many religious fanatics use this verse to justify their own homophobia and violence, never realizing that the original meaning of this Bible verse is anything but clear. The Hebrew wording of this verse is a little ambiguous and has caused scholars to scratch their heads. A more literal translation of Leviticus 18:22 might be: *"And with mankind you shall not lie in the beds of a woman (or wife)."* The same instruction is being given in Leviticus 20:13 as well, with a wording that seems to imply an issue with men having sex with men in their 'marriage' bed.

At this point, many Biblical scholars believe that both verses in Leviticus are not condemning what we would think of as homosexuality. Instead the law may be stating that if a man wants to have sex with another man, it is wrong and 'unclean' to do so in the same bed that the married man shares with his wife. It may also be condemning a man who would bring another man in to have sex with both him and his wife (basically a threesome). I'd be remiss to not point out that there is no law against a man having sex with more than one woman at the same time, something that likely happened frequently as men were allowed as many wives and concubines as they could afford!

In the ancient world homosexual sex was actually very normal. There are many depictions and accounts of men having sex with other men and even long lasting romantic 'friendships' with other men. In many armies this 'brotherly love' was encouraged. Celtic, Roman, and Japanese cultures all glorified the love between men because it was seen to solidify loyalty and camaraderie between soldiers. This mindset may have even existed in ancient Israel, for there is enough romantic (even erotic) wording in the Old Testament book of 1 Samuel about the friendship between the future

King David and Jonathan (the son of King Saul) that many
scholars now believe David to have been bisexual. Too many
references to the 'friendship' between David and Jonathan are
written in ways that ancient readers would have acknowledged
as being sexual. Nowhere else in the entire Bible is a
'friendship' spoken about with such intimate language. We are
told that Jonathan strips down naked, giving David his own
armor as an act of love. When David defeats Saul for the
throne and Jonathan is killed in battle, David rends his own
garments and loudly laments that his love for Jonathan was
greater than the love he would ever feel for any woman:

*"I am distressed for thee, my brother Jonathan: very
pleasant hast thou been unto me: thy love to me was
wonderful, passing the love of women!"* 2 Samuel 1:26, KJV
*"I grieve for you, Jonathan my brother; you were very
dear to me. Your love was wonderful, more wonderful than
that of women!"* 2 Samuel 1:26, NIV

Why would David even need to make that kind of
corollary, that Jonathan's love surpassed the love of women?
King David was notoriously sexual and his love affairs with
women would become high drama for the royal court of Israel,
so for David to make this statement makes it apparent to many
scholars that David and Jonathan shared the kind of
homoerotic 'friendship' that was common to young unmarried
men and even soldiers. Few people realize that bisexuality is a
normal part of humanity and of nature itself. Whether a person
insists on seeing nature as the result of intelligent design or
simply evolutionary processes, the fact is that many animal
species exhibit bisexual behavior. Bonobos monkeys have
been shown to have sexual intercourse not just for mating, but
with their own gender solely for pleasure. If these monkeys

were created by the God of the Bible as so many insist, then God had no problem creating a species that takes pleasure in having homosexual orgies just for the kicks of it! Many other animals have shown the same capacity, from male dogs who will happily copulate with another male to species of invertebrates that even change their gender! Apparently the verses in Leviticus cannot be forbidding homosexual love between men if the greatest ruler of Israel who was chosen by God himself was able to freely love Jonathan!

In Leviticus 20:13, even the translation of 'blood guilt' is misleading. The translation could just as easily and correctly be written as 'they shall be cast out of society' instead of giving them a death penalty. If all of this logic and reason is not enough to convince the more rabid fundamentalist believer, then I ask them to consider that the 'death penalty' being proposed in many Bible translations is the same penalty given for another commandment in Leviticus, that of children who dare to curse their parents!

Even if Leviticus 20:13 is taken as a reason to do harm or even kill homosexual men, then the same religious literalists are guilty of picking and choosing with the Word of God because only four verses before, in Leviticus 20:9, the same sentencing of death is placed upon any child who dares to insult or curse their mother or father.

If a person is to hold so tightly to believing in the literal interpretation of this verse and believes that it should be binding in today's age, think of how many young Christian people are disobedient, insulting, or disgraceful in their behavior towards their parents! If we followed the Bible on this verse the same way so many religious people insist on following the verse about homosexuality, there'd be no Christian teenagers left in the Western world! The same

Levitical texts have a long list of 'abominations to God' aside from what many have interpreted as homosexuality. Technically tattoos, shellfish dinners, and garments made from sewing two different kinds of cloth (polyester) are all called 'abominations'! Now when I see anti-gay protesters touting the Levitical verses, nothing is more ironic than picking out the one who has a tattoo of Christ on their arm while wearing a polyester shirt. They have no idea they might as well condemn themselves to hell too, especially if they go and eat some shrimp or pork chops later that day!

I don't think I can ever stress it enough to the reader that these books were meant to be historical points of reference that were followed by the people of that day and culture. All cultures have different standards and choose their own beliefs based upon their own best interests. What we do as spiritual human beings is done not because it is the best for the culture, but because it is the right thing to do when we come to an understanding that we are all created equally with a desire for love and a need for compassionate understanding.

12. A Sexually Diverse Ancient World

The ancient world was sexually diverse, pure and simple. It was diverse before the Israelites ever entered the Holy Land - the vast Middle Eastern swath of land that covers modern day Turkey, Syria, Israel, Palestine, Iraq, and even Saudi Arabia. Sexual experience in the ancient world from the European continent to Northern Africa remained diverse and inclusive all the way into the Roman Empire and beyond. There was no real definition of homosexuality as we now know it. Ultimately there was just sexuality! What I mean by this is that no sexual 'labels' existed in the way we see today.

A person's homosexuality or heterosexuality did not define them or limit them the way modern Western society has treated sexual preference. Marriage for love is a relatively modern concept. In the ancient world marriage was a legal state that occurred as a means of forging families together for wealth, power, and protection. Marriage was also necessary for establishing a concrete hereditary line of children who could inherit their father's wealth and carry on the family legacy. It was rarely a means of proclaiming emotional love (not to say it never happened). And yet the ancient world was filled with love and desire between people just as it is today.

Love between men, both platonic and sexual, was common throughout the Middle Eastern empires and the Greco-Roman world; even the world of the ancient Celts was familiar with the love that frequently occurred between two men. Our modern world may have coined the term 'bromance', but its concept and meaning stretches far back into antiquity. Sexual love between women was also extremely common in a society where women were often treated as property and in the

Greek and Roman worlds were restricted to their own households with very little freedom. Most women were under their father's, then their husband's control. Given this stifling atmosphere, it should not be surprising that in a society where marriage was more of a business deal between a father and future husband, women often found emotional intimacy and sexual gratification in each other. If anyone thinks this is not the case, I challenge them to do a quick internet search of the name 'Sappho'. They will soon discover that this ancient bisexual woman left behind an incredible body of poetry glorifying the intense bonds of romantic love that commonly occurred between women. The strong bonds that came with sisterhood frequently developed into sexual relationships as well. As I said in the previous chapter, bisexuality was absolutely normal. None of this was seen as disgusting, immoral, or unnatural in the ancient world.

The great cultures that interacted with the Israelites were anything but backward and uneducated. The Phoenicians, Egyptians, Assyrians, and Babylonians were all contemporaries whose cultures were filled with art and beauty, religion and spirituality, but also power and prestige. Their religions were not only polytheistic, but infused with a great passion for life. This passion for life meant that the sexual and sensual were considered vital and thoroughly infused their everyday world. Entering into the great ancient cities like Alexandria in Egypt or Athens in Greece would be little different in its metropolitan atmosphere and diversity than walking around great modern cities like New York or London. Perhaps nowhere was the literal lust for life more evident than in the temples of the ancient world where priests and priestesses often engaged in sex. This sacred prostitution often saw money going towards temple funds that not only supported the clergy, but others in the community as well. What we think of as 'hetero' sex was common in these temples, but so was homosexuality.

No matter how 'pure' a society tries to keep itself, there will always be a need for escape. A reading of the Biblical books by the Prophets makes it apparent that a lot of young Israelite men had fun by cavorting to these temples and having sex (both straight and gay). What's the big deal? Just boys being boys, right? Perhaps anywhere else in the ancient world, but not for a society that was trying to isolate itself into something different and keep a reign on the younger generation. In our world overpopulation is an issue we all face. We take for granted just how important having children was for ancient people.

Even only a century ago, if you were a farmer whose livelihood depended upon tilling the soil, you needed every child you had to help work the land and bring in a living. Family becomes everything, not only for emotional reasons, but because having a large family ensures that there are enough hands to get all the work done that ensures prosperity and survival. This was even more important in the ancient world, especially for a small nation like the Israelites who discouraged intermarriage with anyone outside of their religion. Not only did they need a labor force, they needed a strong army to keep back bigger empires like Assyria and Babylon. Strict homosexuality was an immense threat to such a need. Not only were Israelite men spending money at these temples that the Levitical priests would rather see tithed to their own community, they were wasting their energy and their semen in a very unorthodox way.

In light of this the prohibition on male homosexuality, but the total lack of concern over lesbianism, makes an immense amount of sense. Because women of Biblical times were viewed as little more than property, even a complete lesbian would have had no choice but to marry and produce children with her husband... but a man who has no desire whatsoever for women and cannot physically fulfill that duty becomes a liability to this Levitical social order. This is why even to this day Orthodox Judaism will turn a blind eye to a man who is gay as long as he marries, has children, and does not act upon his homosexual desires. It is also why a man who admits the truth and refuses to live with a lie by coming out as gay is quickly turned out from the community. He has become a threat to its solidarity and procreation.

While many of the Levitical laws make common sense and have their basis in older laws of the Middle Eastern cultures (like the older law codes of Hammurabi), other laws, such as the supposed decree against male homosexuality are obviously rooted in religious and political agenda. These are the concerns of men in power; men who had an agenda for the purpose of growing their numbers so that no one could destroy their personal belief system in the God they worshipped. To add a little more food to thought is the fact the Dead Sea Scrolls, which are currently the oldest source we have for these Biblical texts, has neither of these Levitical verses (18:22 or 20:13) in them. Neither are found in the Book of Leviticus that is recorded in the Dead Sea Scrolls. The Dead Sea Scrolls are looked to as the earliest known texts of the Old Testament and their book of Leviticus chapter 18 begins with verse 16-19 before picking up again at verse 27 after a big gap. Similarly, Leviticus chapter 20 goes from verses 1-8, has a gap, and picks up at verse 30.

The scholastic belief is that these missing portions deteriorated with time, but the impact here is that we technically have no evidence one way or the other from the

Dead Sea Scrolls about what these verses originally meant about homosexuality or if they were even originally there at all or added on later by other writers. May I just take a moment to point out the irony that neither of the two verses that supposedly condemn homosexuality managed to survive? If they were so important to God one would think He could have kept the cave worms and time from eating away at them. What if these verses did get added at a later time in Israel's history? It could have been brought in at a time when Israel was suffering a major identity crisis under the rule of the Greek Empire.

Because of the great conqueror and emperor Alexander the Great, the land we call Israel came under Greek rule around 332 BC. Though the Greeks allowed the nations they conquered to keep practicing the religion of their choice, Greek influence ended up permeating the conquered territories with all things Greek. Scholars refer to this as 'Hellenism', meaning Greek art, architecture, philosophy, and religion. Just as American pop culture has saturated many parts of the world (think of the iconography of McDonalds, Coca Cola, Apple, etc., that can be found throughout the world), Greek culture thoroughly infused the nations it ruled. For most of the ancient world this was not a problem and was often welcomed. The Greeks brought advanced learning like engineering, architecture, mathematics, and philosophy wherever they went. For Jewish culture this was a very big problem. Many young Jewish men were becoming Hellenized. They attended Greek schools, spoke Greek, enjoyed Greek perks like theater, bath houses, and, yes, the openness of Greek sexuality which extolled the virtues of sexual love between two men.

While Judaism seemed fine with adopting useful things like Greek mathematics and philosophy, this open sexual tolerance created the same problem faced by earlier generations and, again, we see a strong insistence against homosexuality. This was not because they viewed homosexuality as being wrong in and of itself, but because it was something that threatened Jewish identity. Just imagine a young Jewish man telling his parents he did not want to get married and have children with a good Jewish girl, but instead was going with his Greek male 'friend' to study at the Greek academy and relocate to Athens, forsaking the family business of kosher butchering to become a free loving Greek philosopher! His parents could have overlooked their son's infatuation with the Greek boy, but they cannot forgive or tolerate him turning his back on the family and their entire culture. This still happens even in our modern world, so how much more so in the ancient world?

Perhaps that is the one thing that many religious people do not understand. Despite the laws in Leviticus, Judaism never says that homosexuality is wrong… not if you are not a Jew. You see, the whole point of Israel trying to separate itself from its neighbors was that they truly believed in one kind of law for their own people and leaving the rest of the world to its own beliefs. In fact, in Judaism's eyes, as long as non-Jews (Gentiles) abided by a set of common sense moral laws (referred to as the Noahide laws) like not murdering each other or brutalizing an animal, than in their belief non-Jews were absolutely fine with God. This meant that technically God was only upset with the homosexual Jewish man who refused to bed his wife, but did not care what the non-Jewish gay man did.

It should be becoming clear that the law against male homosexuality is something that was more of a concern to the Jewish ruling authority than it ever was to 'God'. This is why you do not see any Orthodox Jewish people joining in to picket against homosexuals or holding up signs proclaiming the Levitical verses like we see with certain extreme Christian groups. They know that their own religious beliefs are supposed to be theirs alone, and even then only for those who insist on the strictest Biblical observance of Biblical law.

13. Sodom and Gomorrah: Seeing What Isn't There

The only other example that is dug up in the Old Testament to be used against homosexuality is the story of Sodom in the book of Genesis. For those unfamiliar with the story or perhaps a little rusty in their Bible reading, the story goes like this:

After Abraham (supposedly the first monotheist) settled in the land of Canaan with his wife and family, his nephew Lot decided to take his family, animals, and wealth to move into the city of Sodom. Sodom was a large city, supposedly full of vice and wickedness, much as religious people might view a big city like Glasgow or New York. After a time, God let Abraham know that He intended to destroy Sodom and its sister city of Gomorrah. Abraham pleaded with God, asking if there was at least a few righteous people in the city if God would spare the populace. God agreed, but apparently not a single righteous person could be found in either city and so the plan for destruction was carried out. Apparently even the infants were somehow wicked, since God insisted the entire population would be wiped out.

As a favor to Abraham, God supposedly sends three angels in the guise of regular men to warn Lot of the impending doom and help them get out of the city in the dead of night. When the 'angels' come to Lot's house, he gives them food and the hospitality that is due to guests. In the midst of their visit, a large gang of men suddenly begin to bang on the door demanding that Lot turn the men over to them in order that the men of the city might 'know them' (a Biblical phrase that intends sex). Lot pleads with the men to not do such a horrible thing and offers them instead his own two virgin daughters. The men outside do not accept this peace offering and start to break in. Lot does manage to escape with his wife, daughters, and the 'angels' just before Sodom is razed to the ground in fire and brimstone as punishment for its utter wickedness. This entire narrative can be found in Genesis 19.

For a long time it was assumed that the great sin of Sodom was homosexuality, because of the men of the city insisting on wanting to have sex with the male 'angels' who had come to save Lot. Some religious factions go so far as to insist that Sodom was full of nothing but homosexual men and this is why God had to raze it to the ground, killing everything and everyone. But, as with the verses in Leviticus, meaning is being read into the story that is simply not there.

The text relates at least twice that Lot's daughters are engaged to men in the city, blowing away the theory that only homosexual men lived in Sodom. Obviously Lot would not have married his daughters off to husbands who were not going to beget children with them. It is also referenced that God destroys everyone in Sodom from the young to the old. There is no way this is possible unless people are procreating in the city, meaning that there are plenty of married couples living in Sodom. So, safe to say, not every man in Sodom was homosexual.

The biggest issue is that most people who read the story of Sodom have no idea that we have entirely lost its cultural context. Anything that is written in the past must be understood in light of the culture and people it was written for. A good example is that the works of William Shakespeare are still widely read. Even though a modern reader can understand the jest of his poetic work, most of his books now come with added reference guides to help the reader understand certain terms and phrases. Everything Shakespeare wrote and all of the innuendos and inside jokes and wording would have made complete sense to an audience in England in the late 1500s, but much of those terms and phrases do not exist anymore in our modern world and need to be explained to readers. The Bible as a whole is a work that is over three thousand years old, and yet most readers are expected to understand and interpret it without any added historical context or explanation.

In the issue of homosexuality and the story of Sodom, it is vital to understand that in the ancient world (not just in the Middle East, but also in Greece, Italy, and even Celtic lands) there was a well understood law of hospitality that applied to all visitors and travelers. Traveling in the ancient world was long, arduous, and often perilous, but utterly necessary for trade routes and the building of vital economies for large kingdoms and empires like Egypt, Babylon, Greece, and eventually Rome. A common sense rule developed as a corner stone of many of these cultures in which travelers and visitors were always expected to be treated with the utmost hospitality as honored guests. At the very least a guest was to be given food, drink, lodging, and, if possible, supplies or even gifts.

To this day in Middle Eastern cultures, to be invited into someone's home is an immense honor and is never taken lightly. Whether the family is rich or poor, they will share whatever they have with you. I can personally attest to this generosity and kindness having had the honor of being invited into the homes of Persians, Afghans, and Turks. This kindness is expected to be reciprocated should the host ever travel to the land of the guest. To break this unspoken law was seen to be a slap in the face of all that was decent and right. In this light of understanding, the actions of the men of Sodom would have been seen in the ancient world to be a horrendous breech of honor and ethics.

Not only are the men of Sodom being extremely rude, they are threatening male guests who should have been shown kindness and respect. Because the men of Sodom are so bold in their aggression and threats, it shows that they have likely acted this way with other travelers and guests before. To not show kindness and hospitality to guests in a city that was considered to be wealthy was a sign of cruelty, stinginess, and hard heartedness that anyone reading it in the ancient world would have been outraged. On top of this, the threats made against the guests in Lot's house is not homosexuality as we understand it today.

In our modern world we understand homosexuality as the inclination towards the desire of the same sex, with the result being a union of two people of the same gender having consensual sex. This is blatantly not what is intended by the men of Sodom. The men of Sodom threaten abuse, violence, and rape at its most base. Not only are they not abiding by the laws of hospitality, they are guilty of being sadistic sexual predators. Throughout the world, but especially in third world prisons, it is not uncommon for male prisoners to suffer torture and rape from their male prison guards. This is not an act of homosexuality, but an act of sexual violence meant to establish dominance over the victim and inflict degrading humiliation. Similarly, it has been proven that violent rape perpetrated on women tends to have little to do with sexual attraction and everything to do with fulfilling a sadistic need for dominance, power, and total control over the victim. This is the kind of male on male sex that the Bible references in the story of Sodom and Gomorrah, not the kind of consensual homosexual relationships we see in our culture today.

If the men of Sodom were not strictly homosexual, why did they not take Lot up on the offer of his daughters? This seemingly odd fact has been used often to try to prove that the men of Sodom were gay, but, once again, we are dealing with a cultural misunderstanding. The offer of Lot's daughters is an empty one and may have had more to do with trying to rile his potential son-in-laws into action than actually throwing his daughters to the wolves. Because his daughters were already engaged to men in the city, they were technically not his to offer. Remember, we are dealing with a time and culture in which daughters were the literal property of their father and kept in the home or married off at his behest. Once engaged to another man, they were technically the property of their fiancé even if they still lived under their father's roof. The men of Sodom would have been aware of this fact, so of course they were not going to accept them for their sexual gratification because doing so meant they would violate the property of two of their own group.

Even in later portions of the Bible when Sodom is brought up by different prophets as an example of God's divine judgement, homosexuality is never given as the explicit reason for the city's destruction. Instead, the 'sin' of Sodom is that its people were cruel, stingy, hard hearted, and willing to commit the worst sort of violence against people who cultural law demanded be cared for and shown respect. Nothing in the story of Sodom or Gomorrah had anything to do with condemning two people of the same gender who care for one another and have consensual sex.

The word 'sodomy' came into frequent usage in the Middle Ages around AD 1250-1300. It is worthwhile to point out that while most people assume the word sodomy refers only to anal sex (or male homosexual sex), the word was used as a catch all by the Church to refer to any kind of sexual relations that were considered 'unnatural'. This included not only anal sex, but also oral sex and even masturbation. Any kind of sex that would not result in potential pregnancy was seen as 'unnatural' and could result in a charge of sodomy whether it was a man or a woman, straight or gay. It is just another example of how meanings change over time and what is 'perverted' and 'unnatural' to one culture and time becomes normal and acceptable for future generations and cultures. After all, how many straight, married couples reading this just realized that they have engaged in numerous acts of 'sodomy' in the course of their usual sexual routine together?

14. Jesus' Silence Speaks the Truth

The New Testament references homosexuality in only three places. Ironically, the issue is never addressed or raised by Jesus Christ. Considering that homosexuality was widely practiced and openly visible in the Roman Empire, one could think that the son of God incarnate would have seen fit to remind humanity of the sins of men sleeping with other men. As the direct representative of God (if not God himself), you would think he would have spoken very openly on this issue just as he did about other topics. For homosexuality being such an 'abomination' and dominating issue for so many churches today, these believers need to stop and ask themselves why the son of God never saw fit to condemn men and women who were romantically involved with their own gender.

For those familiar with modern Bibles, it is, after all, common to print the words of Christ in red ink to emphasize the importance of his teachings. Nowhere in red is there any remark whatsoever from Christ on the topic of homosexuality. It is a fact that should give any Christian a moment to pause and reflect for themselves. Hopefully it will be a revelation that can guide those who insist on Biblical perfection to a greater enlightenment. If anything, a believer should follow the words of Christ above all and use their common sense, love, and compassion to accept and show kindness to all human beings.

The first mention of homosexuality comes from the words of the Apostle Paul in the New Testament book of Romans. We'll get to that a little later, but for now let's focus on Jesus Christ. Jesus was born into a Jewish world that was under the dominion of the Roman empire. Jewish identity was becoming fractured between those who insisted upon holding tightly to their religious culture, and those who felt they could live in both worlds by being both Jewish and Roman. This is a struggle we still see frequently today with the 'Westernization' of many parts of the world and the battle between embracing our culture or resenting it. Consider the Taliban of Afghanistan, who deplore anything they see as 'Western' including movies, books, foods, fashion and ideas. It does not matter if Western medicine can make their lives better, fanatical Taliban Muslims will bomb a van filled with life saving polio vaccines rather than let 'evil' Western technology or ideas compromise their religious ways of life.

The Jews of Jesus' time were also seeing many of their children embracing Greco-Roman modes of thinking, fashion, ideas, and culture and it threatened their own religious identity. Because of this, Jewish philosophy was already fracturing between competing schools of thought. As I briefly mentioned in a previous chapter, two of these schools belonged to thinkers named Hillel and Shammai. Both of these philosophical schools were still high profile during Jesus' time and it was not uncommon for the followers to get into heated, even violent, arguments. Many scholars believe Jesus was influenced more by the school of Hillel and that many of his altercations with other Jews and the Pharisees were because these people followed the thinking of Shammai.

To paint the differences as basically as possible, Hillel taught that Jews and Gentiles could live peacefully together and that Gentiles and Jews were equally saved in the eyes of God. Shammai, on the other hand, taught a very strict form of Judaism with emphasis on keeping minute Levitical laws. He emphasized that the Jews needed to remain separate from the Gentiles because the Jewish people alone were saved by God.

In a world where the Jews were feeling increasingly oppressed by Rome, Hillel emphasized peace through brotherhood, while Shammai emphasized a potential holy war for Jewish autonomy based on strict Jewish religion.

Jesus seems to have preached a kind of revitalized and reformed Judaism that emphasized a personal connection with God over the need for oppressive and restrictive religious laws. When Jesus is quoted in Matthew 15:11 as having said: *"It is not what enters into the mouth that defiles the man, but what proceeds out of the mouth that defiles him."*

Jesus is purposely challenging any school that espouses strict religious laws, including Shammai's followers and the Pharisees. That statement alone was blasphemous to Jewish religious authorities whose entire political structure was built on following the intense Levitical laws that forbade eating certain kinds of food (like pork and shellfish) and even enforced to the tiniest detail what a person could and could not do on the Sabbath. To this day Orthodox Jews will not turn on a light switch or even boil water on the Sabbath, so strict is their belief in these modified ancient laws.

It was these kinds of requirements and laws that Christ saw as hypocritical and oppressive on the Jewish people as well as a hindrance to relations with non-Jews. Christ went even further in Matthew 22:37-39, declaring that even with the Ten Commandments, the two greatest and most important to follow were: *"Love the Lord your God with all your heart… and the second is like it, Love your neighbor as yourself."*

This was a teaching that broke down the walls of isolation between Jew and non-Jew. Throughout the four gospels, there are many important sticking points with which Jesus concerned himself, yet homosexuality is never addressed. One would assume that, being the son of God, and so many believing God had condemned homosexuals to death because of Levitical law, that Jesus would have made this a priority. After all, homosexual behavior was prevalent in the Greco-Roman world around him, yet he never deems it necessary to even bother with the issue. Perhaps because he understood that the Levitical law did not mean homosexuality as we now know it and as I have, hopefully, thoroughly explained.

So, having addressed the Old Testament issues and raised the significant fact that Jesus never seems the least bit bothered about homosexuality, why do so many Christians seem to feel that the New Testament also condemns gay people? For that answer we have to look at Paul and three different books and passages. But first, it's vital to have some basic understanding of who Paul really was.

15. Homosexuality and Paul

Paul is a major figure in the Christian tradition. This is something I never really bothered to question before my awakening. As I began to truly study the New Testament deeply and critically, I found that almost all of the Christian dogma that we associate with the church comes from the books supposedly written by Paul. I had to ask myself why a religion that insisted it was following the teachings of Christ seemed instead to follow the teachings of Paul? This became a tremendous turning point for me. I had always considered myself a Christian, a devoted follower of Christ, and yet I found myself realizing I was blindly following the teachings of the Apostle Paul. Paul is incredibly important to this discussion because not only do we get the only three mentions of homosexuality in the New Testament from him (or at least two of the three), but long passages that have been used to repress the role of women in the Church are attributed to him as well (which will be discussed in Chapter 18 *A Christian Revolution?*).

Paul never actually met Jesus. The Apostle Paul also lived the first part of his life as a devoutly religious Jew named Saul. As a staunch religious Jew, he admits to having persecuted those of the Jewish faith who chose to follow the teachings of Jesus. The reason for this being, as I mentioned before, that Jesus had preached a variant form of Judaism in which Jews and Gentiles alike were able to have personal relationships with God and have salvation without having to abide by the incredibly restrictive Levitical laws. Somewhere along the line Paul experienced a profound encounter with a vision of Christ that converted him to Christ's teachings.

The great persecutor of the faith became its greatest champion and went out as a missionary, successfully leaving new churches in his wake all across the Roman Empire. All of this is recounted in the book of Acts, which tells the stories of Peter and then Paul. Contrary to popular belief, Biblical scholars believe the book of Acts was not written by Paul, but by the same Luke that wrote the Gospel of Luke. The rest of the books of the New Testament are not meant to be historical accounts, but are instead letters written by Paul to individual churches in different cities of the empire like Corinth, Ephesus, and Rome.

This is important to remember because it means that these books were not written as meticulous records of Christian faith. In other words, the letters are not Paul's intent to create a concrete list of do's and don'ts that establish exactly what Christians should and should not believe. Instead these books are one sided conversations in which Paul is responding to concerns brought up by these individual churches about issues that were specific to each place. Unfortunately we only have Paul's response, which means we do not know exactly what the churches were asking or what their responses were to Paul's letters. Imagine if you had written a letter to your best friend and someone finds it twenty-five years later. This future person reads the letter stating your love for your best friend, but because they do not have your friend's responding letter, the person might feel right in assuming that you and your friend were actually gay (when in fact the relationship was platonic and 'Alex' is a woman and not a man, and you are straight, and married with four kids!). The point is that with only one side of a conversation, the reader doesn't know any of the context of what they are reading and they jump to assumptions and conclusions that are often wrong. This is no different with trying to piece together the letters of Paul.

Today we would understand this parallel when we insist on
hearing 'both sides' of the story in a court of law before we
dare to make a judgement. We know that we cannot truly
understand the situation without all the facts, yet this is what
has happened with the interpretation of Paul's letters by many
Christian clergy.

Two of these letters are the source of thinking
Christianity forbids homosexuality. In the book of Romans,
written by Paul for the Romans, we also have the first
addressing of female homosexuality:

*"Because of this God gave them up unto vile affections
for even their women did change the natural use into that
which is against nature. And likewise also the men, leaving the
natural use of the woman, burned in their lust one toward
another; men with men working that which is unseemly, and
receiving in themselves that recompense of their error which
was met."* Romans 1:26-27, KJV
*"Because of this God gave them over to shameful lusts.
Even their women exchanged natural relations for unnatural
ones. In the same way the men also abandoned natural
relations with women and were inflamed with lust for one
another. Men committed indecent acts with other men, and
received in themselves the due penalty for their perversion."*
Romans 1:26-27, NIV

In this portion of Romans, Paul is starting out with an
overview of the things that the Gentiles do that are seen as
unnatural and strange to Jewish eyes; he chalks this up to the
fact that the Gentiles do not know the true God. He says it is
for this reason that the Gentiles (Romans in particular) were
'given up' to these 'unnatural' sexual practices, and this is

interpreted to relate back to the Levitical laws against male homosexuality. In other words, God did not give that particular law to the Gentiles, so before they became Christians it was not a concern. The word 'unnatural' in this verse is a loaded one, at least in our English meaning of the word. Most people who read this verse interpret the word to mean something that is wrong or disgusting, but this is not what the word means that Paul uses.

In the Greek translation of this text (bearing in mind that the New Testament was written in Greek, not Hebrew), the word used to mean unnatural is *'para physin'*. *Para physin* does not carry the meaning of unnatural in the sense of something wicked or heinous, instead it literally means 'not the normal way'. This was the natural view of anyone who had been steeped in Jewish culture because their religious laws dictated that sex was for the primary purpose of procreation and hence occurred between men and women only (though, as I pointed out before, women with women were exempt).

Despite appearances, Paul is not condemning the practice of homosexuality because he is not addressing it as something that is evil or wicked. Instead, he is simply recognizing that homosexual relations are not something that his personal culture sees as being normal. Some argue that this is a kind of condemnation in itself. After all, he does say of the men (again the emphasis is more on the men than the women) that they 'received in themselves the due penalty for their perversion'. Notice that he does not say that God punished them, smote them, or was in any way the source of divine 'penalty' on these men. It is fair to suggest that Paul is making a commentary on the kinds of problems that naturally arise from any kind of promiscuous sex. Sexually transmitted diseases existed as readily in the ancient world as they do today and were an unfortunate byproduct of unprotected sex for gay, straight, and bisexual people alike. There may also be a hint in this text at the horrors of forced male prostitution, an issue that will become very important when we look at the next verse that discusses homosexuality. Why do I feel that this interpretation is justified?

Because when you go back to the rest of the verse and read what comes immediately after, it says in verses 28-32:

"And even as they did not like to retain God in their knowledge, God gave them over to a reprobate mind, to do those things which are not convenient; being filled with all unrighteousness, fornication, wickedness, covetousness, maliciousness; full of envy, murder, debate, deceit, malignity; whisperers, backbiters, haters of God, spiteful, proud, boasters, inventors of evil things, disobedient to parents, without understanding, covenantbreakers, without natural affection, implacable, unmerciful: Who knowing the judgement of God, that they which commit such things are worthy of death, not only do the same, but have pleasure in them that do them." Romans 1:28-32, KJV

"Furthermore, since they did not think it worthwhile to retain the knowledge of God, he gave them over to a depraved mind, to do what ought not to be done. They have become filled with every kind of wickedness, evil, greed, and depravity. They are full of envy, murder, strife, deceit, and malice. They are gossips, slanderers, God-haters, insolent, arrogant, and boastful; they invent ways of doing evil; they disobey their parents; they are senseless, faithless, heartless, ruthless. Although they know God's righteous decree that those who do such things deserve death, they not only continue to do these very things but also approve of those who practice them." Romans 1:28-32, NIV

This is where Paul gets fired up and addresses things that he sees as being the most wrong and evil in Roman culture. Notice the list: envy, murder, strife, deceit, malice, gossiping, slandering, God-hating, insolent, arrogant, boastful, disobedient to parents, senseless, faithless, heartless, and ruthless. These are the things that Paul recognizes as deserving death according to God's law... but nowhere in that list did homosexuality come up. Paul had just addressed homosexuality a few verses before, so he could have easily reiterated it into this list as well. This is more apparent when you stop to consider that a repeated theme in Paul's writings is the need to remind both himself and his brethren that the Levitical laws no longer hold sway.

God's salvation is open to all regardless of religious laws because of belief in Christ's teachings. Considering this, it is more than reasonable to assert that Paul is not condemning homosexual relationships. Remember that we are reading Paul's response to a letter that he received from Rome. We have no idea what the church in Rome was asking that prompted Paul to even bring the issue up. What matters is that Paul is simply stating that women being with women and men being with men was something that was foreign to him because of his own ethnic background. Remember that in Judaism even if men or women had homosexual inclinations they were still expected to marry and produce children, whereas it sounds like the relationships the church in Rome was coming across was women and men who were refusing to live a lie and instead lived with each other in a manner that we may recognize today as same sex partnerships.

Paul's second addressing of homosexuality comes up in his letter to the Corinthians:

"*Know ye not that the unrighteous shall not inherit the kingdom of God? Be not deceived: neither fornicators, nor idolators, nor adulterers, nor effeminate, nor abusers of themselves with mankind, Nor thieves, nor covetous, nor drunkards, nor revilers, nor extortioners, shall inherit the kingdom of God. And such were some of you: but ye are washed, but ye are sanctified, but ye are justified in the name of the Lord Jesus and by the Spirit of our God.*" 1 Corinthians 6:9-11, KJV
"*Do you not know that the wicked will not inherit the kingdom of God? Do not be deceived: neither the sexually immoral, nor idolaters, nor adulterers or male prostitutes nor homosexual offenders, nor thieves, nor the greedy, nor drunkards, nor slanderers, nor swindlers, will inherit the kingdom of God. And that is what some of you were. But you were washed, you were sanctified, you were justified in the name of the Lord Jesus Christ and by the Spirit of our God.*" 1 Corinthians 6:9-11, NIV

This is one of the verses where it is worthwhile to read the King James Version and compare it with the New International Version, because there is a big difference in how the two versions translate this text. One defines 'effeminate' and 'abusers of themselves with mankind', while the other translates it as 'male prostitutes' and 'homosexual offenders'. Some sources do not even identify this wording with gay men but referring to men who are habitual masturbators. The reason for this odd variation is that the Greek words used to imply these issues are two words that scholars have great trouble nailing down a concrete definition. Both the terms 'effeminate' and 'male prostitute' are interpreted from the Greek word '*arsenokoitai*'.

Biblical and Greek scholars are left scratching their head on this one because it is not the same word that Paul uses in Romans when he refers to homosexuals, but it is a word that seems to imply some kind of male with male sexual act. Another problem is that this Greek word occurs very rarely even in other Greek works and so there is not a lot of reference for understanding this word. When it is used, it seems to refer some kind of horrible, illegal act; it can be translated as 'male prostitute', but it carries a much deeper meaning than this. As I have shown, in the ancient world (and especially in Greece), consensual homosexual sex was normal. The act of rape being committed by one man upon another man was seen as an instance of sexual violence that was done not just for perverse sexual gratification, but as a form of domination and humiliation. What the Greeks are likely implying with the word *arsenokoitai* is not just a man who has sex with other men, but a man who gets off on degrading, violent sex with other men. In modern terms we would see this as someone who is sexually turned on by sadism, masochism, bondage, and the hurt or humiliation of their sex partner. Scholars believe that this interpretation may be the most accurate because of the Greek terms that immediately follow in the Corinthians verse.

The words 'abusers of themselves with mankind' or 'homosexual offenders' are being translated from a related Greek word '*malakoi*'. This particular Greek word is a derogatory term that literally means soft and is intended as an insult towards a man. Remember that while homosexuality was permitted in these societies, Greek, Roman, and even Jewish cultures were still obsessed with masculinity and men were still expected to behave as men. Women were seen as soft and meant to be dominated during the sex act, something which emphasized masculine power. Sadly, there was no greater insult to masculinity than to be forced into the degraded position of a woman. In this case *malakoi* may refer to men who are allowing themselves to be used like women by being degraded and abused sexually for money.

This concept is not so foreign to us in our modern world. While there is nothing wrong with two adults engaging in consensual sex, we are still faced with the sad reality of those who prostitute themselves (male and female) often because there is no other way to survive or because they have been forced into sexual slavery. Even to this day there is a thriving underground market in which human beings - men, women, and children - are sold for the sex trade. If it is still a problem in a 'modern' and educated time like ours, how much more prevalent in the Roman world where the slave trade was rampant? Just as we are disgusted and appalled when we see the horrendous sexual crimes committed against these victims, so too was Paul and others. The kind of sexual activity that is being addressed in this verse is, again, not the idea of homosexuality we have today where we see loving couples of the same gender building a life of commitment and sacrifice that is no different from straight couples. In 1 Corinthians what we are being shown is not the act of consensual sex between two adults, but the act of one man in power choosing to violently degrade another man sexually.

This meaning is asserted again in the third instance of the New Testament that addresses homosexuality, the book of 1 Timothy. The majority of Biblical scholars who specialize in the writings of Paul agree that 1 Timothy is a letter that was written in Paul's name by an anonymous Christian leader living a century or two after the real Paul. Because of this, 1 Timothy should be taken with a grain of salt in terms of interpreting it, and it is doubtful that it has anything to do with

Paul's personal views or writings.

Some Bible readers may be scandalized to hear that some of the books in the New Testament were not written by Paul, but in the ancient world it was not uncommon at all for religious leaders to write their own documents and forge the name of a respected authority like Paul in order to lend weight to their own beliefs. There is also the issue that because surnames did not come into use until our recent modern times, there wasn't much that could be done to separate the identity of one Paul from another. It certainly doesn't help that the name was quite common in the ancient world, just like John still is today. The people who did this did not see their actions as blasphemous because they felt that they had the right interpretation; by forging Paul's name they thought it would help clarify issues that they personally felt Paul would have agreed with… of course the problem with this is that everyone's interpretation is different and there is no way to know if Paul would have agreed with them at all. I will go far more in-depth into this issue of Paul in Chapter 18 *A Christian Revolution?*, but for now understand that even if this letter is not written by Paul, it has become an important part of the New Testament. This verse has been a factor in the condemnation of homosexuality by some Christian sects. It reads:

"But we know that the law is good, if a man use it lawfully; knowing this that the law is not made for a righteous man, but for the lawless and disobedient, for the ungodly and for sinners, for unholy and profane, for murderers of fathers and murderers of mothers, for manslayers, for whoremongers, for them that defile themselves with mankind, for menstealers, for liars, for perjured persons, and if there by any other thing that is contrary to sound doctrines; According to the glorious

gospel of the blessed God, which was committed to my trust."
1 Timothy 8-10, KJV
"We know that the law is good if one uses it properly.
We also know that law is made not for the righteous but for
lawbreakers and rebels, the ungodly and sinful, the unholy
and irreligious; for those who kill their fathers or mothers, for
murderers, for adulterers and perverts, for slave traders and
liars and perjurers - and for whatever else is contrary to the
sound doctrine that conforms to the glorious gospel of the
blessed God, which he entrusted to me." 1 Timothy 8-10, NIV

Again we have a big discrepancy in how these verses are
translated. The King James Version insists on the words
'whoremongers' and those 'that defile themselves with
mankind', while the New International Version insists on
using 'perverts'. The reason for the discrepancy is that we run
into that rare Greek word again *arsenokoitai* and *malakoi*.
Some believe that the inclusion of 'kidnappers' and
'menstealers' right after these two terms in the verse help to
identify those two words as being related to the idea of sexual
slavery. In the ancient world, many poor and foreign peoples
were kidnapped by 'man stealers' who then sold them to
Roman citizens for the express purpose of sexual slavery and
prostitution. In effect the verse is addressing a triad of 'sin':
the sadistic men who pay to commit sexual violence on
another, the male prostitutes who may (or may not) be
allowing this for the sake of money, and the slave traders and
kidnappers who keep the market going by forcibly
imprisoning and selling other human beings. Clearly what is
being condemned in the New Testament is the sadistic sexual
acts committed by free men with money and power, and the
stripping away of the free will and soul of those that are forced
into the role of prostitution. Again, none of which bears any

resemblance to today's homosexual relationships which are based upon consensual sex and intimacy between two men or two women. Christian protestors would do well to forget using this verse as fuel against homosexuality and return it to its rightful place as condemning anyone who partakes in rape and forced sex trafficking even in our modern day.

In the midst of this another issue needs to be raised. Though the Greek words being used in these verses imply a kind of sexual violence between men, there was another issue in Greece and Rome that may have been a cause of concern and disgust to leaders of the early Church. The reason for so much emphasis on sexual 'perversion' was because sexuality infused every aspect of Greek and certainly Roman life. Many religious purists try to compare our modern culture in America with that of Rome, claiming that we have become a nation with too much sexual freedom and perversion. The truth is that even with all our freedom, we are still nowhere near the Roman model. Not only was sexual rape and violence a normal 'privilege' for wealthy free Roman men to commit upon women, male slaves, and female slaves, there was an even darker side to Roman sexuality.

Since the time of Greece, it was commonplace for wealthy free men to take young boys under their wing. In the process of becoming a father figure and mentor in teaching these young children, it was also recognized that the male mentor had absolute right to the child sexually. This relationship was known as 'pederasty', and while society was well aware of the reality, the children had no say in this. This system was so common it was not even viewed as sexual abuse even when it occurred within a family environment between uncles and nephews! An example of the damage inflicted upon these boys and their helplessness can be seen in

an account of the mentally psychotic Roman emperor
Caligula. Renowned for his own cruelty and perversions,
Caligula had been 'mentored' by his own uncle and was
subjected to cruel physical and sexual abuse at the hands of a
man who had even taken one of the young boys under his
charge and murdered him by throwing him out a window.
Today we recognize that anyone who has sexual attraction for
children has a mental illness and is classified as a pedophile
and sexual predator.

Interestingly, this mindset may have begun to develop in
the Christian church by seeing such damaging and abusive
relationships for what they were. As a survivor of childhood
sexual abuse I want to take this chance to make something
clear: pedophilia and homosexuality have no relationship to
each other! Every time I hear someone spouting their
ignorance by saying that they feel allowing a gay man or
woman to be around children is the same as a pedophile, it
makes me ill. I suffered at the hands of pedophiles. I
witnessed other children in my family suffer horrendous
sexual abuse at the hands of men we were related to. It did not
matter if the child was a boy or a girl, they preyed on both
genders. None of these men were homosexual. So please, I
pray if the reader has ever entertained that damaging notion
that they will discard it immediately. Pedophilia has no gender
and it has no sexual orientation; it is a mental illness that must
be rooted out by society and brought into the light.

In a society like Rome where having money and power
allowed Roman men to do whatever they wanted to another
human being, it is no wonder that a religion like Christianity
became popular amongst the masses of slaves and
downtrodden who found in the teachings of Christ a sense of
worth, salvation, hope, and equality. I tried to make it clear in

the opening of this book that I have never had any interest in bashing religion or getting rid of faith, and this is one place where I will sing the praises of a religion like Christianity. While it is true that the fanatical sects of Christianity that would later come into power would do a great deal of harm, in the very beginning of the faith it was indeed a powerful tool for good. It was the first faith in the Roman empire that really united thousands of men and women who had no hope and no sense of worth because of living in a society that had enslaved them and stripped them of all rights. It was not until Christianity was legalized by the Roman Emperor Constantine that it would evolve into something so highly political that it became an excuse for exclusion, oppression, and even physical abuse under the accusation of heresy.

It is incredibly sad to me to see Christian sects that have made issues like homosexuality, abortion, and sex their fanatical sticking points. In doing this they have essentially chosen to place themselves on the same level as God. They condemn and judge using words from a book that they do not even fully understand. They use translations that Biblical scholars know are faulty or incorrect. They are operated under the leadership of clergy who have their own religious or political agendas. Sensationalizing homosexuality, giving already prejudiced people a religious license for their hate, emphasizing the dehumanization of gays, lesbians, or transgenders, has become a quick method for some churches and clergy to call greater attention to themselves. In doing so they benefit from increasing the amount of money that comes into their coffers. They act from a place of fear that has completely ignored not only reason but the knowledge of what the Bible really says. Faithful believers take for granted that the person speaking from the pulpit knows what they are talking about when, in fact, many clergy have never even studied the Bible in its original language. Sadly, many clergy who do have a background and know these things often stay silent because to try and fight against the ignorance of more popular sects may invite outright wrath and even financial ruin.

16. LGBT: A Blessing To Humanity

I have chosen to write extensively on this issue simply because I have recognized the need to do my part in rectifying what has been so blatantly painful for so much of humanity. Even as the tide has turned in the popular opinion of the LGBT community in the United States and Europe for the last fifteen years, the Western world cannot rest on these small victories. Lesbians, gays, and transgender people face horrific cruelty, prejudice, and outright violence in many parts of Africa, South America, and the Middle East. As the spotlight of the world came upon Russia with the advent of the 2014 Sochi Olympics, the former USSR was exposed for implementing a radical legal measure of homophobic propaganda. Even as modern Russia seeks to find its place in a world of technology and advancement, it has proven that it still holds a Dark Ages mentality when it comes to the spectrum of human sexuality. In a smear campaign that has its roots in the religious mentality of the Russian Orthodox Church and is endorsed by Russia's own government, homosexuality and pedophilia are presented as one and the same. This notion is ridiculous.

No one should ever support relationships that are not consensual. Pedophilia, bestiality, and any form of sexual relationship with a partner unwilling, unable, or too young to understand what is going on, is flat out **rape**. Any sexual activity with a human being, male or female, young or old, without their consent is **rape**. **Rape is never acceptable**, but the consensual activity of two mature adults, be it men with men, women with women, or women with men is not something that should be judged or oppressed by the ignorance of others.

People have a right to believe whatever they wish, but they do not have a right to enforce it upon another human being, and especially not through violence or religious oppression. In Russia, gay men and women are routinely 'hunted' in a sick parody of sport by vigilantes insisting they are simply punishing 'pedophiles'. Homosexuality is seen as a mental disorder by the majority of Russians, and any attempt to fight back against the violent, sadistic torture of these vigilantes is quickly halted thanks to Russia's 'anti-gay propaganda' measure. Any attempt to stand up for gay rights, or to educate the public about the normality of homosexuality is instantly halted and protestors risk the kind of jail time that their homophobic persecutors will never see. The wonderful work of organizations like Human Rights Watch and documentaries like *Hunted: The War on Gays in Russia* are helping to expose these atrocities, but what of so many other places in the world where this persecution continues?

In all of these places one fact remains: homophobic persecution is sanctioned, enforced, and spread thanks to a religious mindset which chooses to read the Bible's scant passages on homosexuality as incontrovertible truth. I have tried to expose the fallacy of this mentality by showing the real history of these Biblical texts with the sincere hope that it can help change this mindset. For those who feel they are so righteous in their faith, I hope their certainty has cracked and they open their hearts to the knowledge that these human beings are not abnormal or deviants or any other name which implies that their desires are somehow unnatural. For those who are on the fence, I pray this has shown you a path to understanding and compassion. For those who are part of the LGBT community, may the information here not only illuminate your path, but serve as a powerful weapon against the ignorance of others. Only good can come into this world by embracing the energy of consensual Love in all its forms. It is the job of every human being, whether they are gay, transgender, bisexual, or straight to stand up for the right of human beings to bring Light into this world through the expression of Love.

It is at this point that I wish to make a special recognition of the transgender community. Transgender men and women are human beings born into this world with an intense recognition that despite being born as one gender, their true essence and soul is the opposite. I honestly believe that these individuals have been born into this world to teach the rest of humanity something that society has forgotten: gender is fluid and was never meant to be a rigid role for human beings to be forced into. Because of the separation of the sexes and thousands of years of oppression placed upon women, gender roles became something that were politically and religiously charged. The worship of all things masculine and the insistence that masculinity somehow embodies perfect gender qualities is a mindset that has damaged the soul of humanity for far too long. It not only has oppressed women, but has oppressed the expression of feminine qualities like compassion, understanding, nurturing, peace, and a recognition of the power of nature. We forget too quickly that while women are the most obvious victims, any man who dared to cherish a more feminine mindset and actions was often just as badly ostracized and victimized by a violent society.

I have seen the issue of transgender be accused of being a completely 'modern' problem, but the truth is that a look at history shows that the transgender impulse has existed in human beings since the dawn of time. There are plentiful records in the ancient world of men who desired so strongly to serve alongside venerated priestesses in service of goddesses like Ishtar (the Middle East), Artemis (Greece), and Cybele (Turkey, Rome, and Northern Africa), that they actually made themselves into women the only way they knew through what we would call genital mutilation. Men seeking to become women and serve with women willingly became castrated and, in some societies, even underwent the extreme of having their penises split or partially removed. If that is not the same impulse that modern transgender men undergo when they seek gender realignment surgery by removal of their genitals, I do not know what is. Examples of women dressing and acting as men are also prevalent, even in Native American societies where such individuals were believed to be marked out by the spirits to become shamans.

In so many cultures transgender and gay individuals were viewed as gifted and kissed by the spirit world. They believed that a man who could actually live with the energy of a woman, or vice versa, was a soul who had come into perfect balance between masculine and feminine energies. These people were gifts to their communities. It was not until the advent of cultures who denigrated the feminine that perspectives began to change. In cultures like Greece and Rome where homosexual sex was glorified, the idea that a man would 'debase' himself by acting feminine began to impact the culture. By the time Christianity became a dominant religion, it is this Roman misogyny that will eventually lead to the fear and outlawing of all sexual 'perversions' in the Middle Ages. It is worth noting that transgender does not always mean homosexual, and many in the transgender community are bisexual.

I never understood until I embarked on these studies that bisexuality is truly a normal state for humanity. It is natural for women and men to think or fantasize about both genders. The truly rare are those who are absolute heterosexuals or absolute homosexuals in feeling no sexual response in the least for the respective gender. But again, in this sense, it is only about sex and sexual attraction. What I am speaking of transcends simple attraction and is elevated into the realm of love. In this respect more than ever I recognize them as souls that can teach us to look beyond the physical body and understand that love and identity are not limited by what genitals a human being is born with. They embody a simple fact about humanity that has become forgotten: men are born with feminine energy, and women are born with masculine energy. Both sexes have both kinds of gender hormones in their bodies, and qualities like love, strength, intelligence, and compassion are not the sole right of any single gender. Perhaps no group understands the reality of this more than transgender individuals and the gay community.

I say this to anyone reading this work who is openly gay, transgender, or bisexual: I see you as soldiers in the fight for the freedom of the human Soul. You who love without the blinders of the Ego have come to possess the true meaning of love. So many in the LGBT community have sacrificed themselves in our military so that we can live in a democratic country. Anything other than a hero's welcome by this nation is the real 'sin'. I thank you, and I pray that you will always come to the conclusion that you are an individual who is ready to love and accept yourself for who you are and not for who others want you to be. Happiness and love are the greatest gifts you can possess in the face of prejudice and those who would insist on living in ignorance.

For those who have chosen to stay hidden, whatever your reasons may be, I hope and pray that you will be able to come out and stand with so many who are ready to support and encourage you. It is only through the energy of those willing to take a stand for what is so instinctive in the human Soul that change can come to those who live with their closed minds. Being gay is not a disease. It is not some disorder, phase, or rebellion, and it is certainly not an abomination. Being gay, in my eyes, means simply being a human being, no better or different from anyone who is heterosexual. However, you have become stronger from standing in the face of the ignorance and lack of love exhibited by those who feel so certain in their righteousness. I ask you to rejoice, come out, and join those that have made the choice. Show your family members and loved ones that you are not a mistake of God. To the contrary, you are a gift from the Creator of humanity! If there is anything from this chapter that you can use, either for your own inner peace, or to arm yourself with knowledge against those who would shove a Bible in your face to make you feel ashamed, then my soul can rest in the knowledge that I have at least made some difference with my work.

For those who face the unique challenges of being transgender, may you find the happiness you deserve in asserting your identity to yourself and to the world. For the bisexuals, may you be more than a sexual identity and show the world that love has no gender. For the heterosexuals, consider yourselves blessed that you have come into this world unrestricted by the beliefs of man. You have been given the ability to coexist and love openly without condemnation because of your relationship with the opposite gender.

Remember that this is a blessing that should not be taken for granted, and may you never see it as a right that is yours alone, to be denied to those who would love just as passionately and beautifully with their own gender. I truly wish that humanity could see itself as I see everyone that has crossed my path.

We are souls that are here for a short time, inhabiting physical bodies that are the epitome of the Ego, but if humanity can allow the Soul to look into the souls of others it will be able to find the meaning for its lifetime. It will be able to embrace a spirit that can bring balance with peace and love guided by the Light of the Soul. All will be well within humanity when it allows the Soul to come forth and translate the meaning of life for themselves and not by the dogmas of man. I believe that as long as human beings educate themselves and follow the common sense of the Light that is carried in their souls, they will always know deep within themselves that being different does not mean anyone is ever an abomination to humanity. Quite the opposite, they will discover that the majority of the time, being different presents itself as a gift to humanity.

Unfortunately, for far too long in humanity's history, anyone different from the approved model decided by a religion was demonized. Too many times I have sat and listened to a religious cleric insist that Satan is behind so many of the 'evil' things going on in the world. How sad that into this mix is lumped homosexuality, transgenderism, bisexuality, and even feminism! As long as Satan is made a scapegoat, religion will never, ever take responsibility for the ignorance and damage it perpetuates in the name of God. While Satan gets the blame for truly atrocious things like murder, torture, illness, and evil, there comes a time to recognize that somehow almost the whole of human sexuality has also been laid at this so-called Fallen Angel's feet. In Chapter 21 *Satan, the Devil, and God: A Human Trinity* we will discover who Satan really is and why he was made to appear to be so evil. Exploring this topic will help you understand one of the greatest truths about humanity and the true source of evil. Perhaps nowhere and for no one does the adage 'the truth will set you free' apply more than to Satan himself, for he is the last bastion of ignorance that ties down so much of humanity into righteous hatred for the demons within themselves and what they deem to be 'demonic' in anyone else.

I am aware that with all I have written here that there will still be many who have a difficult time with what has been shown Biblically on the issue of homosexuality. Because neither my daughter nor myself are gay, I realize that this is an issue I could have easily steered clear of for the purpose of self-interest, but I speak honestly when I say I have felt no other choice than to expose myself to the kind of backlash and criticism that comes with even addressing any of this. I recognize now that homosexuality was never meant to be viewed by humanity the way that some religious sects portray so many of these beautiful human beings. I will always find it fitting now that the word 'gay' is applied to this community because it is a word that originally represented happiness. Yet for most of these men and women's lives they have experienced nothing but hell on earth thanks to people who have chosen to follow a misguided interpretation of a doctrine that was written thousands of years ago by men who had their own cultural and religious agendas.

Many people in the Western nations look at third world countries in the Middle East and feel that these people have stayed stagnate in their development because of their extreme religious beliefs… and yet many of the people who feel this way are stagnate in their own religious beliefs in choosing to judge others (especially the LGBT community) according to laws and doctrines that never originally belonged in a world of democracy, equality, and technology.

I beg anyone on the fence with this issue to look closely and see that when you look at so many in the gay community you will see human beings whose hearts are filled with so much love for their partners. I beg humanity to look beyond the physical body because the energy that is being displayed here is the energy of the soul itself. In all my studies and meditations, I truly believe that the soul makes a promise before it is born, acknowledging that it will find its soulmate in this lifetime regardless of gender. This can only happen in a society that recognizes that it is normal and natural for a person to be attracted to another human being regardless of gender.

This beauty only intensifies when it blossoms into the fullness of a family. Too many LGBT couples suffer the prejudices of people with quiet dignity, but it is another matter when their children are drawn into the cross fire. Some LGBT couples are blessed to have their own biological children and I have watched in horror as some religious fanatics insist these children would be better off in foster homes than be in a 'homosexual' environment. Never mind that these parents have never done a single thing that would warrant the removal of their children, but this is how extreme some people's religious homophobia is. Perhaps even sadder are those who put up roadblocks for LGBT couples to adopt. With so many thousands of parentless children constantly going in and out of the foster system, it is just unconscionable to me that anyone would deny a child a home filled with love just because the parents are of the same gender.

While I acknowledge the many wonderful heterosexual parents, I have witnessed something about many LGBT parents that makes my heart soar. One instance came when my daughter and I witnessed two women together with their young son. The little boy was rambunctious and one mother took him by the hand and reprimanded him more sternly, while the other mother coddled him. In his play, the little boy fell and began to cry. Both mothers were united in their reaction of comfort as the boy was scooped up into a family embrace. He was too young to articulate, but the interaction of these two mothers was so nurturing that the little boy immediately stopped crying and relaxed. It was if I was witnessing a mother's energy increased twofold. The little boy was so loved and so happy, it was as if he knew that there was no greater security than in the arms of his two mothers. Though the one woman had first behaved with what society deems to be 'masculine' fatherly behavior, while the other portrayed traditional 'feminine' behaviors, ultimately as they held their child I saw how they had brought the Light of true balance between the energies.

Our second experience occurred at an art museum. Two men came around the corner pushing a large black and pink stroller, and in the arms of one of the men was a beautiful little Asian girl. They stopped at each art piece, both doting and in utter devotion to this little girl they had adopted. Neither man dressed in an overt manner. They were both very traditionally 'masculine', and only the tender way in which they held hands or embraced showed that they might as well have been married. In watching them, I saw the feminine aspect so clearly presenting itself with such reverence from these two men. As with the lesbian women and their child, it was sheer love in its most beautiful form. Two men imbued with masculine energies had come to balance with the feminine and the Light was visible to anyone who could appreciate it. Both my daughter and I walked away in complete awe.

My third relevant experience was at a grocery store. A 'normal' husband and wife with three children came down the aisle. One young child was crying and the father looked at his wife and sternly asked her to keep him quiet. The mother looked tired and frazzled, but leaned over and comforted their youngest son. She put her arms around the little one while the other two held closely to her skirt. Her husband on the other hand paid no attention. As they were leaving after paying, the little one began to cry again. He turned around and snapped at the child to be quiet, and again the mother sought to comfort the child. As they left, he pushed the cart ahead of her while she lagged behind with the three children in tow. I have seen this scenario far too many times. Maybe it's taken for granted and I'm sure there are gay couples who would act the same way, but what I can honestly say is that I have not yet witnessed it.

I realized then that what I was seeing in many heterosexual couples like this was the energy of the soul out of balance. The father held no feminine energy whatsoever and he had left the balancing entirely to the woman. This lack of harmony was so dreadfully apparent and it was obvious that the man held little regard for what he saw as 'woman's work' when it came to dealing with the children. I did not see this attitude in the gay couples. In spite of being the same gender, I have truly seen more balance of the divine Masculine and Feminine between LGBT couples than in most heterosexuals. This is a lesson for all of humanity. This is the Light that loving members of the LGBT community carry.

This is where love truly begins, not in how you look or what your gender is, but in how you see one another. In the physical body we will always see what is before our eyes, which is often a human being that lives, thrives, and survives in the Ego so that it can be accepted in this world. But in the Soul of each individual exists an energy that calls to one another beyond the physical boundaries. This is why the wisdom persists that love is blind. Love sees no figure. It does not condemn the color of the skin, nor ethnicity, nor gender. How incredible it truly is for the human being who allows their Soul to fall in love with someone without prejudice or expectation and truly finds their soulmate! To me, this potential is one of the greatest gifts that was given to humanity.

Part III: Restoring the Light

*"The human Soul will only find its Light
when the Ego gives it permission."*
- C.C. Campbell

*"We can easily forgive a child
who is afraid of the dark;
the real tragedy of life is when men
are afraid of the Light."*
- Plato

17. From Old Misogyny To New

Since ancient times, misogyny (the disdain, resentment, and hatred of women) has been at the core of women's oppression and downfall. When the Bible is read through the eyes of faith, you may as well be reading a censored version. Somehow the importance of all the violent and unpleasant passages of the Bible become neutered when religious leaders skip over them to exhort the beauty and positivity of the more uplifting stories. Not only did I have my blinders firmly in place, looking back now I have had to admit that I could read verses about horrible things and be completely unphased, verses like:

"Happy shall he be, that taketh and dasheth thy little ones against the stones." Psalm 137:9, KJV

"Now go and smite Amalek, and utterly destroy all that they have, and spare them not; but slay both man and woman, infant and suckling, ox and sheep, camel and ass." 1 Samuel 15:3, KJV

And this gem from the New Testament that was used extensively to support the institution of slavery in Europe and North America prior to each country passing emancipation laws:

"Slaves, submit yourselves to your masters with all respect, not only to the good and gentle, but also to the cruel." 1 Peter 2:18, NIV

I read these verses, never once considering their implications as I swiftly returned to read over and over again the happier verses about God's love and Christ's redemption. I have two words for that: brain washing. Much as it pained me, and thoroughly sickened me, to come to that realization, there was no other explanation. In these past two sections I have shown the verses of the Bible that were the most shocking and have caused some of the worst suffering for humanity over the last few thousand years. The truly dreadful moment came when I realized that I had read all those verses at one point or another my entire life, and yet I had acted as though the impact they carried for humanity meant nothing. The light of religious righteousness isn't just blinding, it is searing, and it washes out all reason and clarity when it comes to seeing the world as it needs to be seen.

For most of my life, I had been deluded into thinking my soul was somehow in need of redemption, when really I had no idea that what my soul was really feeling was the suffocating weight placed upon it by the dogma of manmade religion. As a woman, I felt that weight so much more acutely than many can imagine. No matter how much religious men professed to feel the weight of their God-given 'burden' to be righteous leaders of their homes and communities, it was a joke compared to what they had insisted the Bible laid upon women. One of the great tenants of Christianity is this insistence that Christ came not only to redeem humanity from their 'sins', but to bring redemption through grace. This poetic phrase is meant to mean that while the Jews had followed their ethnic-religious laws for thousands of years in order to feel they were pleasing God, Christ had supposedly taught that all those oppressive laws were over and done with.

I had been taught that Christ came to show that a personal knowledge of God was available as long as one believed and followed his teachings, accepting his sacrifice on the cross. From the pulpit I often heard this Good News and how much it applied to women. I was reminded that women were so much better off because of Christ, that our burden of acknowledging a loving husband as head of the house was nothing compared to the ill treatment of women prior to Christ. But none of this was true. Granted, Christ seems to have had a revolutionary view of women, but insisting that somehow Christianity made life better for women than Judaism had was a fallacy. What is true, is that once Christianity came into a power sanctioned by the Roman Empire (and with it the texts of the New Testament) there was a big shift in how women were viewed. Not only was the change not positive, it had almost nothing to do with the teachings of Christ, but everything to do with the authors of the New Testament.

I have gone to great lengths to try to get across something crucial about the Bible, especially the Old Testament: it was written by Jewish religious men over three thousand years ago for Israelite men!   Because of this, all the laws over women come from men who are concerned with one thing and one thing alone when it comes to sexuality: the creation, stability, and continuation of a people. In an ancient world where it was rare to live into one's forties, the need to see sons grow up and take over the family business, or serve in the nation's army, or work the nation's land, was vital to the existence of a small ethnic nation like Israel. Considering the numerous times the Israelites were attacked and invaded, the survival of their ethnic-religious way of life depended upon women who could keep the population viable.

These were not the concerns for the men who wrote the New Testament, yet the early Church's view on sex became no less restrictive. Part of this is because they inherited this view from the Old Testament, but also from the influence of the Roman Empire. I will tackle the Roman influence a little later, for now I want to make a point about the Jewish influence on the notion of sex and women.

As I have shown, sex is far more prominent in the Bible than one would think (as is bloody violence). In the Old Testament, laws concerning sex are centered around one great concern: children. In the end, there is no higher law in the Old Testament than when God commanded Adam and Eve to be fruitful and multiply. So important is this mandate that any woman that was barren could expect to see her husband resort to impregnating the household female slave or handmaiden if it would give him an heir. A childless, widowed woman could expect her husband's brothers to get in line to sleep with her so that she could become pregnant with a son to carry on her dead husband's name and property since she was denied the legal right.

One of the stories that exemplifies this issue is the story of Lot. You may remember that Lot is the crucial figure in the story of the destruction of Sodom (way back in Chapter 13 *Sodom and Gomorrah: Seeing What Isn't There*). According to the story, Lot's wife disobeys the command of the Lord delivered by the angels to not look back at Sodom during the destruction. When she does, Lot's wife becomes the infamous pillar of salt, leaving only him and their two daughters to flee into the wilderness. Lot and his daughters take up shelter in a cave, and it is here that one of the most infamous stories of the Bible takes place:

"*... And he dwelt in a cave, he and his two daughters. And the firstborn said unto the younger, Our father is old, and there is not a man in the earth to come in unto us after the manner of all the earth. Come, let us make our father drink wine, and we will lie with him, that we may preserve the seed of our father. And they made their father drink wine that night: and the firstborn went in, and lay with her father; and he perceived not when she lay down, nor when she arose. And it came to pass on the morrow, that the firstborn said unto the younger, Behold, I lay yesternight with my father: let us make him drink wine this night also; and go thou in, and lie with him, that we may preserve the seed of our father. And they made their father drink wine that night also: and the younger arose, and lay with him; and he perceived not when she lay down, nor when she arose. Thus were both the daughters of Lot with child by their father.*" Genesis 19:30-36, KJV

"*... He and his two daughters lived in a cave. One day the older daughter said to the younger, "Our father is old, and there is no man around here to give us children - as is the custom all over the earth. Let's get our father to drink wine and then sleep with him and preserve our family line through our father." That night they got their father to drink wine, and the older daughter went in and slept with him. He was not aware of it when lay down or when she got up. The next day the older daughter said to the younger, 'Last night I slept with my father. Let's get him to drink wine again tonight, and you go in and sleep with him so we can preserve our family line through our father.' So they got their father to drink wine that night also, and the younger daughter went in and slept with him. Again he was not aware of it when she lay down or when when she got up. So both of Lot's daughters became pregnant by their father.*'" Genesis 19:30-36, NIV

This story brings up an interesting and often ignored area of Levitical law. Despite all of the laws concerning sex, especially who can have sex with whom, there is no law in any of the Torah prohibiting incest between fathers and daughters. There is a prohibition against sons sleeping with their father's wives, but this has nothing to do with incest and more to do with the son daring to usurp his father's power and property (since that is what the wife was: property). Some Biblical scholars argue that the reason incest is not addressed is that it was a common sense practice to avoid inbreeding in the population, and that the insistence upon a daughter's virginity at marriage would ensure no such act was committed by a father. Still, the fact remains, that were it to happen, there was no Levitical law condemning it.

There are deep problems with this story and this text. Remember that this is the same Lot who offered these same virgin daughters to be raped and assaulted by the men of Sodom in place of his male guests (again, an issue thoroughly addressed in Chapter 13). These daughters are often painted as the aggressors, and the evilness of their conception is laid at their own feet while their father is shown to be an innocent victim. The interpretation of this story has always been one that has kept me thinking: How was it possible that the father could not be aware that he was actually having sexual contact with one of his daughters? To begin with, no matter how drunk the daughters got their father, it seems more than eyebrow raising that Lot is able to still perform sexually not once, but twice. One would think by the time the second daughter got him drunk the next day that he'd have been so hung over from the excessive intake of alcohol, that he would never have been able to impregnate his daughter.

According to the scripture above, Lot is so wasted from drunkenness that he is basically unconscious. How could an unconscious man get up enough sexual drive to successfully impregnate a woman, unless he was aware that a woman was with him and that woman could have only been his daughter. There is no way that Lot is simply blissfully ignorant of his actions. Even if one insists upon this insidious interpretation, when Lot awakens he must be aware of what transpired, and he certainly could not play dumb when both of his daughters' bellies began to swell with child! Nowhere in the following scriptures is there ever any kind of condemnation upon Lot or the daughters for the act of incest or of the children born of the union. Notice the emphasis in the story: preservation of the family line. I question this story, like I question all stories now from the Bible. Perhaps this story more than any delivered a major blow to my faith in the Bible.

Because this story is recounted in Genesis, religious traditions state that the author is supposed to be Moses. But this is not possible. Moses is supposed to have lived thousands of years after the events of Genesis. The religious minded will instead insist that God revealed all these stories to Moses, so it could be argued that Moses by the magic of God was given the ability to witness what transpired in that cave and recorded it. If this is true, it means the God of the Bible watched Lot's daughters and their evil action, so why didn't God smite down this incestuous family at that moment? After all, Lot was someone that God had just saved from the destruction of Sodom! Thinking of this, I had to wonder why God did not bother to toss in some divine commentary about how wrong He felt incest was while recounting it to Moses!

Later in my studies I discovered just why this story was
kept in Genesis. The son each daughter gave birth to ends up
becoming founders of two sects of peoples who were enemies
of the ancient Hebrews. In essence, this story served as a way
for ancient Hebrews to degrade the origins of two of their
enemies, while elevating their own ethnic status. Still, as
always, it is the image of women that is sacrificed in order to
make this point. Over and over again in my mind as I studied
and learned, I had to wonder how on earth the God of the
Bible had become so venerated for being all knowing,
especially in terms of the future of humanity. In spite of this,
this God seemed completely unwilling to intervene in
moments like these, but as I learned about the mythology of
Yahweh as just another god of war, it made sense. A war god
has little regard for the sensitivities of the female sex when the
divine emphasis is on conquering and national domination by
the men who venerate him. Lot's daughters are just another
casualty, a means to an end, as all women in the Old
Testament are, their greatest importance lying only in their
child bearing value or as propaganda tools. The rampant
moral contradictions and stories of injustice show the reality
of how one book with many authors has taken the soul of
women as prisoners for the ego of men.

Judaism would eventually develop a fascinating stance
on female sexuality because of the overwhelming importance
of procreation in keeping Jewish identity alive. While many
oppressive laws remained such as women having to be virgins
upon marriage, to dress modestly and cover their heads and
resigning to being only wives and mothers, etc., there came a
slow shift in the mindset that began to be revealed when a
fascinating body of work entered the Jewish mindset: the
Talmud. In AD 70 the Jews of Palestine made a final violent

effort to overthrow Roman control of the region, and the Roman war machine responded by starving out the people of Jerusalem, slaughtering the rebels, and ultimately destroying the great Temple. As punishment most of the Jewish remnant was scattered throughout the vast empire. It would seem the mythological war god Yahweh kept getting trounced by the mythological war gods of whatever empire was in charge at the time. When I made this remark I once had someone say to me that the reason for this was because the Jews kept disobeying him. I responded that that excuse was even worse as it implied that Yahweh basically abandoned them. I've seen human parents manage to stand by and uphold their children through the worst rebellions and crises, so shouldn't a divine god be able to do the same? Needless to say, I didn't get much of a response.

In an effort to continue the tradition of Jewish learning and to establish a uniform religion regardless of where Jews lived, religious bodies began to write a massive book of commentary and expanded laws known as the Talmud. The Talmud was written by Jews in both Babylon and Palestine, becoming a massive codex of laws and Jewish commentary upon the Tanakh. Basically, where rabbis felt the Bible left a question mark on certain issues, groups of men in religious authority got together, hashed out hypotheses and wrote them down until most were agreed upon as further rules for religious Jews. Despite the fact that, once again, women had absolutely no say in these new laws whatsoever, a recognition does arise that may surprise readers: Sex is a good thing and not just for babies!

While it really can't be said that any of these men went to any great lengths to enlighten others about female sexuality (or consult any females), the Talmud and Jewish religious laws recognize that while the main purpose of sex is for procreation, it is also meant to be a sensual blessing upon both men and women. It insists that a woman has a right to her desire and that a man has a responsibility to awaken desire in his wife (adding the incentive that bringing one's wife to climax may help ensure the conception of sons). Though the body must be covered up for modesty sake (a rule applying to both men and women), it is not because the body is somehow dirty or sinful, but because it is powerful and sensual. It is to be enjoyed only behind closed doors between a husband and wife.

Significantly, women were not allowed to read or study the Talmud, nor participate in its writing, so again women were blocked from having any input in Talmudic law about their own sexuality or bodies. In spite of this, the fact that the Talmud insists on the glory of the body and sexuality would become a vast contradiction to the stance Christianity would end up taking and which I will address in the next chapter.

When it comes to sexuality, contradictions abound in the Old Testament between the strict Levitical view of sex and what may have really happened in daily life. A fantastic example can be found in the book of Ruth. It tells the story of a Jewish woman named Naomi and her two sons who marry foreign women, one of whom is Ruth. When both sons die, Naomi releases her daughter-in-laws to return to their father's households, but Ruth insists upon staying with Naomi and returning with her mother-in-law back to the land of Judah. Ruth, Moabite born, is a picture of humility and loyalty as she cares for Naomi, scavenging grain from fields to feed them both, until she comes to the attention of a kind and wealthy land owner named Boaz. Naomi eventually gives Ruth an interesting order:

"And now is not Boaz of our kindred, with whose maidens thou wast? Behold he winnoweth barley tonight in the threshing floor. Wash thyself therefore, and anoint thee, and put thy raiment upon thee, and get thee down to the floor: but make not thyself known unto the man, until he shall have done eating and drinking. And it shall be, when he lieth down, that thou shalt mark the place where he shall lie, and thou shalt go in, and uncover his feet, and lay thee down; and he will tell thee what thou shalt do." Ruth 3:2-4, KJV

"... Boaz, with whose women you have worked, is a relative of ours. Tonight he will be winnowing barley on the threshing floor. Wash, put on perfume, and get dressed in your best clothes. Then go down to the threshing floor... when he lies down, note the place where he is lying. Then go and uncover his feet and lie down. He will tell you what to do." Ruth 3:2-4, NIV

Many people read this story and never realize that there is a whole level of meaning to Naomi's orders than they ever imagined. Hard as it may be to comprehend in our modern world, the phrase 'uncover his feet' was a euphemism for sex in the ancient world. In fact, many references to the handling of feet in the Old Testament are symbolic for sexual intercourse. Consider for a moment just how many ways we have of referring to sex in our own modern times! Someday far in the future there may be people reading stories written by current writers and when they see a phrase like 'he wanted to bang her', they will scratch their head and wonder why he wanted to blow her up! This is the kind of problem modern readers will always encounter with an ancient text like the Bible, but the problem is that very rarely do theologians or clergy ever bother to point out this pitfall.

Ruth, a character often exalted from the pulpit for her submission and loyalty, does everything that Naomi asks, right down to 'uncovering his feet'. Ancient Hebrews reading this story would have chuckled and nudged one another, recognizing the truth that Ruth had ensured her future by sleeping with Boaz, an older man of prestige and a redeemer of Naomi's family. And yet, this is sex outside of marriage! According to Levitical law, shouldn't she have been stoned or cast out? Ruth is now one of the most celebrated figures of the Old Testament and a constant model for Biblical women for her goodness, yet how many pastors and preachers would sing her praises if they knew that she is guilty of enjoying premarital sex with Boaz?

When Boaz discovers Ruth 'at his feet', she says to him:

"Spread therefore thy skirt over thine handmaid; for thou art a near kinsman.' to which Boaz responds with a hearty, "... And he said, Blessed be thou of the Lord, my daughter, for thou hast showed more kindness in the latter end than at the beginning, inasmuch as thou followedst not young men, whether poor or rich." Ruth 3:9-11, KJV

"Spread the corner of your garment over me...The Lord bless you, my daughter, this kindness is greater than that which you showed earlier. You have not run after the younger men, whether rich or poor, and now, my daughter, do not be afraid. I will do for you all you ask..." Ruth 3:9-11, NIV

How did Boaz know that she was requesting his protection and legitimacy of marriage if she had not offered herself sexually? In a Hebraic society where the two genders were kept separated, requesting anything as intimate as having him put his garment over her and 'uncovering his feet' could only intimate that Ruth and Boaz became intimate (especially when she must then sneak away back to Naomi before anyone else is awake). Boaz's enthusiastic response and awe that a beautiful young woman like Ruth would come to an older man such as himself, and lay with him sexually was indeed something Boaz was grateful for and I can just imagine many Jewish men reading this tale with a knowing smile.

Things turned out well for Ruth and Boaz, and yet the real meaning of this interlude between them has become entirely lost for modern readers. How much irony there is in the condemnation of two people having premarital sex when right in this passage one of few great female characters of the Old Testament has her fate determined by sleeping with a man she is not married to! Today there are many who condemn women like her, and yet Ruth is chosen in the Bible to be one of the few women mentioned in the ancestry of King David and eventually Christ in the New Testament. Whatever pitfalls of misogyny ancient Israelites can be accused of, the truth is that the view that would evolve in Judaism of human sexuality was made to look gloriously healthy when contrasted to the views that would evolve in Christianity.

18. A Christian Revolution?

As the early Church evolved into the Catholic Church, a strange fanaticism began to take hold concerning celibacy, sinfulness, and the inherent 'dirtiness' of human sexuality. Along with this view began a systematic campaign by later writers of the New Testament against all things related to women and the female gender.

Regardless of Jesus' teachings, later books of the New Testament record what would become a prevalent viewpoint of the early Church thanks to verses such as:

"But I would have you know, that the head of every man is Christ; and the head of the woman is the man; and the head of Christ is God. Every man praying or prophesying, having his head covered, dishonoureth his head. But every woman that prayeth or prophesieth with her head uncovered dishonoureth her head: for that is even all one as if she were shaven. For if the woman be not covered, let her also be shorn: but if it be a shame for a woman to be shorn or shaven, let her be covered." 1 Corinthians 11:3-6, KJV

"But I want you to realize that the head of every man is Christ, and the head of the woman is man, and the head of Christ is God. Every man who prays or prophesies with his head covered dishonors his head. But every woman who prays or prophesies with her head uncovered dishonors her head - it is the same as having her head shaved. For if a woman does not cover her head, she might as well have her hair cut off; but if it is a disgrace for a woman to have her hair cut off or her head shaved, then she should cover her head."
1 Corinthians 11:3-6, NIV

I would like to make some commentary on this infamous verse. The first portion of this address, which is believed to have been written by the Apostle Paul to the early Church at Corinth, deals with the question of head coverings. This verse has been used to shame modern women into being overtly conscious about their hair and has forced many women in certain Christian sects to wear head coverings while in church. What modern readers do not realize is that this command has more to do with the cultural customs going on during Paul's time and nothing to do with how modern women should behave.

In both Roman and Jewish cultures, a woman's hair was always seen as a symbol of her sexuality, and in ancient Rome women who had severely cut hair or shaved heads were often associated with prostitution or sexual slavery. For this reason, Paul recognizes that a woman who has become part of the Christian community must put this kind of life behind her if she is going to be a part of the church. By covering her hair, a woman is acknowledging the desire to leave behind her former life of prostitution or slavery. Covering her head would also avoid unwanted attention by those who might realize she came from such a profession, but also the covering of hair was something Paul (a former religious Jew) would have endorsed from his own cultural preferences. Ultimately, while the command of this verse made perfect sense for the era it was written, it is a shame that it is used in our modern time to shackle women to a custom that has no place or reason in our modern world. The truly problematic verses come next:

"For a man indeed ought not to cover his head, forasmuch as he is the image and the glory of God: but the woman is the glory of the man. For the man is not of the

woman; but the woman of the man. Neither was the man created for the woman; but the woman for the man."
1 Corinthians 11:7-9, KJV
   "A man ought not to cover his head, since he is the image of the glory of God; but woman is the glory of man. For man did not come from woman, but woman from man; neither was man created for woman, but woman for man."
1 Corinthians 11:7-9, NIV

If the New Testament's stance on women could not get any clearer, Paul puts a deeper nail into the coffin of the hopes of women for any kind of recognition or equality in the body of Christ:

   "Let your women keep silence in the churches: for it is not permitted unto them to speak; but they are commanded to be under obedience, as also saith the law. And if they will learn any thing, let them ask their husbands at home: for it is a shame for women to speak in the church." 1 Corinthians 14:34-35, KJV
   "Women should remain silent in the churches. They are not allowed to speak, but must be in submission, as the law says. If they want to inquire about something, they should ask their own husbands at home; for it is disgraceful for a woman to speak in the church." 1 Corinthians 14:34-35, NIV

Ironically this verse seems to be in direct contradiction to a verse in Galatians in which Paul asserts the equality of those who accept Christ:
   "There is neither Jew nor Greek, there is neither bond nor free, there is neither male nor female: for ye are all one in Christ Jesus." Galatians 3:28, KJV

"There is neither Jew nor Gentile, neither slave nor free, nor is there male and female, for you are all one in Christ Jesus." Galatians 3:28, NIV

Either Paul is bipolar on his view of women, or perhaps he is just writing what he thinks each particular church wants to hear. I addressed most of the Apostle Paul's history in Chapter 15 *Homosexuality and Paul* because most of the verses used to condemn homosexuality in the New Testament are attributed to him. The argument I made there bears repeating here. For those unfamiliar with the history of Christianity, the Apostle Paul was believed to be a man who had once been a devout religious Jew and had borne a personal vendetta against the followers of Christ. He himself never met Jesus, but he supposedly had a metaphysical vision of Christ that made him convert to Christianity and become its most avid missionary. Though Christianity claims to have been founded on the teachings of Christ, nearly every tenant and belief of the Christian religion originates with Paul and the rest of the writings of the New Testament.

Only four Gospels tell the story and words of Christ, and yet Christianity built itself upon twenty-three books and letters written by men who may have never even met or personally conversed with Jesus Christ. I have to admit, I often began to ask myself why on earth anyone bothered to called themselves Christians when it was apparent that strict religious Christians follow the words of Paul far more closely than the words of Christ! I suppose 'Paulianity' just wasn't as appealing a title. One of the problems with Paul, is that from what little is known about him, he appears to have been a man of contradictions. On the one hand it is believed he was raised as an educated and deeply religious Jew, well versed in his own dogma and religious laws, but on the other he was also a man educated in Greek (the language of the New Testament) who was so familiar with the Hellenized culture of Greece and Rome that he often recast Christ's teachings and stories to appeal to a Greco-Roman audience. Why that is so important will become clear later.

Something began to seem so wrong when I realized that almost all the rules of Christianity were created and set forth by Paul. The very foundation of the Catholic Church (the first organized form of Christianity) and all Christians sects that were to come after are built on the teachings of Paul and Peter. If Jesus had truly meant to create a Church, wouldn't he, as the son of God, have taken the time to truly elaborate upon how he wanted his followers to continue worshipping him and building his Church?

For those at this moment who feel I have deeply erred in this line of reasoning because of the New Testament verse of Matthew 16:18 in which Jesus gives his disciple Peter the missive to build his church, I will return to that argument later. Even if one wishes to hold onto this command by Christ, I want to point out that most of Christian law is still owed to Paul more than any other - a man Jesus himself never spoke of in spite of the fact that he could have prophesied about him to his disciples had he cared to.

At the end of the day, the fact that Christ did not take the time to establish his own religion should make every person who calls themselves a Christian reconsider their own beliefs and ask themselves whether they truly follow the teachings of Christ, or are they allowing the opinions of Paul to dictate how they live their religious lives? I know for myself, I had to admit that I had been living more by the words of Paul than of Christ. In essence, I have come to recognize that only those Christians who can discard the works of Paul and follow the teachings of Christ have any right to call themselves

Christians.

Indeed, a solely Christ based religion would have no higher calling than to love God and to love your neighbor, to feed the hungry and help the poor, heal the sick and reach out to the dying, and treat all other human beings without judgement. When he said: *I am the truth, I am the way, I am the Light*, his words should have been made evident to every Christian. The Truth is that he showed how to love humanity unconditionally. The Way represented the choice each one of us would have to make if we truly wanted to change the way the world treated human life, animals, and the planet. The Light is how he tried to illuminate for humanity what was happening in the world around him. Ultimately, he exemplified the divine light that was given to all of us. The heart of these teachings are what Christianity was always supposed to be, but two thousand years of Church history has shown this is not what happened. To make matters worse, as I began to truly study the history of the New Testament, I discovered a shocking truth: Half of the works attributed to Paul were never written by him!

I glanced over some of the methods used by Biblical scholars to study ancient texts and investigate their authors back in the first section of this book. Incredibly talented women and men who have devoted their lives to studying these ancient texts (often without any kind of religious prejudice of their own) have been able to use many methods to learn about the writers of the Bible. The world owes a great debt to these scholars, because without them people like myself who wanted to learn the truth would never have been able to discover the reality and history of the Bible (not to mention there would be no works to reference in my bibliography). These scholars look at every detail of how the

206 The Stolen Light Of WoMen

work is written, going back to the earliest sources they have. In the case of the New Testament, these sources are almost always Greek, and by looking at the way the author repeats certain phrases, favors certain words, uses particular inflections, they pick up on the author's personal writing style - a kind of literary signature. In the case of the man Christianity calls Paul, Biblical scholars feel comfortable in declaring that the New Testament books of Romans, 1 and 2 Corinthians, Galatians, Philippians, 1 Thessalonians and Philemon were, indeed, written by Paul. The book of Acts, which intends to tell the story of Paul and Peter, is believed to have not been written by Paul, but instead by the same person who wrote the Gospel of Luke. The other books of the New Testament attributed to Paul (1 and 2 Timothy, Titus, 2 Thessalonians, Ephesians, and Colossians) are believed to be outright forgeries.

This might sound shocking to those who are still entrenched in their religious beliefs.
I sympathize with your indignation and shock. I felt utter outrage when I discovered this and it took some time and much deeper studying before I would even accept it as truth. In time I learned that this actually wasn't surprising. In the days of the early Church, Christianity was still a young religion and viewed by both the Jews and Romans as nothing more than another 'crazy cult'. I like to emphasize the word 'cult' because since Christianity became the dominant religion of the West, its leaders have made a habit of singling out and slandering other systems it deems 'cults', forgetting that at one time Christianity was viewed as a strange and dangerous cult as well. Because of this many early Christian leaders wrote their own letters and would forge the names of noted Christian heroes like Paul and Peter. They did this in order to lend legitimacy to their views, and likely believed that what they

wrote is something that the early founders would have agreed with anyway. The problem is that this completely undermines any Christian sect that would insist upon reading every word of the New Testament as being the inerrant word of God and seeing every verse as binding truth for how human beings should live their lives.

Knowing this, it makes the use of verses to exclude and control women all the more sickening. Two verses in particular, one in 1 Timothy and the other in Ephesians are now known by Biblical scholars to be forgeries that were never written by Paul. The first example borrows ideas from Paul's words in 1 Corinthians, but notice that it adds significantly to it, not only silencing women but addressing them with resentment and asserting a damaging belief about the salvation of women that would echo through the ages:

"Let the woman learn in silence with all subjection. But I suffer not a woman to teach, nor to usurp authority over the man, but to be in silence. For Adam was first formed, then Eve. And Adam was not deceived, but the woman being deceived was in the transgression. Notwithstanding she shall be saved in childbearing, if they continue in faith and charity and holiness with sobriety." 1 Timothy 2:11-15, KJV

"A woman should learn in quietness and full submission. I do not permit a woman to teach or to assume authority over a man; she must be quiet. For Adam was formed first, then Eve. And Adam was not the one deceived; it was the woman who was deceived and became a sinner. But women will be saved through childbearing - if they continue in faith, love and holiness with propriety." 1 Timothy 2:11-15, NIV

"Wives, submit yourselves unto your own husbands, as to the Lord. For the husband is the head of the wife, even as Christ is the head of the church: and he is the savior of the body. Therefore as the church is subject unto Christ, so let the wives be to their own husbands in every thing." Ephesians 5:22-24, KJV

"Wives, submit yourselves to your own husbands as you do to the Lord. For the husband is the head of the wife as Christ is the head of the church, his body, of which he is the Savior. Now as the church submits to Christ, so also wives should submit to their husbands in all things." Ephesians 5:22-24, NIV

If anyone would argue that these verses did not have a negative impact on women in Christianity, I would like to bring back the words I quoted from the influential early Church father Tertullian, in quoting Genesis 3:22, he also echoes the sentiment of the verses in 1 Timothy and Ephesians when he declares of all women: *"In pain shall you bring forth children, woman, and you shall turn to your husband and he shall rule over you. And do you not know that you are Eve? God's sentence hangs still over all your sex and his His punishment weighs down upon you. You are the devil's gateway; you are she who first violated the forbidden tree and broke the law of God. It was you who coaxed your way around him whom the devil had not the force to attack. With what ease you shattered the image of God: Man! Because of the death you merited, even the Son of God had to die... Woman, you are the gate to hell."*

For ages, these last two verses were brought up by clergy and used as the basis for many Medieval laws concerning marriage. Because of these verses, it was not considered a crime for husbands to beat and rape their wives, to deny them access to education or socialization, and exclude them from any significant positions of legal authority or autonomy. Even more damaging, the verse from 1 Timothy expanded Paul's words in 1 Corinthians to insist that a woman's salvation was found in childbirth. While we may recognize this as being shaky theological ground because it should be obvious that Christian women found salvation through Christ just like men did, this damaging verse was used over and over again by the Church to outlaw birth control and even deny women any kind of pain killer during the agony of childbirth well into the modern era (an issue addressed in Chapter 5 *Eve*).

While it seems that early Judaism removed rights from women in marriage, early Christianity took it to an extreme. But why? This question pounded in my head as I searched for how it was possible that a religion that was supposed to be built on the words of Christ had somehow adopted practices that Christ never spoke of or endorsed, especially concerning women. I would find my answer, not within the texts of the New Testament, but in books dealing with the culture that was in charge while Christianity was first developing: the Roman Empire.

The Roman Empire was not a friendly place for women. While history may remember Rome for its architectural marvels, advancements in politics, warfare, and academics, it was actually one of the most restrictive and stifling cultures for women. The Romans built their culture on the foundation of the Greeks who had come before them; they adopted Greek philosophies, Greek mathematics, Greek architecture, even Greek religion by absorbing all their old gods and giving them new Roman names. Unfortunately, the Romans also adopted Greek misogyny and, like most other things, took it to a new extreme.

Rome venerated the masculine to an extreme. All things associated with the male gender were seen to be the epitome of goodness, reason, and advancement. All things associated with the female gender was seen to be weak, feeble, and backwards. Phallic worship was rampant with statues, monuments, and even jewelry commemorating the venerable power and potency of the penis. Women were commodities and had little to no rights of their own, nor any say in their own lives. As in Middle Eastern cultures, a woman was the property of her father until she was wed to whomever her father chose, and then she was under the authority of her husband until his death or her own.

As mentioned in the previous section, love between two men was glorified, and homosexuality was normal. Unfortunately, even when men violently sexually abused or raped another man, it was painted in the light that the weaker man had taken the position of the 'woman'. There was no greater insult to any Roman man than to be compared to a woman, that is how much shame and disdain was placed on the female body and feminine qualities.

So intense was this denial of the feminine, that Roman doctors, expanding on damaging Greek beliefs, insisted that women did not even have any real part in the act of conception! To them, only the semen of the man carried any kind of life force. In their eyes, the woman was nothing but 'fertile soil' into which a man planted his seed. Mothers were carriers and nothing more. Ironically, nine months and the pain of childbirth counted for little in the eyes of a Roman man. For this reason, women had no legal rights to their own children whatsoever, whereas the father had the legal right to do whatever he wanted to his children, even sell them into slavery or prostitution if he wished to. This is the hateful atmosphere that Christ's message of love and peace came into.

I wish at this moment to make something clear about Christianity. Though I no longer count myself among the religious, I recognize that Christianity (as Christ taught it) was revolutionary for its time. There is good reason for why Christ's teachings found fertile soil in which to grow and why it became so popular. In an empire that thrived on the backs of slaves and violent suppression of men and women who were treated like animals, the words of Christ would have been a blessing! After all, here was a man preaching about rising above the dogmas of restricting religious laws as well as the suffocating control of dictators, who decreed that there was a loving God who was ready to embrace both Jew and Gentile if only a person loved God and their fellow man.

I do not doubt that it was in this spirit of love and charity that the early churches managed to reach out to those who had no hope, those who had been so badly beaten down, the men and women who suffered all manner of abuse at the hands of their Roman masters. In this spirit, I recognize that Christianity began to become a force for goodness and change in an empire dominated by violence, bloodshed, and sexual terror. The problem is that most Christians have no idea that this early church was anything but unified. Early Christians did not read the New Testament that we read today. Just as the Old Testament (Tanakh) was a work in progress for hundreds (if not thousands) of years, so too the New Testament came together in an equally rocky way.

For many years Biblical scholars believed that early Christians read holy texts that were no longer part of the New Testament, but they had no proof until the discovery of a large cache of writings were discovered in 1945 in an area of upper Egypt called Nag Hammadi. Buried in the desert sands, the

Nag Hammadi library would shine a light on a period of history that had been forgotten. Perhaps nowhere does the phrase 'History is written by the winners' apply more than the history of Christianity. For ages, Biblical scholars had assumed that Christianity had evolved in a direct manner from the teachings of Paul into what would become the Catholic Church.

However the early Church started and continued, the movement was fractured until the empire began to persecute Christians, seeing them as threats to the Roman government hierarchy. Under Roman law, rulers were often seen at the same level as gods and were to be worshipped, something that both Jews and early Christians refused to do. The Jews, as punishment for the Jewish revolt in AD 70, had seen their temple destroyed and the remaining survivors had been scattered throughout the empire. Christians, for their heresy, started to be persecuted legally and physically. The persecutions ceased when an emperor named Constantine came to power. Recognizing that the Christian religion was not going to go away, and realizing a chance to unify his broken empire, Constantine 'miraculously' had a vision of a cross in the sky and as victory was given to him on that battlefield decided to become a Christian. It is because of Constantine that Christianity became the official religion of the Roman Empire.

Many Christians know this little part of their history and rejoice for it. I know I once did. But as I studied historians who had no personal religious beliefs to sway them one way or the other, I soon discovered that the story was not so clean and clear. To begin with, Constantine was a Christian only in name and when it was politically expedient. He was a horrible man who committed numerous atrocities and while he gave lip service to Christian leaders, continued to worship his own personal Roman gods. Despite professing being a Christian, he was not baptized into the faith until he was on his deathbed! It is significant that Constantine recounted his vision as being of a cross instead of Christ, for the cross is an ancient symbol that was well known to the Romans (and the Egyptians, and any ancient culture for that matter) which represented the Sun. For Constantine, heartfelt faith had nothing to do with his championing of Christianity. Instead he was seeing his empire tearing apart because of religious and political differences and he saw in the structure and hierarchy of the Church a marvelous opportunity to marry Roman politics and religion in one fell swoop.

The problem was that the only way to have a unified empire was to make Christianity a unified faith, and at the time it was anything but. So fractured were Christian beliefs that Constantine had to gather all the Christian bishops from around the empire to a Council in Nicaea in AD 325 for the purpose of solidifying Christian beliefs once and for all. I want to interject at this point the irony that at this time in history Constantine was still not a Christian, but paid service to his Roman pagan gods as well. The God of the Bible did not call this council together, but instead a human man who was sitting on the religious fence (and apparently had both 'God' and other gods inspiring him). Because of records from this council, Biblical scholars knew that early Christians were reading and endorsing far more holy texts than the twenty-seven that were finally agreed upon in Nicaea, but the texts just didn't seem to exist anymore. That all changed with the Nag Hammadi discovery in 1945.

The Nag Hammadi library was painstakingly restored, studied, analyzed, and translated over several decades, but when it was finally revealed to the public it painted an amazing picture of the beliefs of early Christians and shed light on the battle for the soul of Christianity. Scholars discovered that early Christianity had many, many sects with beliefs that would shock mainstream Christians today. Beliefs about reincarnation, the equality of women, even the belief that Jesus had been nothing more than a mortal man, were common. Though these texts would come to be called 'Gnostic', they represented sects of Christianity that were every bit as vibrant and strong as traditional sects would become. I will address these beliefs later, but suffice to say that these alternate beliefs threatened the image of Christianity that Constantine wanted to create in order to be of use to the Roman Empire.

Under the control of Constantine, Christianity ceased to be a religion of diversity and became forced into the mold that he and his authorized clergy legalized it to be. Soon the hierarchy of the Roman Catholic (a name chosen based on Constantine's insistence that his Christianity was 'Universal') Church was an almost mirror image of the hierarchy of Roman religions and politics. The two began working hand in hand. It is because of this marriage of faith and politics that the sanctioned view on women became the same view Rome had always had on women: they were property, they were to be silent, and they could not even dare to imagine a life outside the control of men. And yet the role of women and their importance could not be extinguished. Nowhere did this become more evident than in the identity of the most important woman in the New Testament: Mary. As the prayer is spoken on the lips of millions of Christian faithful to this day: Mary, the *Mother* of God.

19. Eve and Mary: The Sinner and the Redeemed

In the New Testament and the history of Christianity, no woman is as important or visible as the woman who bore the son of God. It is a story that is relatively well known amongst all Christians because of its recitation during the Christmas season, but I'll give a quick overview for the less religiously inclined. Mary is a young virgin girl engaged to be married to an older man named Joseph. One day an angel of the Lord (tradition holds it to be Gabriel) appears to Mary and informs her that out of all the women in the world she has been chosen to carry and give birth to the savior of mankind, the son of God, Jesus Christ. With utter humility and submission, Mary accepts this news (as if she had a choice). As can be expected, Joseph is bewildered to discover his virgin fiancé is suddenly pregnant, but the angel of the Lord clears the air with him as well. Jesus is born in Bethlehem in a stable as the familiar narrative goes, because there was no room at the inn, the shining star high above to guide the Wisemen on their way to bring gifts.

We are never told much about whether Mary suffered through hours of labor pains, or how exactly she survived the agony of birthing a baby through a virginal birth canal. In this divine birth, there is no room for the reality of birth that all human mothers have gone through, only the sudden and miraculous appearance of this infant who is supposed to be God incarnate. Of course Joseph does not leave any written account either. No one witnesses Jesus' birth except Mary and Joseph, for the shepherds are in their fields and the Wisemen are still far away. One would think that if such an incredible miracle was occurring that God bringing forth himself in the form of his own child into this world would have made certain there was a human audience to acknowledge the greatness of God's work. Upon witnessing this, even the greatest enemy of Israel would have to bow down in trembling worship and fear filled awe. Why was everything so secretive? Ultimately Mary is just the carrier in this narrative, it is Jesus who is the center of the whole story. Of the four gospels, Mark and John do not bother recounting Jesus' birth, Matthew begins with Jesus' genealogy and only briefly addresses that Mary was impregnated by the Holy Spirit, while it is in the gospel of Luke that we receive the traditional Christmas narrative complete with an appearance by the archangel Gabriel.

The book of Matthew, which comes first in the New Testament, chooses to give the reader an overview of Jesus' genealogy and scholars believe that Matthew is written with the intention of reaching out specifically to Jewish readers. Because of this, the author includes the genealogy in order to prove to Jewish readers that Christ is the Messiah they have been waiting for. For the Jews, the Messiah was supposed to come from the line of King David and Matthew's list of Jesus' ancestors served as 'proof' that Christ was indeed descended from King David. There's just one little problem hiding in plain sight.

How I never saw this as a devout Christian I will never know, but when I returned to the gospels with critical eyes, I remember reading each chapter and verse and realizing that I might as well have never read these books before. My cup of coffee in one hand and the other holding a pen, I found myself staring at the verses and awakening to the truth. Just as I was aware of the warmth of the coffee mug in my hand and the cold metal pen in the other, my mind began to blossom to the fullness of reality. My Soul now was in control. It was pointing things out to me that I had never seen before simply because I had allowed my Ego to only see what the Ego of man had white washed over for its own gain.

According to Christian doctrine, Jesus is the only begotten Son of God. Mary, an untouched virgin, was impregnated through an immaculate conception by the 'Holy Spirit' of God. Because of this, it stands to reason that any physical blood Jesus has and any family line Jesus has would come solely from his human mother Mary. Though Joseph weds Mary, ultimately Jesus is only an adopted son who shares no literal blood with Joseph whatsoever.

Yet, the genealogy given in Matthew ends with:

"And Jacob begat Joseph the husband of Mary, of whom was born Jesus, who is called Christ." Matthew 1:16, KJV

I remember distinctly slapping my forehead as I read that line over and over again. If Jesus is not Joseph's blood related son, why on earth would the author of Matthew feel the need to establish Jesus' descent from King David through a man he had no blood relation to? Why hadn't the genealogy been counted through Mary's father's ancestors, for only that would have made sense!

Another discrepancy stopped me in my tracks. In Matthew 1:22-23, the author recounts the angel of the Lord speaking to Joseph and tells him the child Mary carries will fulfill a prophecy made in the Old Testament book of Isaiah:

"Now all this was done, that it might be fulfilled which was spoken of the Lord by the prophet, saying, Behold a virgin shall be with child, and shall bring forth a son, and they shall call his name Emmanuel, which means 'God with us'." Matthew 1:22-23, KJV

Only another line down, the author states: *"Joseph knew her not till she had brought forth her firstborn son, and he called his name Jesus."*

In all of my research I have never found a satisfactory answer for this contradiction. The angel of the Lord tells Joseph that the child Mary carries will be named Emmanuel. Some argue that Emmanuel was simply meant to be a title, but that makes no sense because the name Emmanuel was being used as a proper first name during the time that Christ was born, and yet that is NOT the name given to the child. Instead, he is named Jesus.

While we're on the topic of Jesus' birth name, it's important to point out that Jesus' original Hebrew name was Yeshua, a name which does mean 'salvation'. Yeshua when translated into English is the proper name of Joshua. The name Jesus came into being when the Apostle Paul and others began to proselytize to the Greeks and had to find an equivalent to Yeshua's name in Greek. The closest they could come was the Greek name of Iesous, which evolved into our modern word Jesus during the Middle Ages in Europe. Either way, the name bears no resemblance to Emmanuel.

Why on earth did Joseph and Mary decide to apparently circumvent the will of God by naming their child something other than what the angel told them to name him? Even more interesting is that the angel of the Lord contradicts itself, saying in Matthew to Joseph that the Son of God's name is Emmanuel, yet in Luke 2:21 it says:

"And when eight days were accomplished for the circumcising of the child, his name was called Jesus, which was so named of the angel before he was conceived in the womb." Luke 2:21, KJV

So which name did the angel insist upon, Jesus or Emmanuel? The prophecy the angel refers to in Matthew 1:22-23 brings up a vital point about Mary. A prophecy was made in the Old Testament book of Isaiah stating:

"Therefore the Lord himself shall give you a sign; Behold, a virgin shall conceive, and bear a son, and shall call his name Immanuel." Isaiah 7:14, KJV

There is something far more problematic going on than just the contradiction of Jesus' name. In the verse from Isaiah, the word 'virgin' is a mistranslation. In the original Hebrew text, the word used in Isaiah is *'almah'*. *'Almah'* in Hebrew is a word that signifies a young woman or girl who is unmarried, but it does not explicitly mean 'virgin'. Its emphasis is on the youth of the woman, not on her physical state of virginity. Lacking a word for this, when the Hebrew text was translated into a Greek version of the Tanakh known as the Septuagint in the second century BC, translators chose the Greek word *'parthenos'* which does mean a literal virgin. Therefore, Mary is indeed an *'almah'* in that she is young and unmarried, but whether she is a virgin before or after the conception of Christ is open for debate.

Why is this so important? Because even though mainstream Protestant Christianity has largely left Mary to the simple role of giving birth to the son of God, Mary has been a figure of immense importance in the development of the Church and the history of Christianity. Protestant Christianity has only existed since the stirrings of reformation began in the 1500s, prior to that, all questions of faith and dogma were under the interpretation of Catholicism. The early Church was already in existence prior to Constantine's Nicaean Council in

AD 325, but by the time it was done, Roman Catholicism was the only orthodox branch of Christianity and would remain the authorized version of the faith until the birth of Protestantism in the 1500s. Because of this, it does not matter what denomination or sect of Christianity a person belongs to, the source of their beliefs and the evolution of Christian doctrine lays at the feet of the Roman Catholic Church. In the previous chapter and in the very first section of this book, I showed how Roman culture's disdain for women and the feminine became ingrained into what would become orthodox Christian doctrine. This is not to say that there were not opposing viewpoints, but those will be dealt with in the next chapter concerning Mary Magdalene and the Gnostics.

As Christianity began to truly break away from its Jewish roots, early Church fathers were left with the sticky problem of how to approach what they called the Old Testament (formerly the Jewish Tanakh). Many leaders made the choice to view the stories of the Old Testament as a mixture of Biblical history and allegory. They plumbed through the ancient stories, picking and choosing pieces they felt were relevant enough to apply as either supports for the New Testament, or as contrasts to the New Testament. One of the Old Testament figures that would be resuscitated into dubious importance was the first woman ever created: Eve. I examined Eve and her part in the Creation story of Genesis thoroughly back in Chapter 5; to spare a lengthy retelling, I urge the reader to go back and review that chapter if they feel they need to.

Writings by the likes of Clement of Alexandria, Tertullian, and Augustine (all of whom became cornerstones of Church doctrine and whose venomous quotes can be found in Chapter 4 *A Woman's 'Place'*), constantly show a disdain for women as they assert over and over again that all women are under the punishment of God because of Eve's disobedience in the Garden of Eden. If Eve's treatment under Jewish interpreters was maligning, she became outright reviled by early Church fathers who blamed her for the loss of Paradise and every ill that had befallen humanity!

The reason for this, again, comes down to the influence of Greco-Roman beliefs upon Christianity. The belief in these other gods was still very strong during the birth of Christianity, and the worship of these gods remained prominent all the way to AD 381 when 'pagan' beliefs were made illegal in the empire. Even then, these stories and beliefs remained influential throughout the Middle Ages and into the European Renaissance. Stories were shared between nations and in Greco-Roman religion there also existed a story about a first woman who caused the entire world misery and suffering by her actions. She may even have influenced the story of Eve, as the ancient Jews would have certainly heard this tale from their Hellenistic neighbors and trading partners.

This woman was known as Pandora, and in Greek religion she was the first woman created on earth when Zeus (king of the gods) ordered his divine craftsman Hephaestus to create her out of water and earth. Pandora's name roughly means 'imbued with all gifts', for the gods endowed this first woman with beauty, music, persuasion, and every wonderful thing imaginable. Pandora became a pawn of Zeus when she was wed to the brother of a god named Prometheus who had disobeyed Zeus by helping humanity. Angry that Prometheus had stolen divine fire in order to make humanity's life better, Zeus arranged for Pandora's wedding and gave her a 'gift'. The gift was a beautiful jar, but the gift came with a command: It must never be opened. Because Pandora had been given intelligence, she was naturally curious, and opened the jar. The moment she did, a whole host of evil energies representing every possible misery, illness, and harm was unleashed upon the earth. Though she tried to close the lid, the damage was done and humanity would forever suffer. Only one thing remained in the bottom of Pandora's jar, and that was Hope.

The parallels between this well known myth of the Greek and Roman Empires and the Biblical Eve are truly startling! Not only are both supposed to be the first created woman, they are created by a divine King and warrior god, in this case Zeus and Yahweh. They are both created, not for themselves, but for man. Both are given impossible temptations: for Eve, it is the fruit of the Tree of Knowledge which she may see but never taste, and for Pandora it is a jar which is put into her hands but which she must never open. Both have their fates sealed by the actions of a being that possesses a truth they are not supposed to have.

For Eve, the Serpent represents wisdom and speaks an unthinkable truth: God has lied to her and Adam, for they will not die when they eat the fruit, but instead will have their eyes open and become like divine beings who understand good and evil. As I made clear when I addressed Eve in the first section, the great irony is that the Serpent becomes demonized and yet every word the Serpent said was true! It is significant that Christianity would adopt a belief that the Serpent was really Satan in disguise, causing Eve to sin and bring about the Fall of humanity from Paradise, but we will come to know Satan better in a later chapter. For Pandora, it is her unintentional relationship to Prometheus that sheds light on the connection.

Prometheus in the myths was known as a 'light bringer' ('*lucifer*' in Latin), for he angered Zeus and the gods when he disobeyed a divine command and stole fire from

Olympus. He gave the divine fire to humanity, for the story goes that before him humanity was lost in darkness, unable to do much more than survive. Once they had fire, they were able to learn and the spark of imagination led humanity into a golden age of advancement. Enraged, Zeus punished Prometheus by chaining him to a rock where he was condemned for all eternity to have his liver pecked out by an eagle, dying only to have to awaken to the hellish torture all over again come morning.

Apparently punishing Prometheus was not enough, for the innocent Pandora is given her mysterious jar and sent to Prometheus' brother. So, perhaps not as intimately as Eve and the Serpent, Pandora is still connected to Prometheus as the second phase of Zeus' punishment. Eve eats of the tree and gives to Adam, causing them to be exiled from Paradise. Eve's action of daring to gain knowledge was believed to be the entire reason for the suffering of humanity in an imperfect world full of pain and misery. Likewise, Pandora is a woman too intelligent for her own good, and her desire to know (her curiosity) caused her to disobey Zeus and unwittingly unleash every horror onto the world that humanity would have to suffer with for the rest of its existence.

Neither Eve nor Pandora die for their disobedience, but both are turned into the scapegoat for all the miseries of the world. For eternity, they become the model to which all women are held, the reason all women are punished for daring to become educated and seek a life of independence free of the control of men. It is little wonder that men who had already grown up in the misogynistic atmosphere of the Roman Empire were unable to shake the disdain and mistrust of women that Pandora had taught them, especially when they readily found her Biblical counterpart in Eve.

Sadly, both Eve and Pandora are indeed lessons, but not about female stupidity or disobedience. Again, we are dealing with stories that were recorded and sanctioned by men who were happy to have a ready scapegoat for their inbred fears concerning women. Nowhere in discussions about Pandora or Eve did the men studying the tales ever bother to place the blame where it truly belongs: Zeus and Yahweh. Pandora does not ask to be created and she certainly does not ask for a jar of hideous horrors. It is not Eve's fault that the God of the Bible seems to enjoy placing something wondrous and beautiful right in their midst and yet puts a 'Do Not Touch' sign on the tree. Both women use their divine given reasoning: Pandora recognizes that there is no sense in being given a jar that is a wedding present if it is to never be opened. Eve realizes that the Serpent is speaking the truth, for what sense does it make for there to be a Tree of Knowledge right in their midst if it is not to be eaten from?

The actions of Zeus and Yahweh, are not the actions of loving, wise, Creators, but instead reflect the petulant and vengeful attitude of divine Dictators . Both deities could have struck down the women who 'disobeyed' them, but instead they punish them by punishing all of humanity which is to come. Where is the wisdom in that? Neither deity has any interest in fairness or mercy. They do not care that Pandora and Eve, and through them all women to come, will shoulder man's resentment for the loss of Paradise. But it is the last similarity between them that should make the reader think.

For Pandora, in spite of all the damage done, one thing remains in her jar: Hope.

For Eve, in spite of God's curse upon her (and all women) to experience the agony of childbirth and be under the control of man, Christian leaders read her story and saw something that they felt was hopeful when God says to the Serpent:

> "*I will put enmity between thee and the woman, and between thy seed and her seed; it shall bruise thy head, and thou shalt bruise his heel.*" Genesis 3:15, KJV

In these words, early Christian fathers felt there was a sort of divine prophecy of hope, that the future figure who would be capable of defeating Satan (who they associated with the Serpent though the Jews never did) could only be foretelling the coming of Christ. While many Church fathers chose to see Eve as the ultimate sinner, it was in this prophecy that they saw the foreshadowing of Christ's redemption of mankind. But Christ could not enter into the world without the divine actions of another human woman: Mary.

The Roman Empire may have been the perpetrators of an incredibly horrific view of women, but it could not escape the fact that women were a vital part of the empire. Aside from all the work women were burdened with when it came to caring for home and families, there could be no empire without the fertility of Roman women. It has always been the dreadful irony of misogyny that while men may resent, beat, and abuse their wives and daughters, a special place of honor is often reserved for their mothers. This was true in many ancient cultures and is an unfortunate truth even in cultures in today's modern world. Male dominated societies may strip women of their individuality and purpose, but the identity of the mother is almost always venerated. I wish it could be said that mothers used this influence to make life better for other women, but just as we see in certain cultures in our time, women who are brain washed into accepting a male dominated culture usually only help perpetuate it.

I have heard many horror stories from female friends who originally lived in Afghanistan, India, Saudi Arabia, South America, and even Mexico or Russia, recounting that not only were they physically beaten and abused by their husbands, it was often done in front of their mother-in-laws or even incited by their husband's mother. There is nothing sadder in the plight of women than the disgusting truth that patriarchy and misogyny thrive not just by the will of men, but by the compliance of women who have become too brain washed and bitter to dare fight against it. For them, the love of their sons who have been taught since birth that they can do no wrong is paired with the constant instilling of the belief that women somehow always ask for or deserve abuse. This is one of the greatest roadblocks to helping the oppressed women of our modern world. In this respect, Rome and much of the Mediterranean was no different in its viewpoint. As I have stressed before, this is not to say that there were not pockets of ethnic groups or people who had cultures that were matriarchal or in which women were valued and thrived! There is evidence this did exist, but unfortunately they were usually the exception to the rule.

In direct contradiction to the overwhelming preference of Romans towards anything masculine, the empire was full of the worship of female deities! When Rome conquered foreign groups, they often allowed the cultures to continue worshipping their own gods and goddesses. If the religion was popular enough, it might become transplanted to other parts of the empire. For example, many people have no idea that the religion of Buddhism came into existence 400 years before the birth of Christ and there is textual evidence that Buddhist as well as Hindu monks traveled throughout the Empire and set up groups of worship. This might explain why many of Jesus' teachings parallel Buddhist teachings, and there are those who believe that Jesus' so called 'missing years' were likely spent traveling to India and back… but that is a topic for another book. Under the protection and advancement of Rome, trade routes thrived all the way from India and up into the British Isles. Just as ideas, religious beliefs, and stories had traveled throughout the Middle East during the time of the Israelites, the belief in certain gods and their stories took root in places far from their original homelands. One of the best examples and the most pertinent to this discussion was the goddess Isis.

Today we read about Isis and think of her as just another mythological figure. Modern readers forget that Isis was a goddess who was deeply beloved and who people honored with as much heartfelt love and devotion as any modern follower of God or Christ. She was venerated and worshipped in Egypt for thousands of years. When Egypt was conquered by Alexander the Great as part of the Greek Empire, Isis was soon imported into Greece and found loyal worshippers. The same occurred when Rome absorbed Egypt. Not only did Isis have a temple in Rome, her image and worship spread to areas in modern Spain, France, and even Great Britain where temples and statues of this Egyptian goddess have been found. In Turkey (known at that time as Anatolia), a similar female deity was worshipped known as Cybele. She had much in common with Isis, and like her Egyptian counterpart, Cybele became worshipped in the far reaches of the Roman Empire.

Isis and Cybele were both venerated as the ultimate divine mothers who offered compassion, mercy, and healing to humanity. Isis was frequently shown sitting with an infant to her breast (her divine son Horus) or seated on her lap. This imagery is identical to images created of Mary holding the infant Jesus to her breast or on her lap only a few centuries later. Cybele also had a divine son named Mithras (born on Christmas day), and when Mithras met his death to save humanity (an act which took place around Easter), Cybele was often shown cradling her dying son, just as later images would come to show Mary cradling the dead body of Jesus after the crucifixion. There is too much similarity here between these figures and the story of Christ for any Christian to ignore, but for those still in denial I will fully address this in Chapter 21 *Satan, the Devil, and God: A Human Trinity.*

Both goddesses were known by beautiful titles such as: Mother of God, Queen of Heaven, Redeemer of the World, and Holy Mother. The love for these Goddesses ran deep and the devotion of their followers went back for generations. Today we hear their names and we think of museum relics or simple myths, but these deities were every bit as honored, loved, and fiercely worshipped as any religious person today honors the God of the Bible. Take a moment to read these words of worship from ancient writers, pay attention to the dates, and ponder for a moment if they do not record the same kind of devotion being expressed by modern men and women.

The ancient writer Apuleius, through his character Lucius in Book 11 of *Metamorphoses* gives his love to Isis: "*Hail, holy one, eternal Savior of the human race, ever cherishing mortals with your bounty, you who extend a mother's tender love to the sufferings of the unfortunate. Not a day, not a night, not a fleeting second passes in which your goodness is not at work... The gods above worship you, the gods below revere you: you make the earth revolve, you give the sun its light, you rule the universe, you trample hell under your feet. Obedient to you the stars rise and set, the seasons return, the powers rejoice, the elements perform their service... I shall keep and contemplate your divine*

countenance and your holy power in the secret recesses of my heart forever."
This hymn to Isis was written in AD 200, well into the time that the early orthodox Church was forming.

In their beautiful book *Inanna*, Diane Wolkstein and Samuel Kramer translate an ancient Akkadian hymn to Inanna (Ishtar of the Sumerians) dated somewhere between 2334-2218 BC. The worshipper speaks with an almost identical reverence for the divine Mother: "*I say Hail to the Holy One who appears in the heavens!... I say Hail to Inanna, Great Lady of Heaven!... You who fill the sky with light! You brighten the day at dawn!... Mighty, majestic and radiant, you shine brilliantly in the evening, You brighten the day at dawn, You stand in the heavens like the sun and the moon, Your wonders are known both above and below... To You, Inanna, I sing!*"

Notice that the devotional love in these two hymns for the Queen of Heaven are separated by over *two thousand years*, proving that the heartfelt worship and reverence for the Divine Feminine did indeed exist and was prolific amongst humanity in the Western world... until the rise of the orthodox Church. When Roman Emperors began to marry their political power to the Church's religious power it was obvious that these female centered religions had to be wiped out. Remember that the dominant view of the early Church fathers was to see anything feminine as distasteful, and there was nothing more disgusting to them than the sight of woman being worshipped or usurping their Father God and the Son. Sex, politics, and religion had no separation in that day and women paid the price then just as they do now in nations still ruled by male religious authority.

Many Christians see the history of their religion through rose colored glasses. When I was a believer, I sincerely thought that Christianity began as a persecuted sect, was divinely raised by God's will through Constantine to be the true religion of the Roman Empire, and that was the end of it. The Church sent out missionaries to the ends of the Empire and slowly but surely Europe became a Christian nation because even pagans came to know the truth of Jesus' love and redemption. If the reader is getting tired of hearing how shocked I was, imagine how weary and tired I was becoming of having to dismantle the fallacies my whole worldview had been built upon!

In reading this, you have experienced only a fraction of my journey. If the information seems excessive, it is only a tiny portion of the knowledge that is available and which my daughter and I have devoted ourselves to. While I'm past feeling avalanched by information, I do sympathize with anyone who, like friends of mine, insist that this is all too overwhelming. It was overwhelming for me too, but I got over it, dusted myself off, and kept going. For anyone who truly wishes to know the truth of their faith and begin a path of spirituality that centers on the heart of their beliefs (not its dogma or religious politics) there is no other way than to open yourself to this information and let it guide your beautiful Soul back to its Light.

Needless to say, this peaceful view I held of Christianity's birth and rise to power is nothing like the truth that is painted by history. Even though Constantine declared Christianity legal and the official religion of the Roman Empire, he never outlawed other religions. Because of this, a kind of civil war began to brew. Christian leaders who suddenly found themselves in seats of power instead of persecution were quick to lay judgement upon all other faiths which they deemed 'pagan'. On a side note, the word *pagan* comes from Old French and its meaning was 'country dweller', nothing more or less. Is it not ironic that the very people once persecuted suddenly decided to become the judge and juries of persecution instead of following Christ's model of peace and forgiveness? Perhaps had they done so, they might have actually converted more pagans instead of alienating them and causing what amounted to a great deal of bloodshed and destruction for the next few centuries.

Today most religious minded people hear the word pagan and think that the people of the ancient world were simply uneducated individuals dumb enough to worship anything that moved like lightning or the sun, or violent barbarians slitting the throats of their enemies in order to slake the desire of their bloodthirsty gods. While it is true that some pagan groups did practice animal sacrifice, human sacrifice had been illegal throughout the Greco-Roman world for some time. In fact the greatest thinkers of the Hellenistic world were what we would consider pagan: Aristotle, Plato, Pythagoras, Epicurus, and on and on down a list of genius philosophers, mathematicians, architects, historians, and artists. The great achievements of Egypt, Greece, and Rome were built on the foundation of their 'pagan' religious beliefs. Meanwhile, it was not long after Christianity became the official religion of the Roman Empire that the empire began to go downhill.

Ponder that for a moment.

If God was pleased with the foundation of a Christian empire, why did it not enter into a new Golden Age of peace and prosperity?

Instead, the legal domination of Christianity heralded the four hundred year period of European history known as the Dark Ages - a time of ignorance, violence, and oppression.

Violence erupted between fanatical Christians who insisted that all other gods were evil, that anything that came from pagan hands was worthless (including mathematics, science, and philosophy), and that pagans should be forced to convert even if it was at the end of a sword. Pagans struck back with equal vehemence and one of the most notorious cases of Christian violence and destruction took place in Egypt in the great center of learning of Alexandria. Often pagan women had more freedom and choice with their pagan beliefs and fought tooth and nail against the silence and submission Christianity began to demand of them. I will return to this decisive moment in Chapter 20 *Magdalene: Saint or Harlot?*.

I have taken the time to paint this picture to make the point that the early history of Christianity is just as bloody and violent as the history of any other religion or nation. It has never been an exception to the rule or a miraculous change in the history of humanity. The 'pagan' gods, but especially the goddesses, were deeply loved and that love did not just miraculously vanish when Constantine made Christianity legal. 'Paganism' still held the hearts and souls of many in the empire centuries later when an emperor named Theodosius officially made any kind of pagan belief illegal in AD 381. Even after this law made any other form of faith an act of heresy worthy of torture and death, the expansive beliefs of 'paganism' continued to live and would resurface over a thousand years later during the reawakening of Light of learning in the Renaissance.

How does this come back to Mary you may be asking? I promise I did not tangent off topic! You needed this information to comprehend what I am about to describe. The Mary of the gospels is referenced only a few times. She is seen asking Jesus' help when a wedding party they are attending runs out of wine, to which he miraculously turns water into wine (John 2:1-12). At one point she and her other children ask to see Jesus, but Jesus refuses to see her, insisting to his disciples that those who follow him are his true 'mother, brothers, and sisters' (Mark 3:31-34). Lastly, she makes an appearance at the foot of the cross of Jesus' crucifixion and is joined with Mary of Magdala (John 19:25-27). After that, she mostly vanishes from the New Testament. This might be the end of her role in the gospels, but it was just the beginning of her role to believers and the Church.

Women and men alike who had been forced to adopt Christianity either under threat of physical violence or economic and legal intimidation, saw in Mary similarities to their own beloved holy Mothers. Mary was a virgin. While the Church saw virginity as being defined as the physical inexperience of a woman who had never had sex, pagans had a different definition. The pagan world was full of Virgin goddesses like Artemis, Diana, and Athena. They called them 'virgin' and yet myths abounded of the goddesses having sex! The reason became clear when I discovered that 'virgin' could also refer to divine women who had so much power that they could refuse to be married. Once married, a woman lost all personal identity and power to her husband. As long as she was unmarried and had the power to do as she pleased, she was technically in a state of divine virginity. A friendly reminder that all of these tales existed for ages before the birth of Christ or the Bible.

Also, stories abounded in Egypt, Greece, Rome, and the Middle East, about human virgin women who so entranced a male god that he descended and magically impregnated her. These stories existed hundreds, sometimes thousands, of years before the birth of Christ. The child born of this union was both human and divine, a man and a god, capable of great acts of heroism, sacrifice, and miracles. So, when pagans read about a virgin Mary being impregnated by a male god, and then giving birth to a divine son who could walk on water, turn water into wine, magically feed thousands of people, carried words of enlightenment, was murdered, resurrected after a stint in hell (the underworld) and finally ascended into heaven, they immediately felt right at home!

What did not set well for these converts was that the Church was trying to undo all the customs, holy days, and cultural rights that made these people who they were. The pagans fought to keep their beliefs and traditions alive, and eventually the Church had no choice but to absorb these elements just to stay alive. After all, the Church had to quiet pagan outrage somehow considering that every time a wealthy pagan temple or town was consecrated to Christianity, all the gold, jewels, and wealth of the area suddenly found its way into the coffers of the Roman Catholic Church.

Holy sites that had once housed temples to Isis and Cybele suddenly had their statues rededicated to Mary. Soon it was Mary who held such titles of veneration as Queen of Heaven and Mother of God. The Church did fight back, but people who had been used to worshipping the feminine found Christianity to be a cold religion that made little sense. For people who were tied to the fertility of the land, whose whole existence resided on the changing of the seasons and the miracle of conception be it animal or human, they recognized that without the feminine there was no life and renewal. Male gods had never been able to fully take the place of Female goddesses when it came to the laws of nature or its beauty. Yet this was exactly what the Church tried to enforce with its doctrine of the trinity: God the Father, Christ the Son, and the genderless Holy Spirit (all of which were somehow the same deity).

Even Judaism was not so devoid of spiritual feminism as Christianity was. Judaism had insisted that God had both male and female qualities and certain spiritual branches were comfortable with seeing Him in the role of Mother. Also, the Holy Spirit in Judaism was known as the 'Shekhinah' and was seen to be the Feminine creative force of God (something Christian writers ignored as they insisted that the Holy Spirit had no gender). For pagans, many of their gods came in trinities, but even then trinities included male gods and female goddesses (often the trinity was a family unit, made of Father, Mother, and Child). Against this norm, Christianity insisted that the Trinity was male, but pagans recognized it was senseless to believe creation could exist without the Female life force. Into this male dominated Trinity and Church hierarchy, Mary became the peace offering.

Not without immense debate, Mary was crowned with the title '*Theotokos*' (God Bearer). But this presented a problem for the Church. Mary had simply been a normal human girl, which implied she was just as sinful as any other human being since the Fall. To compensate, the Church began to write and certify more and more elaborate doctrines and commentaries, establishing that Mary herself had been born without sin. They also quashed the common sense recognition that Mary likely had sex with Joseph and gave birth to other children. They claimed Jesus' siblings were Joseph's children from a previous marriage and that Mary had indeed remained a physical virgin her entire life. Once this was done, it paved the way for a doctrine which stated that Mary herself did not die, but ascended into heaven where she sits at the hand of her divine son. In this place, Mary took on the role of much needed intercessor. The God of the Bible was a terrifying figure and often vengeful, and while people were told they were saved through Christ, they began to fear for their sinful souls. Also, the masculine God of the Bible often seemed remote and lacked the loving touch people associated with women and motherhood. Once again, Mary stepped into the role of a caring, loving, eternal Mother who would intercede on the behalf of imperfect humans by taking their cares straight to her son.

As Queen and Intercessor, Mary was even declared to be a 'co-redeemer' since she had been the physical bearer of God in the form of Christ. Once this happened, Mary had come full circle into the roles of goddesses before her such as Isis, Cybele, Ishtar, and Asherah. Except, of course, that she is never called a goddess. I cannot be the only one to see that for any woman to give birth to a god, she herself must be a goddess, simply because it defies all the rules of the realm we live in where a body is formed, lives, decays, and dies whereas the body of a god or goddess lives on. For the Church to add on that Mary never truly dies absolutely puts her on par with her own child. Apparently all common sense has been lost in the translations of religious writers and the doctrines they kept making up to try and solve these nonsensical theological problems.

More aggravating is that the Church elevated her to this role to meet a need, yet backed off just shy of addressing her as a Goddess. Mary came into the same kind of strange limbo that all women were placed in by the Church: she was intercessor and divine, more than human and yet unable to be called a goddess. She never creates on her own and is relegated as the submissive womb that nurtured God in human form. Why would God even bother to use a woman at all? After all, he supposedly made the first woman out of the rib of man (something Church fathers would lord over women and which is still cited by modern Biblical evangelists), so why not make his own Son out of the rib of a chosen prophet? We all know God was more than capable of doing this in his all powerful majesty and glory, and yet he doesn't. These are theological questions that will never be addressed simply because they are too problematic for the Church and get passed over with the excuse of it being a divine mystery. Over and over again, the woman is elevated to meet the theological needs of men but is allowed nothing more to her identity than what is given by male clergy.

None of this is to say that Mary evolved overnight. Her identity was debated on and fought over by Christian leaders for centuries. But once Mary became a co-redeemer and viewed to be without sin, she suddenly became a mirror image for Eve. To the credit of some men in the Church, Mary was seen as a figure who could redeem women from the 'sin' all women bore because of Eve. Though Eve did not begin so, writers like Augustine and other pro-celibate Church fathers began to interpret Eve as having been very sexual, even equating the Fall as having had to do with the first time she and Adam had sex, so her disobedience was seen as the epitome of female wickedness. Mary's total virginity and utter submissiveness to God became a new model to which all women were expected to aspire if they were to find redemption in the eyes of the Church.

As caring and wonderful as Mary was in the role of Mother, in many ways she became a double edged sword for human women. On the one hand, she was the only divine figure women could turn to in their hour of need. She was the great comfort for women facing the terror of pregnancy and motherhood. On the other hand, she was a standard no human woman could live up to. The worship of Mary made little impact on how real human women were treated and the abuses and domination of husbands over wives, fathers over daughters, and male Church clergy over female parishioners remained unchanged and unchallenged. Just as men in ancient times and modern have often idolized their mothers while treating other women horribly, so too did many men pay utter adoration to Mary while still subjecting women as a whole to total oppression and submission. Mary also presented a significant problem in the Church. Not only was the Church male centered and dominated, but the only female representation was a perpetual Virgin. While goddesses like Isis, Cybele, Ishtar, and Asherah had been Divine Mothers, they had also been wives and sexual beings in their own right. They taught women and men alike how to appreciate the sensual gift of sexuality that resulted in the ultimate miracle of life and renewal.

As the insistence upon celibacy and virginity grew in the Church, women began to face the persecution of men who were not only imbued with religious and political power, but the brunt of their own self-inflicted sexual frustrations. Women could never be Mary unless they willingly surrendered their lives to the Church and lived celibately in nunneries. For the majority of women who did not have this option, they lived in a dreadful limbo where their own sexuality became the battle ground for religious control. A male society began to develop that had been imbued with a God complex on one hand, while being taught that their sexual desires could only be channeled into creating children and nothing more. Instead of controlling themselves, masculine resentment turned to women who were blamed for inciting their lust and sin. No figure in the New Testament bears greater proof to this than Mary Magdalene and she holds the startling truth that at one point Christianity and women could have had a far different religious fate. Now follow me, and let me introduce you to the real Mary Magdalene.

20. Magdalene: Saint or Harlot?

The real Mary Magdalene in the gospel of John is not the same Mary Magdalene that pop culture became fascinated with thanks to a recent blockbuster movie and novel. I had barely begun contemplating that the Bible might not be the perfect word of God when a scintillating and controversial novel hit the market: *The Da Vinci Code*. Because I was still in the shadow of my religious convictions, I did not deign to follow the hype and read the book when it first came out. I heard enough about it on Christian websites, reviews, and morning programs. From the side of the religious, the book was vilified and the only thing I knew about it was its blasphemous assertion that Jesus Christ had been an ordinary man who had been married to Mary Magdalene.

I have to admit, my curiosity grew at every mention of her name. After all, in the gospel of John it had been Mary Magdalene who had come upon the resurrected Christ for the first time. It was Magdalene who had gone to embrace Jesus when he warned her that he had not yet ascended to his Father and could not be touched:

"The first day of the week cometh Mary Magdalene early, when it was yet dark, unto the sepulcher, and seeth the stone taken away from the sepulcher… Mary stood at the sepulcher weeping: and as she wept, she stooped down, and looked into the sepulcher. And seeth two angels in white sitting… And they say unto her, 'Woman, why weepest thou?' She saith unto them, 'Because they have taken away my Lord, and I know not where they have laid him'. And when she had thus said, she turned herself back, and saw Jesus standing,

*and knew not that it was Jesus. Jesus saith unto her, 'Woman,
why weepest thou?' She, supposing him to be the gardener,
saith unto him, 'Sir, if thou have borne him hence, tell me
where thou hast laid him, and I will take him away'. Jesus
saith unto her, 'Mary'. She turned herself and saith unto him,
'Rabboni', which is to say Master. Jesus saith unto her, Touch
me not; for I am not yet ascended to my Father: but go to my
brethren and say unto them, I ascend unto my Father, and
your Father, and to my God, and your God'. Mary Magdalene
came and told the disciples that she had seen the Lord, and
that he had spoken these things unto her."* John 20:1, 11-18,
KJV

 *"On the first day of the week, while it was still dark,
Mary Magdalene went to the tomb and saw that the stone had
been removed from the entrance ... Now Mary stood outside
the tomb crying. As she wept, she bent over to look into the
tomb and saw two angels in white ... They asked her, "Woman,
why are you crying?"*

*"They have taken my Lord away," she said, "and I don't
know where they have put him." At this, she turned around
and saw Jesus standing there, but she did not realize that it
was Jesus. He asked her, "Woman, why are you crying? Who
is it you are looking for?" Thinking he was the gardener, she
said, "Sir, if you have carried him away, tell me where you
have put him, and I will get him." Jesus said to her, "Mary."
She turned toward him and cried out in Aramaic,
"Rabboni!" (which means Teacher). Jesus said, "Do not hold
on to me, for I have not yet ascended to the Father. Go instead
to my brothers and tell them, 'I am ascending to my Father
and your Father, to my God and your God.'" Mary
Magdalene when to the disciples with the news: "I have seen
the Lord!" And she told them that he had said these things to
her."* John 20:1, 11-18, NIV

It was this moment between Christ and Magdalene that had launched my entire quest into understanding the Bible historically and the deeper mysteries of the soul. Every time I heard her being spoken about, I remembered lying in that hospital bed after my adrenal failure, riddling over her inability to recognize the risen Christ and how it had opened the door to think of the soul in new ways. Thanks to the sensationalism of *The Da Vinci Code*, one could not change a channel without having the blockbuster discussed. Just as word hit that it would be a major motion picture, I picked up a copy and began to seriously research its hypothesis.

After reading the novel, I began to realize that Mary Magdalene had been split into two distinct women. On the one hand, the Magdalene of the gospels remained who I had learned about as a child: a repentant prostitute who became a faithful follower of Christ, and in the forgiveness of her sexual sins was supposed to be an inspiration for all 'fallen' women. This image was the only image I had ever known. I was taught that she had been the sinful woman who had loved Christ so much she had taken expensive perfumed oil and used her own hair to wash and anoint his feet. Some sects also insist she is the woman whom Jesus saves from stoning when she is caught in the act of adultery. Her submission and her repentance from a life of ill repute was all I had ever been taught about her from the pulpit.

For non-church goers, they likely see the Magdalene portrayed by *The Da Vinci Code*: a powerful disciple equal to any man who was the wife of Jesus and mother of his child, beginning a secret bloodline that stored the true identity of the Holy Grail. From this perspective has come a renaissance of women who have chosen to see her as a kind of priestess, a symbol of divine sensuality whose denial and persecution by the later church is a representation of how all women were oppressed by the church. Ironically, both of these views emphasize Mary Magdalene's sexuality. One makes her seem like she is a whore who sought redemption from the Son of God, while the other turns her into a woman who had spiritually charged sexual relations with a human Jesus. Both of these identities are so different that I had to wonder if either had any truth.

Magdalene has never been an easy character for scholars to figure out. Early Church fathers and theologians used her as a handy reference to the sinfulness of women and how they could achieve salvation by coming under the submission of the Church which was supposed to embody Christ. Meanwhile, actual biblical scholars and historians had to recognize that they didn't have much real evidence to work with. What they did know came into direct conflict with Church teachings. Even now there is a great deal of disagreement amongst scholars about who the real Mary Magdalene was, what her significance had been in the time of Jesus, and whether or not she should be elevated to a much higher place of importance in religious history and spirituality.

One thing has resonated with me so much in these years of study and it is the recognition that no matter how much disagreement there might be, everyone who has written about these things has done so with a sincere desire to find the truth. For those who are not religious and claim spirituality, Magdalene has become a woman with two different faces. One face is portrayed in the gospels. The other is a woman of power and spiritual wisdom which rivals Jesus based upon information found in a group of texts we now call Gnostic Gospels (which I will address soon). For theologians, she is only whatever their own church denomination says she is.

For scholars she is simply a normal ancient woman to be explored out of curiosity. I have always sought a middle ground between solid scholarly research and the spiritual insights of the soul. Perhaps nowhere was this embodied more than Magdalene.

Every woman in the Bible has been portrayed only from the viewpoint of man. What we know about them is only what the men who wrote the books cared to share about them. Because of this, I have felt so strongly that justice needs to be done by them. That can only happen when real information is brought to light that allows the person reading the Bible to stop and think and wonder what the true voices of these incredible women would have been had they been able to tell their own tales. Hopefully I can do them some justice by helping you, the reader, think about them in new ways, especially Mary Magdalene.

If you take a moment to do a quick internet search with the name Mary Magdalene and then look at all the images it brings up, you will discover that Magdalene has been the subject of many, many artists. She is almost always depicted with flowing locks of auburn or fiery red hair. Though her poses are often repentant, she is also often free spiritedly nude with her long hair covering her breasts. In a day when art was often censored by the Church, depictions of Magdalene were still certain to incite lust in male viewers. After all, the point was that with just one look a person could tell that Magdalene had once been a prostitute. Poor Magdalene always seems portrayed as though she is caught somewhere between praying for forgiveness or posing for a modern boudoir photo to incite a man's desires. I chuckle at the thought that even the most demure woman could be painted in such a state and be mistaken for a prostitute. Sadly, all women should know that they are beautiful when they can see themselves through the mirrors of their Souls. Instead, beauty becomes something illicit and scandalous only when we are made to be seen through the eyes of the Ego of man. This is the fate of Magdalene as she has been interpreted by the unchecked Ego of men who felt it was their right to recast her story.

If one bothers to read all four gospels in the New Testament, nowhere is Mary Magdalene referred to as having been in prostitution, or even adulterous. This may astound some readers who have heard her tale again and again from the clergy and have taken their words to be gospel truth as I once did. Once I actually bothered to study for myself and listen to real Biblical historians and scholars I found that this was not true at all and the evidence stares the reader in the face from the pages of the gospels themselves. The only personal reference to Mary Magdalene in which we are told anything about her is in Luke:

> *"And it came to pass afterward, that he went throughout every city and village, preaching and showing the glad tidings of the kingdom of God: and the twelve were with him, and certain women, which had been healed of evil spirits and infirmities, Mary called Magdalene, out of whom went seven devils, and Joanna the wife of Chuza Herod's steward, and Susanna, and many others, which ministered unto him of their substance."* Luke 8:1-3, KJV
>
> *"After this, Jesus traveled about from one town and village to another, proclaiming the good news of the kingdom of God. The Twelve were with him, and also some women who had been cured of evil spirits and diseases: Mary (called Magdalene) from whom seven demons had come out; Joanna the wife of Chuza, the manager of Herod's household; Susanna; and many others. These women were helping to*

support them out of their own means." Luke 8:1-3, NIV

This is the only passage in the whole New Testament that gives us any kind of information about who Mary Magdalene is as a person. I will refer to Mary Magdalene as just Magdalene to avoid confusion with Mary the mother of Jesus. People do not realize that Mary was an incredibly popular name at this time in ancient Palestine and we see several women named Mary appear in the New Testament... this actually became a source of confusion for later church fathers and made way for Magdalene's bad reputation. I will get to that soon, but for now this brief passage reveals at least a few facts about this particular Mary.

Magdalene was viewed as important enough to differentiate her from these other Mary's by making certain to include the name of where she was from: Migdala, a town on the northwest shore of the Sea of Galilee. The name means 'high tower'. In the ancient world surnames were rare and did not become common until recent history, but everyday people managed to differentiate themselves by referring either to the place where they lived or who their father's family was. So, at least we know where Magdalene hailed from: Migdala.

Many historians recognize that there are not enough accounts of daily life from this time in Palestine to truly know how common or rare it was for women to work outside of the home, but one thing is made clear from this passage: Magdalene and the other women named are women of means. In the ancient world women were constantly working. If the modern woman still feels the burden of cleaning house, cooking three meals a day, caring for more than one child, caring for her husband and his extended family, all while taking on extra work like gardening/farming, animal husbandry, laundry, and sewing, then imagine the ancient women who lived without any electricity or modern conveniences.

For ancient women, work was from sun up and past sun down, with the home and children consuming every waking moment of every day. The rates of death in childbirth were horrifically high and young women who managed to survive giving birth to their children could expect a relatively short life of constant back breaking work. It is little wonder that the life expectancy rarely went into a woman's late thirties while men might live into their forties if they were lucky. The majority of ancient people were in the peasantry, so things like reading, writing, and education were often only in the reach of the highest upper class who could afford to have servants and slaves doing all the menial day to day work. The majority of ancient people were illiterate and women were certainly not expected to learn.

We are told in these verses that Magdalene, Johanna, Susanna, and 'many other' women came from their homes and traveled to see Jesus. Notice that with the exception of Johanna, none of the other women mentioned are married or have husbands that have come with them. Not only did these women have the ability to leave the home, they apparently were free to do so unlike other married women whose husbands' may deny them the privilege. If this were not a strong enough indicator, the verse makes it clear that Magdalene was one of a whole group of women who were financially supporting Christ and the Twelve. We do not know who these women were because male writers didn't feel it was important. The assumption is that the women were Jewish just as all of Jesus' male disciples were, but I readily challenge that by asking how could we know?

With no other information to go on, I'd like to point out that these women could have come from different walks of life. While women being independent and working for themselves seems to have been foreign to ancient Jewish customs, women who hailed from Egyptian, Babylonian, Cretan, or Turkish families would have come from cultures that allowed women far more freedom. Intermarriage was always discouraged, but it happened in the ancient world and especially in the Roman Empire. Israel during the Roman Empire (known as Palestine) was still the same crossroads of cultures it had always been; the Roman Empire engulfed a wide range of people and their native beliefs from Egypt to Britain and even the farther reaches into Iran, possibly India. There are Roman reports that Hindu holy men could be found wandering the empire, so is it so strange to think that the women of Jesus' support group might have hailed from much broader minded cultures? These women may have already had a greater independence thanks to their 'pagan' cultures than many Jewish women of the time did. Also, there was communication between the Jews in Palestine and the sizable Jewish population that had remained in Babylon. Babylonian Jewish women may have experienced more freedoms thanks to the influence of their 'pagan' neighbors whose women often had more independence and autonomy.

Many people have no idea that the Roman Empire was a great hotbed of ideas, thinkers, and philosophers. Thanks to its roads, travel was more frequent than it had been in the past and merchants went back and forth extensively with both goods and teachings. Most of the ancient world may have been illiterate, but good stories and teachings passed by word of mouth easily. Teachings by great philosophers like Pythagoras (whose religious school included both men and women) and Plato were not just academic but highly spiritual and religious in nature. Emphasizing the soul and life after death, they were popular schools of thought and were starting to influence 'Hellenized' Jews enough to anger the religious authority in Jerusalem.

Even though there is so little that we know about ancient women compared to ancient men, one fascinating possibility lies in a religion that had existed during the Greek empire and continued in Egypt and in the Roman empire called the Mysteries. Because the teachings were to be kept hidden from people who had not been initiated, we know only bits and pieces, but one notable fact is that they were one of the few religions that allowed men and women, slave and free person equal membership and imparted an intense belief in the immortality of the Soul. The possibility that the Mysteries influenced Christ has been on the radar of academics for decades, but given the way in which Christ seems to have attracted these prominent women, I believe, makes it an absolute possibility. He was obviously charismatic enough to call their attention and if the women were Jewish, then perhaps they were entranced by his insistence that in the kingdom of God there would exist no marriage or gender. To them, his actions spoke of a deep respect for women compared to the oppressive laws of the religious authority. For many women, the kind of religion Jesus preached would have seemed a far kinder belief than the religious laws they lived with under the enforcement of the Temple or even the rest of Rome.

My whole point in bringing this in at this time is simple: question it all. We will never get all the answers, but if we just take whatever is given to us and told this is it without any proof, then we have done an injustice to these women. If I have learned anything in my life it is that nothing will ever be black or white. It is vital that anyone who chooses to read the Bible (or any religious book) do so with an open mind that will question and wonder about everything instead of taking another person's interpretation as truth. Whoever these women were, they must have had richer background stories than we will ever know, but at least we do know that these were women with some kind of wealth and influence for their day.

The wording of the King James Bible may seem ambiguous to some readers: 'ministered unto him of their substance', but the New International Version of the Bible renders the situation better: 'These women were helping to support them out of their own means.' As many scholars have pointed out, Jesus did not have a day job. Christ's life was consumed with teaching and spreading the word that the world would end and God's 'kingdom' would come to earth, bringing with it an end to the evils of the age (the Roman rule). The twelve disciples who followed him had come from many walks of life and the gospels intimate that in order to follow him they had all given up regular employment such as fishing, farming, or tax collecting. Divine or human, these men had to have some form of resources in order to eat, clothe, and shelter themselves from village to village and this verse solves the mystery by informing us that Jesus was being financed by women. Why women and not men may confirm that Jesus' teachings were as radical as many historians have believed them to be. Because the prominent attitude of the day for ancient men was that women were of inferior substance and little more than their own breeding stock, Jesus' insistence on treating women as equal human beings hopefully proves that not only were women ready to grasp a message of their own worth, but some men of the day were accepting of this message as well. Sadly, the resistance Jesus so often met shows that it was a message the majority of his brethren did not want to hear.

Jesus' reliance on women is often portrayed as groundbreaking, but I would like to put in my own personal view by stating that it was also a brilliant move. Most historians of this age agree that men largely did not socialize with women they were not married or related to. Jesus is shown to be revolutionary by dining with outcasts such as tax collectors and prostitutes, and now this verse confirms he also teaches women since he has gained their financial support. Notice that one of the other women named is the wife of a man who is a steward of Herod - a vital Roman government official! On the one hand, Jesus may be showing the world that it is the most sinful people who should be reached out to, but on the other he has placed himself amongst the people who know the underbelly of intrigues that are really going on between the Jewish religious authority and the hated Roman government. But I digress into matters that will likely be the basis for another book. The point is that we know that Magdalene is a woman of some independence and wealth, but also one other interesting fact: she dealt with demons.

Actually the Greek text of this verse uses a very special word '*daimon*' and does not say she is 'cured' of them the way the evil spirits of illness were apparently cured out of the other women. Magdalene seems to be singled out at this moment for a good reason. I will discuss this subject further in the next chapter, but for right now you need to understand that a 'demon' in the Greek world was not how we define a demon today. Today the word demon is one filled with fear and terror. We have been inundated with horror movies that show hellish creatures possessing people, haunting houses, and ultimately reporting back to hell to serve the great 'king' of demons Satan. None of this was believed by people in Jesus' time and in fact the Jews of Jesus' time did not even really believe in hell as we now know it, nor did they believe in a being that we now call the Devil.

The Greek word used in the text: '*daimon*' referred to a supernatural being that was like a god. Many Greek philosophers and religions believed that every individual had its own *daimon* that guarded, guided, and spoke to the individual (ironically akin to our idea of a guardian angel). Since it seems Magdalene was not suffering an illness, and it says seven demons 'had come out' of her, I would like to give my own theory since every other interpretation about her is as much guess work and here-say as anything else. Perhaps Magdalene was indeed an educated woman who may have previously been a believer in Greek religion and a follower of other gods until she came upon Christ's teachings. The number seven is significant as well, as it is a holy number in both Jewish and Greek religions. For the Jews, there are seven days of creation, but for the Greeks and Romans, there were seven heavenly bodies that were each identified with a god or goddess. I admit that this is all just an educated guess, but I cannot just ignore that the wording is surprising and gets my curiosity blazing because I have studied the ancient practices of Jewish mysticism and numerology (known as gematria).

Some of you will recognize the imprint and importance of numbers all over the Old Testament, but only those who have studied the more mystical teachings of Judaism recognize that every number given is written down in order to give extra meaning. Many centuries later in Jewish mysticism, demons became something that could be controlled and interacted with for the purpose of personal power. In fact many mystical texts would be written that depicted the great Jewish King Salomon as a sorcerer supreme who builds the Temple with the aid of hundreds of 'demons'. Why would anyone think God would ever allow something 'demonic' to have a part in the construction of his holy house unless the word 'demon' has been utterly misinterpreted in our modern time? In this respect, they were not that different from the Greek *daimon*, a being that would often work on the behalf of its human counterpart. This raises fascinating questions about who Magdalene was and what her true profession or even spiritual nature might have been.

What really matters about her being identified as having had seven demons, is that most Christian teachings insist that these 'demons' were what drove her to sexual sin. The problem is that anytime demonic possession or demons are mentioned in the New Testament (or even in other Jewish sources), they never have anything to do with sex or sexuality. So why does Magdalene have this 'bad girl' reputation? You may be asking, isn't she the prostitute who anointed Jesus' feet and the adulterer who was nearly stoned?
Well, no, she's not.

Long, long after the gospels were written and the whole New Testament was voted on and legalized by the religious authority (canonized), a Pope named Gregory gave a sermon about Mary Magdalene. This sermon became the basis for church teaching from the moment he gave it in AD 591 all the way to our modern day. After pouring over the New Testament, he started to notice that not only were there quite a few women named Mary, but there were also a few women who were unnamed.

There is a brief passage in Luke 7:36-39 in which Jesus has an encounter with a 'sinful' woman. While Jesus dines in the house of a Pharisee, an unnamed woman enters holding an alabaster jar of precious perfumed oil. All we are told about her is that she was 'a woman in the city, which was a sinner'.

She approaches Jesus, kneels at his feet, washes them with her own tears, wipes them with her hair, and anoints his feet with the expensive oil. Jesus' host is aghast that he has let this sinful woman touch him. This is such a brief encounter, only three verses long, and the word used for 'sinner' is a Greek word that has nothing to do with sexuality, so the assumption that her 'sinfulness' was prostitution is unfounded. For all we know, the woman's 'sin' could have been petty theft or blasphemy. Jesus does have his feet washed and anointed a second time by a virtuous woman named Mary in John 12:1-6, but this Mary is the sister of Lazarus and Martha, not Mary Magdalene.

The second anonymous woman is a famous story out of the gospel of John 8:1-11 in which Jesus is asked what he would do about a woman caught in the act of adultery. The woman who has been dragged out to be stoned has supposedly been found in the act of adultery and has been cast to the ground so that the men around may stone her for her sin. The religious authority challenges Jesus by asking what he would do. This moment is tricky for Jesus, for his answer could get him into even deeper trouble with the Jewish religious authorities as well as result in the woman's death. We are told he kneels down and writes something in the dirt. His answer is the thought provoking: 'let he who is without sin cast the first stone'. Slowly each man drops his stones and walks away until it is only Jesus and the woman left. Jesus informs the woman that she is safe now because no one else is left to accuse her, he certainly will not either, and she should now go and 'sin no more'.

This story never gives us a name for the woman, and it has always been a powerful moment in the gospels that most people read and take as a message that they should not judge others. What no one realizes is that it's actually more radical than that. Notice that even though the woman is caught 'in the act' of adultery, the man who was with her has apparently been let go and is nowhere to be seen. Instead, all the blame is placed on her and it is a crime worth her life. When Jesus says that only a man without sin should cast a stone, he's not just reminding the men of the crowd that they are imperfect. In that moment, he has made the woman to be of equal standing and worthy of consideration. This was something that did not happen often in religious laws or trials. It's not just a 'feel good' lesson for the reader, it is a powerful statement by Christ about the standing of women and that they have never deserved to be treated as a lesser sex by religious laws.

Both of these are pivotal stories in the gospels, but neither woman is named. Given that Magdalene was treated with such consideration as to single her out in Luke and John, there is no reason to think the gospel writers would have hesitated to make it clear that she was either of these women. Whoever these women were, they were not Mary Magdalene. So why did Pope Gregory decide to amalgamate all their stories together? Some historians think he was just trying to simplify the stories so that they were easily remembered (a theory that doesn't make much sense), but others believed it was a very intentional move in order to discredit Mary Magdalene as nothing but a whore who submissively came to salvation. More puzzling, the 'sinner' who washes Jesus' feet isn't even explicitly declared to be a prostitute and yet this Pope decreed she was! Notice that the sin was declared sexual in nature not because the text says it is, but because male Christian authors automatically assumed they were. Why would any Church leader want to do this to Magdalene? I soon found out the answer hinged on religious politics.

Many sects of Christianity (and Judaism) have differed in their beliefs and in their politics; as a religion it has never been free of dissension. I hope I was able to paint that picture clearly in the chapter before last. I was so blind to really assume that the early history of the Church was some glorious time in which all the leaders and followers believed the same way simply because they had been chosen through the 'Holy Spirit' and that God had given them knowledge and authority. I believed this meant that all believers had come together as one in their minds, hearts, and souls. I believed it was the strength of this unity that allowed Christianity to become the dominant religion of the Western world. Imagine my disbelief when I learned that almost from the moment it started, Christianity was not only a cult, but a cult of many different beliefs and sects that experienced a fracturing between believers almost from the very beginning.

Historians always suspected this. As they dug into the real history of Mary Magdalene they began to suspect Pope Gregory had stitched together the separate women's stories to purposely disgrace Magdalene. The mystery as to why would not make itself clear until our modern age when archaeologists and biblical scholars painstakingly restored and translated an ancient body of texts that we know as the Gnostic Gospels. This collection of writings were written by Christians who valued 'gnosis' (the Greek word for knowledge) and spiritual wisdom instead of the ceremony and hierarchy of the traditional Church. These sacred works were alluded to in the writings of several early Church fathers, but these leaders always made it clear that the books were 'heretical'. The Church actually commanded that all writings, gospels, and books that were not authorized and canonized by the Roman Catholic Church had to be surrendered and burnt. There are so many things I have tried to impart to the reader over the course of this book, but this is one vital situation I request you stop and think about.

Book burning is not a new problem. It has occurred whenever a government (secular or religious) has felt threatened and is trying to establish complete control over people's beliefs. A religion that is afraid of educated people will always lash out and try to suppress information. In our current day and age, I hear so many Americans criticize other nations and cultures. China (a totally secular nation) bans certain forms of free speech and basically controls what can be seen or discussed online, on television, and printed. During the Communist revolution, any books, art, or music deemed too Westernized were put to the fire and anyone who dared to try to save them risked imprisonment or death. Americans hear about this and are horrified that this nation would purposely misinform and oppress its own people just to keep political control.

Meanwhile, in Iran, Iraq, and Afghanistan (nations controlled utterly by religious authority), any books, art, or music that does not teach Islamic propaganda, or dares to criticize Islam, are burned and the people who try to save them also risk imprisonment and death. Americans have watched this with horror and outrage. Perhaps the most infamous book burners of all were the Nazis of WWII, who staged massive bonfires and put thousands of books to the flames. So intense was their hatred of books that could threaten their power and ideology, that anyone caught trying to save or collect these works were executed. Americans who learn about this history are always aghast and sickened by it. It was Franklin D. Roosevelt, the American President in office during WWII, who summed up the true reason for the Nazi fear of books:

"People die, but books never die. No man and no force can put thought in a concentration camp forever. No man and no force can take from the world the books that embody man's eternal fight against tyranny. In this war, we know books are weapons."

No truer words have been spoken about the power of books in our modern age, so how much more so in the ancient world when the destiny of a religion and the political power of a clerical hierarchy depended upon which books they could make people believe were the one and only Truth? Yet many Christians go to Church and read the Bible without ever realizing that in the ancient world the early Church through the power of the Roman Empire acted exactly as these modern nations have in their desire to destroy knowledge and strip humanity of choice.

Books are the life blood of ideas. They hold not just stories, but the souls of the people who write down their teachings and beliefs. A religion (or a government) that truly believes it holds the ultimate truth should never feel the need to suppress and destroy information. One look at the Nazis, Islamic radicals, or the current Chinese political system, should make the reader wonder just how secure the early Church felt. Like these other corrupt systems, it obviously felt it had things to hide and the only way to keep building its wealth and power was by keeping its followers blind and educated only in its own teachings. Shouldn't a religion that really believes it is the ultimate Truth of God, trust their God through the belief that the Holy Spirit will bring followers, rather than feel a need to force others to convert through oppressive laws? Modern Christians flinch with horror when they hear about radical Muslims converting people at the end of a gun, and yet this same technique of threatening violence was used by the early orthodox Church.

This mindset will be looked into even more intensely in the next chapter about the devil, but for right now what's important is that there was enough fear in the early Church to make them declare all other Christian texts as heresies and illegal. Yet these were all Christian ideologies, written by people who felt every bit as inspired and moved by God to write their books. It was the orthodox Church that had gone astray in the eyes of the Gnostics, not the other way around. Historians knew that this had happened, but they never knew anything about these Christians sects because the Church had done such a thorough job of wiping them out. These unknown believers became a mystery with no voice... until 1945 with the discovery of the Nag Hammadi library.

Everybody thinks of Rome when it comes to the establishing of the early Church, but few people outside of historians know that Egypt was also a big center for the evolution of Christianity. Egyptian Christianity seems to have possessed a diverse and accepting view of faith unlike the strict dogma and politicization that occurred in Rome. Long, long before the days of Islam would change people's views of this country, Egypt under Greek and then Roman rule was a nation of diversity and learning. Its metropolitan harbor town of Alexandria had been famous for its massive library (the largest in the ancient world at the time) and throngs of scholars, philosophers, scientists, and knowledge seekers poured in from all over the empire.

Egyptian culture had always had an inherently wonderful view about women. Egyptian women had always possessed independence even in their ancient history. Egyptian women had the freedom to marry who they chose, freedom to divorce, freedom to own their own wealth, and lived in a society that had appreciated female sexuality instead of trying to control it. Even after it was taken over by Rome, Egypt still maintained a distinct atmosphere of acceptance when it came to new ideas, new knowledge, and new religions. Because of this, it was also a place where the battle between those who fought for knowledge came into violent conflict with those who insisted on blind faith.

In AD 180, one of the early Church fathers, the bishop Irenaeus recognized that the beliefs of 'heretics' (by which he means anyone who wasn't orthodox) had spread all throughout the empire - from Gaul which is modern day France to Greece, and even parts of the Middle East. He was irate that, "they possess more gospels than there really are". Because of this, historians know that at least a little over a hundred and fifty years after Christ's birth, there were apparently numerous beliefs being held by Christians. Orthodox Christianity waged a war against 'heresy', declaring that only their definition of Christianity was the truth. Irenaeus devoted five volumes to 'refuting' these beliefs and titled it *'The Destruction and Overthrow of Falsely So-called Knowledge'*. The orthodox Christians and these 'heretics' remained at odds with each other, but when Constantine backed the orthodox interpretation because it lent itself to Roman politics, all other beliefs eventually became banned. Books were ordered to be turned over to orthodox Church officials for destruction and possessing such books was a criminal offense.

These 'heretical' texts are the heart of what was found at Nag Hammadi, Egypt. Someone whose identity (and gender) will never be known found the courage to save these precious spiritual books from the fire and placed them inside a huge red earthenware jar, took it far out into the desert, and buried it. There the jar remained for over 1,600 years until a Muslim man and his brothers accidentally dug it up while collecting soil for fertilizer. After surviving all that time, some of the texts inside were lost forever when the man's mother used some of the paper for the evening fire, but miraculously 52 texts managed to survive. Anyone interested in the deeper history of the discovery can easily read about it online, as well as the many decades it took for the texts to be preserved, translated, and studied. The work of a lifetime, when scholars finally were able to produce modern copies, the world (at least, the non-religious world) soon discovered just what had terrified the orthodox Church so much.

These texts became collectively known as the Gnostic Gospels and they were books that possessed extraordinary spiritual points of view that seemed totally foreign compared to the traditional New Testament Christianity had come to know. There were books that told the story of Jesus as a child and teenager, books that discussed deeper spiritual teachings of Jesus, books that professed the secrets of the Apocalypse, but perhaps most stunning, books that established a reverence and respect for Mary Magdalene and the case for the equal treatment of women in the church.

In these texts, Magdalene was not shown to be a silent financier, but an active and deeply intelligent disciple. It emphasized the power and honor placed upon her as the first person to witness the risen Christ and who obeyed by witnessing to the male disciples. Magdalene even speaks in some of these books, and it is clear that a battle is brewing between those who feel she was given spiritual wisdom by Christ and those who insisted that women must be silent. This particular attack is made against her by the disciple Peter who became responsible for orthodox Christianity. Many of the texts completely set aside any kind of religious law in order to pursue purely spiritual teachings about the soul and the realms of heaven that exist beyond this physical world. Reading these texts, it is not hard to see why the orthodox Church was so enraged and threatened. Not only were women often painted as equals in the church, these texts emphasized spiritual truth over physical rituals, the enlightenment of the soul over literal dogma, and the need for people to find their own truth instead of being dictated to by a religious hierarchy of priest and clergy.

Why were these texts called 'Gnostic'? The word *'gnosis'* in Greek means 'knowing', but it is the kind of knowing that comes from the Soul's intuition and not that which is manmade. It is a knowing that leads to higher consciousness and truth for all human beings and not just a select and chosen few. Whether or not Magdalene was truly a Gnostic Christian will be up for debate for generations to come, but the point is that the Gnostics seem to have chosen her as their symbol. Gnostic teachings tended to emphasize the need for a balance between the masculine and the feminine and often acknowledge that the reason the world is in chaos is because the energy has swung too far towards the masculine. Many of their allegories and stories revolve around humans having to rediscover 'Sophia', the Greek word for wisdom. Here are some examples of these Gnostic teachings:

"… She became the womb of every thing, for it is she who is prior to them all, the Mother-Father, the first man, the holy Spirit." - The Apocryphon of John

"The male is called 'Assembly', while the female is called 'Life', that it might be shown that from a female came the life for all the aeons." - The Sophia of Jesus Christ

In Gnostic teachings, wisdom is a feminine trait. In their eyes, Christ came to this world to help humanity return to this divine Light, but this feminine trait is too often despised and destroyed by those who emphasize only the power of the masculine. Gnostic groups were often made of both men and women who took turns in positions of spiritual authority. Some scholars have even proposed that some Gnostic texts may have been written by women! The Gnostics understood that there is no Light for the Soul without a balance between the divine Feminine and Masculine.

In Gnostic eyes, as the orthodox Christian movement turned into the patriarchal Roman Catholic Church, it would have been the ultimate rejection of female wisdom and the true Light of the soul. In their eyes, it was the Church that was committing heresy against Christ's teachings, not them. It has been said that History is written by the winners, and in this sad tale it was the orthodox view with all its dogma, rituals, and politics that won out through bloody oppression once it had the militaristic and financial backing of the Roman government. Reading these Gnostic words, it is easy to see why the orthodox Church felt so threatened.

When Pope Gregory maligned Magdalene in AD 591, it happened to be at a time when the Roman Catholic Church was finally stamping out these 'heresies'. Magdalene, who never once in any of the 'traditional' gospels was equated in any way with sexuality, was slandered with the charges of prostitution and adultery in order to destroy her credibility once and for all. A fallen woman could become a useful lesson in how women should submit to the authority of the Church to be saved, but she could never again rise to any kind of respectability or place of leadership. In demoting her, all women were put in their place.

Perhaps the most painful thing I had to recognize about how man has shaped the Bible over the last few thousand years, is that this is supposed to be a holy book, yet it does not paint women as being part of that holiness at all. Only the

Mother of God is supposedly hailed in any way as being holy. All other women are just there. The only reason they venerated Jesus' mother is because they knew no man could give birth to him. Ancient writers of the Hebrew Bible may have been able to somehow convince their people of the ludicrous notion that the first woman was made from Adam's rib, just as the Greeks believed that their war goddess Athena was born straight out of Zeus' head in a bloody parody of birth. Apparently the writers of the New Testament knew no one was going to be believe that a second time. And so they venerated Mary, choosing to ignore the fact that accounts say she had other children, they put her on a pedestal of perpetual virginity and holiness that no human woman could ever imagine attaining. From that moment all women were caught in the perpetual earthly trap of being somewhere between a virgin (Mary the Mother) and a whore (Mary the Magdalene).

If there is any chance that you think that all of this sounds too far fetched, from the battles between the Church and its Gnostic siblings, to a purposeful slandering of Magdalene in order to stamp out Gnostic beliefs, or if you are finding yourself in a place of denial over the fact that the early Church was capable of such underhanded acts, then open your eyes to this story of history.

The Gnostic texts in the Nag Hammadi collection are believed to have been created around AD 350-400 (though thanks to Irenaeus we know the content of the books were widely circulating centuries earlier even in AD 180). Historians arrived to that conclusion by testing the papyrus paper and the bindings upon which the Nag Hammadi texts were written on. Remember that these Gnostic texts were written and buried in Egypt. At the same time and place that these texts were being created and hidden, an important woman was born. A woman that my daughter and I came to know through our research. Her life was recently portrayed in a film titled *Agora* and history has told her story as best as it can recollect under the pen of men for the last few thousand years.

I can recall one particular evening when I closed the book in my hands and felt as if I was transported back in time as a witness to the atrocities that were being inflicted upon those that believed in the freedom to think, to choose, and to live with the understanding that all human beings have a purpose to fulfill... but then, as my mind quieted, I was able to leave that painful era behind. I shook and trembled from my tears. I found myself saying, *I am so sorry, so very, very sorry.* As I repeated those words, I knew that the injustice that had occurred to this incredible woman lay at the feet of all those who choose to see life with only blind faith (as I once had) and ignore the reason they were gifted with from the moment they were born. Let me introduce you to one of the most powerful women the ancient world ever knew, her name was Hypatia. Unlike all the other women whose stories I have shown in this book, Hypatia cannot be found in the Bible. Her story is not Biblical, but it is vital that it is told, because no other woman's story is more poignant during the rise of Christianity. She is one of the rare voices that can still speak to us through the ages, and in her life is the sad and tragic fate of women who dared to reach for knowledge in a time when the Christian religious authority made it clear it would stop at nothing to silence them, even if it meant taking the very essence that they felt was a gift from our Creator: life.

Hypatia was a Greek woman born in Alexandria, Egypt. In her lifetime, she mastered philosophy, mathematics, and astronomy and was head of the Platonist school where she taught. The Alexandria of this time would have been akin to our idea of an important, multi-cultural city like London or New York. Alexandria was the center of learning for the ancient world, its library a constant source of knowledge and intellectual debate in the same way one might think of Oxford or Harvard. The Library of Alexandria housed a collection of over a half-million scrolls. Though we do not know of many women who had the opportunity to reach academic excellence, Hypatia remains as a symbol of ancient education and many of her male students had nothing but glowing things to say about her teaching, experiments, and intellect. Hypatia was what Christians of the day (and our time) would have called 'pagan', but this is misleading.

Hypatia belonged to a spiritual sect known as Neoplatonists. Neoplatonism was both a philosophy and a religion (similar to the way Buddhism is today). It was based on the teachings of Plato and those who went to these schools received training not just in philosophy, but in mathematics and science. Ironically, if the Christian definition of 'pagan' is the worship of other gods, then Hypatia was not even that, for most Neoplatonists did not believe or pay homage to the traditional Greek and Roman deities like Zeus or Apollo. In fact, they believed all life emanated from the One and that to find spiritual truth it was important to live a life of balance in all things.

While Hypatia lived and taught, Alexandria became a battleground between fanatical Christians and non-Christians. It became a place of frequent civil war when the empire split between east and west. In AD 391 she would have watched in horror as the last remnants of the great Library were torn and burned down by a Christian mob acting on the orders of archbishop Theophilus in their lust to destroy all 'pagan' temples and centers of learning. The site was rededicated as a

church. To give a timeline of what was happening in the
Church, the official list of books that became the New
Testament were canonized by the orthodox Church in AD 397,
officially giving license to call all other Christian texts
'heresies' and inflaming the battle between Christians who
took the Bible literally and Gnostics who insisted on spiritual
interpretations. This is around the same time the Gnostic
Gospels were buried in the Egyptian Desert to be found over
1,600 years later at Nag Hammadi. This was the climate of
violent religious upheaval in which Hypatia lived. Ironically
her time is now much like the kind of religious-political
upheaval we are currently witnessing in Islamic countries, the
difference being that our world has become much smaller and
now religious fanaticism and violence is spilling into the
West, the threat of indoctrination coming to the doorstep of
modern youth much the way it did in ancient Egypt, Greece,
and Rome. As I watch the turn of the tide that is so apparent in
global news, I am haunted even more by the echo of Hypatia's
story...

　　Hypatia continued a legacy of learning begun by her
father Theon. Not only did she collaborate on his written
works, a vital volume which reiterated and expanded upon
Ptolemy's knowledge is believed to have been written by her
under the guise of her father's name. This has been a technique
used by many women throughout history who knew their own
discoveries would never be accepted by male scholars if they
used their own names. One of Hypatia's most prominent
students who continued to write about her and keep her
memory alive was a young man name Synesius. Synesius
would, ironically, become a bishop in the Church, but insisted
upon shaping his Christian faith with Neoplatonist teachings.

Hypatia was so highly valued as a thinker that the governor of Alexandria frequently sought her council. It was this favor that put Hypatia on a religious hit list by the local Christian zealots. She was blasted for being a 'pagan', a 'heretic', and a sorceress whose 'evil' powers had given her the ear of the governor. As a woman, she was the ultimate insult to the orthodox Church's teaching that nothing was worse in the eyes of God than a woman who held authority the way a man did or who could go toe to toe with men in the area of learning and debate.

What became of this amazing woman? Around the year AD 416, Hypatia was a mature woman in her 60s. She went out, driving her own carriage (a rarity in a world where women were often escorted everywhere by fathers or husbands) when she was stopped by a mob of Christian zealots. The mob was led by a particularly violent individual called Peter the Lector. With no one next to her to defend her or guard her, she was pulled from her carriage and dragged into a church where she was stripped naked, beaten to death, and then had the flesh scraped from her body with sharp shells and tiles. In this supposed place of holiness, her killers made her a bloody offering to a God who was supposed to represent love, compassion, and peace! Apparently the teachings of Christ's mercy had no place in the hearts of these Christians as they tore apart the remains of her corpse and burned the remnant. Onlookers watched in horror and any attempt at intervention was met with the violence of this Christian mob.

I ask the reader to stop and think. This is a woman whose historical existence is **not** up for debate (unlike the people in the Bible). She was flesh and blood, a woman who understood philosophy and respected the ideas of others. Filled with curiosity, she would have examined the beliefs of the Christians who lived in Alexandria. There is no account of her addressing Christians, or speaking badly about their faith. Because of her own beliefs, this is a woman who would have accepted the beliefs of others and made an effort to understand them even if she did not agree. She sought to live, learn, and teach in peace and she would have fought to keep Alexandria a place where anyone could learn. In her own spiritual views, she could accept the Christians and all the other beliefs that existed at that time. Yet none of these religious men (or women) accepted her for who she was.

According to Neoplatonism, her beliefs in her Creator taught that everything and everyone had a reason and a place in this universe. She did not just 'tolerate' this, she accepted it. She understood the evils of the world and its goodness, recognizing that it had to exist side by side to strike a balance. Because some of her students became Christians, she would have been as educated about the Christian faith as any other. Her student Synesius went on to become a bishop, yet held to the Neoplatonist principles she had taught him. This shows that she understood that the philosophies of Christ and Plato had many similarities. What she could not understand and what must have echoed in her mind was the question of how these believers could insist upon total ignorance of everything else. It is the greatest gift and the greatest curse to anyone who has sought truth and enlightenment: you can accept and embrace the world and its differences, but you are never accepted and embraced with the same respect. Hypatia understood all of this through her years of devotion to science, mathematics, history, literature, and philosophy. She is only one of many throughout history who have paid the price of the hatred of knowledge by those who insist on remaining violently ignorant.

After studying Hypatia, I felt such a strong connection to her and understanding of the foundations of her own spiritual beliefs and ethics. I believe at that moment when she was attacked and dragged into a place that was supposed to be holy to these men, that she could not understand the anger and the fear they displayed all because they lacked the knowledge that she did. At that very moment, I wonder if, because of her own beliefs, she could not help but forgive them. She knew that they lacked the ability to understand or comprehend the world they lived in, she knew they had become pawns for the political and religious control of other men.

In that moment, I imagine she would have agreed with the sentiment of the very man her murderers claimed to follow: the moment Christ looked upon those who had crucified him and uttered, *'forgive them Father, for they know not what they do'*.

If she had been given a glimpse of the far future, she would have related to the words of another great leader of peace, when Gandhi said, *"I like your Christ, but I do not like your Christians. Your Christians are so unlike your Christ."*

I know from personal experience that any human being, man or woman, that becomes enlightened with the true essence of this Universe feels so blessed and at the same time cursed. Hypatia knew this. I don't believe she had any bitterness nor anger towards her attackers, though she must have marveled at the energy she was receiving, the complete ugliness of hatred and the destruction it brings. I think of her and I know in my heart and deep in my soul that peace came over her as they tore up her corpse and did whatever they wanted with it. From what I have been shown in my life, the suffering is over once the Soul departs from the human body.

If this brutality was done to Hypatia, how much worse was done to Gnostic women who would have been seen guilty of a horrific 'heresy' in believing in a spiritual Christ and his beloved disciple Magdalene? Does this sound any different from the horrors so many Western Christians are seeing committed in the Middle East and Africa by fanatical Muslims? The West condemns these individuals as sick, twisted murderers who relish the bloodshed of 'infidels' and 'heretics'. Western Christians recoil in horror and condemn these men for their sick brutality, and yet the story of Hypatia shows that in the early history of the Church there were many Christians who were no less fanatical and bloody in their drive to convert the world to their religion. It should be a stark reminder to modern Christians that these people felt more than justified thanks to so many Biblical passages that glorified killing 'the enemy' for the glory of God. In their eyes, it was not murder, but the will of God. Just as right now we are seeing the very same mentality being played out by Islamic zealots who do not blink an eye at murdering hundreds of innocent people with a bomb because it is 'God's will' for the enemies of their beliefs.

The death of Hypatia, scholars have often said, was the death of learning in the West. From that moment, it is as though an iron curtain was put down. Women had no hope whatsoever for lives filled with anything other than marriage and children. I am sure there were women then as now who had no problems with this and saw their own greatest joy and value in their families, but for women like Hypatia who dreamed of a different life, this choice was completely stripped away for all women for centuries to come. While men could dare to continue learning, they were under the constant threat of crossing the line the Church had set and knowledge had to be in accordance with whatever the Church declared as being truth (even if evidence proved otherwise) or else it was heresy. This was the stealing of the divine Light of women, and through them, men as well.

I still remember feeling the tears that burned down my face as I realized that had I lived in that age with the kind of religious fervor I once had, I too would have likely relished the death of a woman like Hypatia. I wept, realizing just how greatly I had been brain washed. I had always believed that my religion had brought Light into the ancient world, but I learned that in the years following Hypatia's murder, as the empire tore itself apart and the Church established its control over men and the domination of women, the advance of learning and new ideas nearly came to a standstill. It was the beginning of the era historians call the Dark Ages.

How wrong does that seem? Should not a religion that follows a God that was the Truth, the Way, and the Light have ushered in a time of peace and utopia? Instead, the domination of Christianity brought in one of the darkest ages of humanity, a time filled with terror, ignorance, constant wars, invasions, and political-religious battling. It is a darkness that would not lift until human beings fought for the Light of learning and the feminine wisdom of 'Sophia' a thousand years later with the birth of the Renaissance.

How strange to see history repeating itself now as the world braces itself against a new wave of religious fanaticism. The same destruction zealous Christians visited upon centers of learning is little different from the insistence of radical Islam that no knowledge or truth matters but that which is from their God. Zealous Christians insisted a woman had no place outside of the home and her husband was her master, so too are fanatical Islamists putting the same obscene abuse upon women. The terrifying difference is that never has there been so much to lose now that access to weapons, nuclear materials, and even biologically hazardous chemicals and viruses have become so easy for religious terrorists to use. If an ancient mob could destroy one of the world's greatest centers of knowledge simply with stones, sticks, and fire, how much more will we lose to religious fanatics who can now amass and use weapons of horrifying reach and impact?

The world is beginning to realize what only a few like Hypatia did in the ancient world: We stand at the crossroads of politicized religious fanaticism and the human capacity for growth and peace through knowledge. Soon, we may have no choice but to fight in order to keep our freedoms. For no one is this more true than for the women of the world who are seeing their rights stripped away bit by bit more than they ever have been. Ironically, all the ills that came to the Western world were never blamed on the corruption of those in religious and political power, instead the Church turned the people's focus to an enemy no one could see but everyone was forced to believe in: Satan.

21. Satan, the Devil, and God: A Human Trinity

The headlines read: '*Iran calls America the Great Satan!*' This phrase was first coined by the Ayatollah Khomeini after his takeover of the Iranian government, effectively returning that nation to Islamic rule in 1979. It is a phrase that has become popular throughout the Middle East and is often written on signs and mentioned in the propaganda of religious Islamic terrorists. I remember the reaction in the 1970's and even more recently after 9/11 when the Western world's focus turned to the Taliban of Afghanistan. So many religious Americans become irate to hear that these zealots would dare to call America by the name Satan. I heard so many said, "Those people are crazy, they think Americans are the Devil!"

I wish I could have told them what I know now, that these Islamic nations are not accusing America of being the Devil the way that Christianity has portrayed the ultimate evil, or a fallen angel, or Lucifer. It is just one case of many ways in which other religious nations understand certain words so differently from the way the Christian mindset does in the West. Christianity has gone through an incredible evolution since its inception over two thousand years ago. Islam has not. In many ways, Islam is still a young religion that is trying to find its way. In examining Christian and Islamic history, it is as though Islam at this moment in time is trapped in the same conflict that Christianity found itself in during the Middle Ages. For Christianity, it was a time when many freethinkers came forward to try to revolutionize the religion in order to bring greater freedom and equality, but those whose political interests were better served by keeping a stranglehold of power via religious authority managed to brutally suppress its own people via the violence and bloodshed of the Inquisition. In that terrible time when reason was suppressed and faith became full of blood and violence, those who fought for peace or were different met their end in torture chambers, burned at the stake, or hanged. Men suffered under this brutal regime of the Church, but women in the tens of thousands paid the price far more frequently and suffered severe sexual and physical torture before death. This is the same kind of atmosphere the world is seeing permeate Islamic nations, as Muslims who try to fight for peace, balance, and equality find themselves betrayed by fanatics who would return their people to the dark ages. Then, as now, women find themselves the greatest scapegoat and are subjects to even greater brutality because of their sex.

I have been privileged to meet many Muslims in this county, and have witnessed the new generation. Many young Muslim men and women who have had the benefit of learning and living in the West have been able to understand the soul of their faith without bringing to fruition the fanaticism that is plaguing their old countries. Just like Christians and Jews who have found balance between their own faiths and the acceptance of all others, they have an understanding about their personal choice in life and believe that everyone must follow their own religious path. I see these individuals, and they give me so much hope as they become human beings who understand the true philosophy behind the God they worship; they are living a life that is filled with acceptance, love, and joy. There is one thing I have noticed about the men and women who profess to still follow their faith and yet have come to peace with those who are different. They do not take Satan seriously. They know that he is merely a symbol for the evil impulse that exists in human beings. They recognize that there is great evil in the world, but they don't feel that people who believe differently are somehow ruled by Satan or the Devil or Lucifer. Yet it is those who profess the greatest fear and belief in Satan who seem to dehumanize humanity by instilling fear and creating chaos wherever they go. These are the people who become the most fanatical, the people who happily pick up arms in order to 'fight' against Satan for the glory of God even if that means the death of innocent people.

When the Iranian government made the remark that America was the Great Satan, they were simply saying that America was their adversary, nothing more. In fact, they used the same term for the United Kingdom and the governments of Europe, while calling Russia and its Communist regime the 'Lesser Satan'. In the eyes of a religious leader like the Ayatollah Khomeini, the Western nations were indeed a 'great adversary'. The freedom that the West possessed thanks to its foundation of knowledge and learning was the greatest adversary there was to a man who was trying to establish Iran as a purely Islamic State run by religious Sharia law. Perhaps the greatest irony is that while the Middle East continues to portray the West as Satan, it is the religious in the West who look upon these Islamic nations as being possessed by Satan!

It seems no matter which religion the fanatics fall into, somehow Satan is always hiding behind the religion of their enemy, but never themselves. Satan has become the ultimate excuse and scapegoat of religion (and man), but this is not who Satan originally was. Instead, Satan is a character with his own complex history, a figure who has always been at the mercy of manmade authority and not the other way around. In order to understand this, I need to take you back in time to a prophet named Zoroaster around 1400-1200 BC. This prophet came from a good family and was part of the culture of Iran long before the Bible came into existence...

Many religious people assume that the oldest organized religion in this world is Judaism. I certainly thought this. In my studies I discovered that Hinduism actually holds that honor. The Egyptian Pyramid texts are technically the oldest known religious writing in the world around 2400-2300 BC, and the Sumerians left a rich religious history behind in numerous clay tablets long before the Hebrews ever existed. While there were religions that predated Hinduism, Hinduism is considered the oldest organized religion. It is the oldest organized religion that has written scripture, known as Vedic. The Vedas are known to be older than any part of the Bible, predating it by anywhere from a few hundred years to even a thousand. Judaism has often claimed to be older by arguing that the religion began with the patriarch Abraham, but religious scholars recognize that Judaism did not come into existence until the writing of the Torah which can only have occurred around 1400 BC at the earliest (but was not actually written down until 950 BC). The Vedas go back to at least 1800 BC, if not earlier. The rules for Vedic priests have shocking similarities to the rules for Levitical priests, but I'll save that revelation for another time and another book.

Around the time the Bible claims the figure of Moses existed, a man was living in Persia who would become a great prophet. For many who have been Christians and have studied the Bible so intently, they never stop to think about anybody else of consequence having existed at the same time as a man like Moses. The Bible never mentions Zoroaster or dares to acknowledge his eminence in the rest of the ancient world, but this is not surprising because the Bible only concerns itself with the story of the Hebrew people and their enemies. My point is that the Bible was written by Jewish authorities with only their own history and concerns in mind, which makes it all the more ironic that Christianity would try to assimilate it as their own when it was never meant to be. So many faiths and spiritual texts are far older than what occurs in the Bible, but those who insist on believing every word of the Bible blind themselves to this reality. They believe that only the Bible matters, when the truth is that for much of the history of the ancient world the Bible held little to no bearing whatsoever.

Though now relegated to only a few thousand worshippers across the globe (mostly in Iran and India), Zoroastrianism was once a major faith, every bit as influential and powerful as Christianity. It is one of the oldest and longest lasting monotheistic religions. Many scholars recognize that it was a major source for Christian doctrines and may have inspired many aspects of Jewish belief as well. Scholars know for certain that Zoroastrian traditions were well established before Christ, but there is not enough textual evidence to firmly say that it influenced Judaism. It is certain though that the Jews who were exiled to Babylon would have absolutely come into contact with Zoroaster's teachings and his followers. Even after the rise of Christianity, Zoroastrianism remained a strong religion until the Muslim conquests, when fanatical Muslims burned the majority of Zoroastrian holy texts and converted believers to Islam by threat of the sword. Zoroastrianism held beliefs that any Jew, Christian, or Muslim would quickly recognize: belief in a single all-powerful God, an evil being intent on making humans sin, an immortal soul, good and bad angels, the coming of a future savior, and a final battle between good and evil that brings an end to the world. The three monotheistic faiths of this age share all these things, but it is fair to say that Zoroastrianism had them first. Whether these ideas were unique to Zoroaster or already part of his Persian culture, scholars do not know.

So who was Zoroaster? Zoroaster was a young man born into a priesthood who seems to have felt that the religion of his day had become corrupt and that ritual had taken the place of spiritual truth (mirroring the Buddha and Jesus Christ). One day this young man began to be spoken to by his God, the God of the Universe, the Wise Lord known as Ahura Mazda. From the moment his Lord spoke to him, Zoroaster knew he had been called to reconstruct and purify the corruption he saw around him. In doing so, many scholars recognize that he was the first to see God as being the ultimate Good and in direct opposition to an entity that represented ultimate Evil named Angra Mainyu. The foundation of Zoroastrian belief is that the battle between Good and Evil takes place in the heart of every human being. Those who dedicated themselves to Truth, Light, and Right Action would be rewarded with an afterlife in paradise because of their devotion to the Wise Lord (does this sound familiar to Christ's words of the Way, the Truth, and the Light?). Those who lied, committed wrongs, and did evil only served to aid Angra Mainyu and would ultimately end up in hell.

I have mentioned before that Judaism does not believe in Satan or the Devil the way that Christianity does. In Christianity, Satan is the figure of ultimate evil. He is an angel named Lucifer who fell from heaven when his pride made him disobey God and he was cast out and into hell. The angels who followed him became demons while Satan became the ruler of Hell, the realm to which those who reject God and his Son spend all eternity in torture and terror. In the Christian tradition, Satan is powerful and his intent is to tempt all human beings into sin and evil. By most standard Christian doctrines, Satan took the disguise of the snake in the Garden of Eden and through Eve caused all humanity to fall from grace (a fallacy that I examined thoroughly in Chapters 5 and 6). Though the Christian view of Satan knows that God will win in the end, they believe it is his intention to take as many human souls into Hell as he can with the time he has. None of this exists in Judaism. The only resemblance the Jewish Satan has with his Christian counterpart is that they share the same name.

In Judaism, Satan is not so much a personal name as a description, and it occurs only eighteen times in the entire Old Testament. Surprising as it may seem, the word *'satan'* is Semitic in origin and in Hebrew it simply means 'adversary'. Literally, anyone who got in the way of something a person wanted to do, or who was seen as an enemy, was called a *satan*. In this respect, evil people like Hitler or Saddam Hussein would absolutely be recognized as being *'satans'* because they made themselves adversaries to the rest of the world. It was never meant to be the name of a single entity, and ultimately it became a kind of job description for a particular angel. The majority of references to this figure occur in the Book of Job (eleven of the eighteen times) and so this is the book that should be looked to when figuring out just who or what Satan is.

The Book of Job tells the story of a man known for his righteousness and faith in God. Job is a wealthy man with many children, many friends, and many resources. In this story, Satan comes before the throne of God and is not in any way considered to be a fallen angel or entity. Instead, Judaism recognized that *'satan'* is a title given to a member of God's heavenly court, and this being is charged with testing humanity. The *satan* speaks to God, pointing out that it is easy for Job to praise the Lord as long as the man is wealthy and content. He makes a divine bet with God that if Job is stripped of all the good in his life, then Job will eventually curse God. God then permits the *satan* to go forth and test Job with the restriction that he cannot kill Job. What ensues is one of the most miserable tales of the Old Testament. Within a short span of time Job loses his flocks, his farm, all of his sons and daughters are killed in a massive disaster, and he is finally beset by a mysterious illness. On top of this misery, all of his former friends turn on him, insisting that Job must be a horrible sinner and needs to confess to God.

His wife is seen to speak the most damning words, advising Job that he should just curse God and die. The Christian father Augustine (an unabashed misogynist) went so far as to call Job's wife 'the devil's accomplice', claiming that Satan left her unscathed so that he could use her to torture Job even more. Augustine, reading his Greek translation, had no idea that the original Hebrew texts of Job 2:9 states that what Job's wife actually said was: *"Do you still persist in your integrity? Bless God, and die."*
Even Jewish interpreters were never certain whether Job's wife was being sarcastic, or if she was pleading with Job to seek death as a merciful ending to their torments. Once again this is a perfect example of how a woman in the Bible ended up being portrayed so horribly by male interpreters and became just another example of the evilness of women they could preach from their pulpits.

Through it all, Job stays faithful to God and insists that he is a righteous man. Satan is proven wrong and at the end of the tale when Job asks God why all this was done to him, God evades the question entirely by reprimanding Job with the reminder that no one can understand the magnificence and ways of God. Apparently God chose not to be honest with Job and neglected to inform Job that his life had become a chess piece in a cosmic bet. Again, I stress, the God of man behaves like man and not like a god that would never put humanity through such suffering for the sake of divine pride. Job is eventually given back everything he lost tenfold (minus his dead children).

Judaism recognizes that God is the only god, which means that there can be no other entity which has power greater than God or which is allowed to act independently of God's will. Judaism does not even interpret the story of Job the way that Christianity does. Jewish interpretation sees Job as a complete allegory in which Job represents the people of Israel. Like Job, Israel suffered numerous times and experienced great losses economically and personally as its people were frequently under attack or overtaken by larger empires like Assyria and Babylon. Through it all, Israel maintained that it was God's chosen people. They must have often wondered if God couldn't deem to choose some other nation for a change. Like Job, the Jewish people throughout thousands of years have survived because of the promise that somehow, someway, God will always restore them even if it seems like he just as often allows great misery.

In Judaism, there are no fallen angels because there is no way the angels could ever undermine God or outthink God enough to plot a rebellion the way Christian tradition believes. If the reader is thinking about a particular verse in Isaiah which Christians interpret as referring to fallen angels, I will address that later, but in Judaism it is not seen to refer to fallen angels. For this reason, 'the *satan*' in Judaism is not some wicked entity of pure evil plotting in the deep regions of hell; instead, the *satan* is a being who works for God and has been given the divine task of testing the will and faith of human beings.

As for hell, the Old Testament does make reference to two different places: Sheol and Gehenna. Sheol was an underworld that was a shadowy place of non-existence, but it was not inhabited by demons or any great evil. Gehenna, on the other hand, was a literal place in Jerusalem where the bodies of executed criminals were often dumped and burned along with trash. Gehenna exists to this day in Israel and is still avoided by Jews and Muslims alike. So, again, neither were places that resemble the Christian concept of Hell. This is one of the reasons Judaism has never been a religion that felt the need to 'save' the souls of other people, because in their religion there is no Hell, Devil, or Satan of which to be afraid. Instead, they recognize that evil exists in the hearts of human beings and is something which can only be fought against by living by the ethical laws of God (a philosophy identical to Zoroastrianism). For them, what is done in the here and now means far more than worrying about an imaginary devil or hell.

Ultimately, scholars had to ask: If Judaism does not believe in the Devil as the ultimate evil, nor does it believe in a tortuous hell, then why does Christianity? Remember that Christianity was started by the teachings of a Jewish rabbi, and began as a branch of Judaism. Jesus was a Jewish man who grew up in Palestine and apparently knew his own religious laws extensively. He would have known it had no belief in the kind of hell or Devil that Christianity does now. The answer lies in Zoroastrianism, a religion whose teachings would have been known in the days of the New Testament writers and the early Church. For Zoroastrians, the world was divided between the Good which came from Ahura Mazda, and the bad which came from Angra Mainyu. In their belief, the battle between Good and Evil was not meant to last forever. They believed that someday the world would end and their Wise Lord would oversee a final judgement that would destroy Angra Mainyu forever, ushering in an era of peace and perfection for all living things.

Like Satan, Angra Mainyu had an entire army of demons at his command that could tempt human beings. But, as with Job, the Wise Lord ensured that no demon could overstep its bounds and inflict a person with more than they could handle. Some people have tried to argue that Zoroastrianism is a dualistic faith and not a monotheistic one. By this they mean that Zoroaster emphasized two gods (the Good and the Evil) and not a single god like Judaism. It may walk a fine line in the same way that Christianity does by insisting that they worship a single God and yet separate him into a Trinity of Father, Son, and Holy Spirit, but ultimately Zoroastrianism is monotheistic. Zoroaster insisted that Angra Mainyu's powers paled in comparison to Ahura Mazda and that the Wise Lord ensured that the forces of Good would always prevail against Evil.

Zoroastrianism insisted that so great was the Wise Lord's compassion that at the final judgement when Angra Mainyu is destroyed, all the souls in hell will be released, purified by fire, and allowed into heaven. This is similar to Christian doctrine which insists that Christ will one day return and usher in the Final Judgement, in which God will punish the wicked, bind Satan and his demons, and begin a thousand year reign of peace on earth. If you are starting to see eerie similarities between Zoroastrianism and Christianity, it's because they exist and there is no coincidence. Zoroastrianism may be a small, struggling faith now, but at one time it rivaled other religions and its timeline proves that it would have been around at the same time religions like Judaism and Christianity were developing.

Zoroaster is believed to have been born around 1400-1200 BC. To give you some point of reference, Jewish tradition holds that Moses and the first oral traditions of the Torah were given around 1250 BC, while scholars know that the first books of the Torah began to be written down around 950 BC. Just like with the traditions of Judaism and Christianity, Zoroastrian teachings were first passed down orally before they were written down. Thankfully there are plenty of firsthand accounts of other cultures and peoples interacting with Zoroastrianism to prove that this religion was highly influential. For example Cyrus the Great, the leader of the Persian Empire, decreed Zoroastrianism the official state religion between 550-530 BC. Obviously he would not have done so if the religion had not already been thoroughly established and popular. To put this in context, the Persian Empire existed well before Rome and was often at odds with Greece. Under Cyrus the Great, the Persian Empire was vast and included the land of peoples like ancient Israel, the entire Middle East, Iran, and Turkey. So influential was Zoroastrianism that even the great Greek philosopher Aristotle showed the Persian prophet great respect by stating that he believed his own teacher Plato to be the "re-embodiment of Zoroaster". This is all evidence that Zoroastrianism had a great influence on many cultures and its teachings had been spread much further than just the country of Iran.

While the Christian Satan and the Zoroastrian Angra Mainyu have a lot in common, even Angra Mainyu was not as evil as Satan has become. There were many aspects about Zoroastrianism that show the religion took things allegorically. Angra Mainyu represented the evil impulse that exists in the hearts and minds of all human beings, as well as the shadow that exists within all of us that we sometimes succumb to. The battle between Good and Evil are the choices that all people make throughout their lives. They even recognized that if the Wise Lord was the embodiment of Good, then it meant that at the end of time all people would be allowed into heaven regardless of their deeds or even if they had been followers of other faiths. Unlike Judaism or Christianity, Zoroastrianism does not seem to have persecuted other beliefs or religions.

The story of Satan as he is known in the West is a complex one and it is written almost exclusively by Christian authors. Just as Pope Gregory took it upon himself in AD 591 to knit together the separate stories of Mary Magdalene with two different women in the New Testament (something I went over last chapter), an assortment of Church leaders took it upon themselves to investigate and create a history that would turn Satan from a simple adversary that exists within all humans (are we not always our own worst enemy?) to a being of ultimate Evil.

In all the books of the Old Testament, the *satan* is only referenced eighteen times. In the New Testament, that number rises to about thirty-four. Satan as a character makes his most obvious appearance in a story that is told in three of the four gospels: Mark 1:12-13, Matt 4:1-11, and Luke 4:1-13. Even though the Gospel of Mark is the oldest of the gospels, Jesus' encounter with Satan is reduced to only two verses:

"And immediately the Spirit driveth him into the wilderness. And he was there in the wilderness forty days, tempted of Satan; and was with the wild beasts; and the angels ministered unto him." Mark 1:12-13, KJV

"At once the Spirit sent him out into the wilderness, and he was in the wilderness forty days, being tempted by Satan.

He was with the wild animals, and the angels attended him."
Mark 1:12-13, NIV

Matthew and Luke go into much greater detail. Like Mark, both accounts state that Jesus was 'led by the Spirit' into the wilderness (a desert area) for forty days in which he fasted. In Jewish tradition, forty was the number of days in which God caused rain to fall on the earth to purify it in Genesis, it was also the number of years the Hebrews were condemned to wander the desert after disobeying God when he had brought them out of Egypt, and Moses had spent forty days with God upon the mountain, so the number forty was always considered a number that represented a time of trial and renewal. All three accounts also agree that Jesus was tempted by Satan, but while Mark gives no clues to the nature of these temptations, Matthew and Luke tell the full story.

The temptation seems to occur at the very end of Jesus' forty days of fasting, and the first temptation Satan presents to him is that of food. He first tempts Christ by reminding him that as the Son of God he has the power to turn a stone into bread, so why not do so?
Jesus responds that a person should not live on physical food alone, but on the spiritual nourishment of God. Satan then apparently transports him to the highest point of the Jerusalem Temple, telling him that if he is the Son of God then he should let himself fall so that the angels of God can save him. Jesus responds with the rebuke that man has been commanded to not test God. Lastly, Satan then transports Jesus to a very high mountain where the great kingdoms of the world are in view and reveals to him that all these are within his power. He will give them to him if only Jesus will worship him. Jesus gives his last rebuke, commanding Satan to 'get behind' him and that it is written that only God should be worshipped. Matthew and

Luke actually disagree on the order of the last two temptations and reverse them, but both then agree that when this trial was over Jesus returned to Galilee and started to deliver his message in earnest.

These texts were written long before Christian theologians twisted the image of Satan. For Christ, Satan would have been the same kind of figure that he was in the Book of Job. None of these gospels actually uses the name 'Satan'. Both Matthew and Luke use the word devil, which in Greek is *diabolos*. For the Greeks, *diabolos* was not the same thing as a demon. The word *diabolos* means 'to slander, to attack, to throw, and to accuse', and current Word Study Greek to English translations of the New Testament verify that both Matthew and Luke use the term 'the slanderer'. Mark uses a Greek word that implies 'one who pressures and tests'. Basically any person in this day and age who stands and accuses another person falsely would be called a '*diabolos*' or a devil!

It should be pointed out that even though I am using this as an example to show the history of Satan, I cannot let this moment slip by to say that this narrative communicates more to me about Jesus than maybe any other moment in the New Testament. Faithful Christians see it as his moment of triumph over evil, but I see it as something which gives me such an appreciation of who the historical Jesus may have been.

If you are like myself and see Jesus as a man, the Temptation does not lose any of its power. Instead I see something so much deeper between the lines. To begin with, Jesus' experience in the wilderness is identical to journeys undertaken in many different cultures. The technique of isolating oneself and going out into a desert or place of solitude is well known throughout time as a way to shed the limitations of the physical body and gain the answer to a question. In Native American tradition, Jesus went on what they would call a 'vision quest'. Isolation and intense fasting for prolonged periods have been the method of holy men and women since before recorded history and there are countless documented accounts of the visions people have had. Some would refer to it as hallucinations brought on by hunger, isolation, and dehydration. Modern science has proven that lack of nourishment to the body can cause the brain to start hallucinating, creating intense visions and sometimes great moments of spiritual enlightenment.

I want to address those who would challenge me by saying that because Jesus was the Son of God he would not have suffered through any of this. He would not be hallucinating or having visions because he was a perfect, divine being. I challenge this belief by asking why he would have bothered to take forty days in the desert at all? If you insist on believing that this is God in human form, why would he ever put his physical body through the hell of the forty days of fasting in the wilderness in order to get in touch with God if he was already God or the Son of God? Why not spend a night in deep contemplation and get the same results? Or better yet, why would he do anything at all since he is already the God who knows all? If this is God in human form, then the challenge of a *satan* that He created makes no sense whatsoever. It only makes sense if he is a human man in a human body.

Jesus knew that by doing this he will push his physical form to the limits and achieve a result that had been mastered by numerous holy men and women before him. Often the very thing these people encounter is a battle with the modern psychological term for 'the *satan*': the Shadow. These visions are often terrifying, aggressive, and people report having to face their deepest doubts and fears. What comes after the great tribulation of these quests is a sense of rebirth and renewal. If the trials were met successfully, people have reported feeling a fearlessness about their chosen paths and futures.

I will always believe that Jesus was an educated man who was well aware that the mystics of his own faith and others went into the desert to seek the Truth. It is telling that both Mark, Matthew, and Luke state that it was the Spirit that drove him to the wilderness and that he knew he would face 'the devil'. Nowhere in the narrative does it say he actually sees the devil, but he speaks with him, as if the dialogue may be coming from within. Have we not all had moments when we find ourselves struggling and arguing with our own inner demons? We are so often unsure of which decision to make, of which path to take, of which choice is right. We talk to ourselves, arguing with ourselves in order to try to find the answer within ourselves.

Imagine what Jesus was struggling with.

Jesus had just been baptized by his cousin John, who was a powerful leader and prophet in his own right (enough so that he ended up imprisoned and executed). The baptism meant that the mission his cousin had begun was about to be passed on to Jesus. Jesus knew how controversial his message was. To spread it, he was going to have to risk everything and leave everything he had known behind him. If he pursued this path, he needed to know he was strong enough to face the public, the Jewish religious authorities, and ultimately Rome.

In reading these passages, sitting and contemplating, I imagined what it would have been like to have that weight on my shoulders. How would I have dealt with such responsibility? Would I be ready? Would I even want to attempt to spread these teachings that will bring such hardship and tribulation to myself, especially knowing that people will believe whatever they want to believe. How would I have felt, thinking about the religious authority of the day and not knowing if I could make any difference, how would I deal with the backlash of those in power? Even now as I write this, I am aware that a backlash may come from daring to write about all these things. If it comes, it will be from those who insist on blindly following religious authority. I know how hopeless I have sometimes felt, so to imagine Christ who had so much more at stake with the threat of imprisonment or execution hanging over his head made me weep for the man.

How would you feel if you were told that you had an ability and message that could help the world? How would you feel if you knew doing so would bring nothing but hardship to yourself... but if you let it all go and tried to live a peaceful life, could you ever rid yourself of the guilt that you did not do what your Soul had called you to do?
With the weight of these thoughts upon my heart, I read the Temptation of Christ with new eyes. In the three temptations, I saw a deeper allegory and inner struggle for Jesus than I had ever seen anyone interpret. What follows may be my own personal interpretation and opinion, but I invite the reader to consider it.

The first temptation of bread to feed his hunger symbolizes Jesus having to recognize that up until now he has had the security of his family. He has not gone hungry or faced poverty, but if he goes on this mission he will have to break all ties to his family. He will live from town to town with no guarantee of food, clothing, or shelter. If he is rejected by his own people because of his radical views, he will end up starving and homeless. The Accuser/Satan within himself is reminding him that he has the power to sustain himself if he really wants to. Jesus rejects this, insisting that he will be sustained by 'the word of God'. For Jesus, spreading his message is all that matters and he has just asserted that he believes it will sustain him somehow, someway.

The second temptation (I'll use Matthew's version since it's older) is when the Accuser/Satan makes Jesus suddenly feel as though he is transported to the top of the Jerusalem Temple. From above, Jesus would have seen the religious world he grew up in with its priests, rituals, multitude of animals in the hundreds being sacrificed upon the altars. The scent of their burned flesh rising up was part of the religious traditions upon which his entire religious world had been founded upon since Moses. 'Fall', the Accuser/Satan within him mocks, 'for does not God say that he will send his angels to you to rescue you?' The Accuser/Satan within him has changed tactics. Since Jesus insisted God would sustain him, Satan now uses the very words of God to tempt him. Satan is asking, 'If God will sustain you, won't God also protect you?'

Who does Jesus have most to fear?

The answer is the Jewish religious authority, which is torn between the Pharisees and Sadducees and has the ability to renounce him as a heretic and have him arrested. If he insists on carrying his message, he might as well pitch himself off of the Temple, for he is turning his back on the very foundations of current Jewish authority: the legal system. It gives order to Jewish life and keeps the religious authority in their seats of power. To undermine that is beyond dangerous. Jesus will not only gain their wrath, but he will lose their influential protection. Without them to intervene, or worse, with them as enemies, he will be open to the wrath of Rome.

Again my mind could not help but wander, thinking of how so little has changed in our modern world and how people who dare to oppose religious authority in certain nations also face the threat of torture and execution. In the West we have been so insulated by our freedoms and the separation of religion and politics compared to nations who still insist on having their religion and their government be one and the same. We have forgotten the truly terrifying task that men and women take on when they dare to fight against religious regimes who have the authority to kill or ostracize them. This is exactly what ends up happening to Jesus when he is put on trial before the Sanhedrin (the Jewish religious court) and handed over to the Roman authorities.

Jesus answers the Accuser/Satan by asserting that he will not test his God. At this moment I realized what Jesus was really saying (though I stress that I know that everything is up for interpretation and again state this is my educated, personal opinion). To my mind, Jesus has just affirmed that he believes he can walk that fine line with the Jewish authorities as long as he does not go out of his way to act foolish. This is why he recounts the verse that you cannot test God. God will indeed provide, but God does not favor those who act foolishly. Knowing this, I believe Jesus is saying that he believes he can spread his message for as long as possible before he has to challenge the Jewish authority outright. As I looked back over his entire story, I realized that Jesus did manage to frequently debate with the Pharisees and Sadducees, but they never outright attacked him. Jesus is an annoyance and unsettles them as he grows in popularity, but they have no cause to officially go after him until Jesus chooses his moment to stroll into the Temple and start overturning money tables, setting free sacrificial animals, and causing a massive scene. All these moments are timed by Jesus and happen according to his plan.

Lastly, the Accuser/Satan within gives Jesus a soaring vision of the kingdoms of the world. Matthew's retelling has the Accuser/Satan say that he can give the splendor and authority to Jesus if Jesus will only fall down in worship. What sense does this make to think the slanderer is referring to himself, since Judaism would have recognized from the start that the power over the world lay only with God? This is not how Jesus reacts. Jesus doesn't even respond to the promise of the kingdoms, instead telling the Accuser/Satan to 'get behind him'.
Jesus gives the final *coup de gras* by saying that worship and honor belong only to the Creator and Master of all.

At that time in history, all the 'kingdoms' that Jesus knew of belonged to the Roman Empire. If he is being tempted with its splendor and the promise of authority, it's because there's a chance Rome could give it to him. Without the protection of the Jewish authorities, there's no doubt Jesus will draw the attention of the Roman officials. I believe Jesus knew that there would come a time when he became enough of a threat that Roman officials might offer him a way out. They might promise wealth if he stops, or if they saw he had sway over the tempestuous Jewish people they may wish to employ him as a mouthpiece. When that time came, to deny Rome would be to court a painful death. His only choices would be to become a Roman informer and become even more ostracized by his people, or surrender himself to Rome's violent mercies. Jesus acknowledges that at this point his fate does not matter because it is in God's hands alone.

The visions worked. Jesus knew he was strong enough and ready to risk it all. When he insists that only God is Master and only God must be worshipped, he is asserting that he will never bow to Rome. His life is in God's hands come what may. Jesus will always put God first, no matter what temptation is set before him by Rome. The vision quest ends. Jesus has his answers and he knows that he has silenced the Accuser/Satan within himself. Whatever comes, he will not waiver and he will not go back. He is ready to spread the message and die for it if need be. More than illuminating Jesus' character, I see the true philosophical role of the Adversary that is within each of our psyches.

Everything that has dealt with this story ultimately made so much more sense to me after I had a foundation in the historical background of Jesus' time instead of just accepting whatever interpretation was given to me from a pulpit. Even the simple fact that Pontius Pilate did not want to be the one to sentence Christ shows that he knew and, I would dare to say, might even have grudgingly admired Jesus. Again, I understand more than ever what Jesus meant when he held a coin in his hand and taught his followers to *'give unto Caesar what is Caesar's, and unto God what is God's'* (a scene recounted in Matthew 22:21, Mark 12:17, Luke 20:25).

Jesus followed the political laws of his land, but he would not obey the religious laws, and therein lies his revolutionary teachings. Rome did not see Jesus as a threat until the Jewish religious authorities needed him dealt with and told Rome that Jesus was calling himself a 'king' (a title Jesus never claims). Roman Palestine of that era faced similar problems to what we see in a nation like Afghanistan today. A person from the Western world could go to Afghanistan and find himself welcomed by many Afghanis who, even though they are Muslim, are open minded and embrace their own beliefs but also the innovations of the West like clothing, music, education, and television. The same American would quickly find himself being threatened by the Taliban, a group which feels that all Western influences are evil and pose a threat to the way of life they feel their entire nation must follow: the strict religious laws of the Koran. It is this stricter minority that has managed to control the majority through violence and fear.

Roman Palestine contained many Jews who had found a balance between their Jewish beliefs and embracing Roman customs, learning, fashions, and ways of life. Many even became Hellenized, choosing to follow other religions of the empire like the Mysteries or Platonism while still holding to Jewish cultural customs. Much as you see many modern Jews who hold their rituals more out of ethnic respect than strict religious belief. This was seen as a massive threat by stricter and more fanatical Jews who saw everything Roman as being completely evil and in opposition to the laws of God. For any religious fanatic, there is no room for other beliefs and only their own faith deserves to exist. From the moment Rome took control of the region, there were those who wished to mount insurrections to overthrow Roman rule and bring Palestine back under the political control of the religious authorities. By the time of Jesus, Rome was aware they could have a full scale revolt on their hands at any time.

The Romans saw Jesus as a threat only when the Sanhedrin found him guilty of blasphemy and insisted he was calling himself the 'king of the Jews'. This charge would have made Rome take notice because it would have meant Jesus might be planning to lead a revolt, and if he had enough followers would have had the strength to do so. Pilate releasing Jesus back to Jewish authority shows that he did not believe this was Jesus' intent. Knowing the way in which most Romans regarded religious Jews as hypocrites and resented their insistence that Roman rule was evil, Pilate would have not cared for the Jewish religious authority in the least. Because religion and politics had to work hand in hand, he knew he had to appease the Jewish court by making the decision theirs. Not only are my thoughts on this pure conjecture, but the truth is that this entire story is conjecture! Romans kept meticulous records and yet there is no record whatsoever for the trial or death of Jesus. Had Jesus truly come to the kind of prominence that would have warranted hundreds of followers to attend his execution, surely the Romans would have happily recorded that they had dealt with such a threat.

Because the gospels indicate that it was the Jewish religious authority that handed Jesus over to be tortured and executed, many church fathers took the stance that the Jewish people had betrayed Jesus. They began to teach an anti-Semitic doctrine that insisted all Jews were allied with Satan and that the Jews and all their descendants were to blame for Christ's death. This ridiculous notion had more to do with the racism of the church leaders than anything else. Basically they blamed an entire people for the actions of a few who were in power. This is the same as blaming an entire state or country for the actions of one corrupt politician, or an entire religion for the violent views of one clergy member. There is no reason to ever blame Judaism or any Jews for the death of Christ! This attitude would be the same as a person feeling that because one Catholic Bishop sexually abused a child that every single Catholic for all eternity should be made to suffer!

Jesus never preached that the Roman government should be overthrown, but he did teach that a time of endings was coming and that people should prepare to live for the kingdom of God. This didn't mean heaven, but instead the apocalyptic belief that the world was going to soon end and people needed to return to spiritual truth and simplicity if they were going to see peace come to this earth. Doing so meant shedding restrictive religious laws that kept people separated: rich from poor, male from female, Jew from Gentile. But I will address more about this apocalyptic view at the end of this chapter. It's fitting that nowhere does Satan reveal its true identity more than with the history of Christianity. Knowing that *satan* was a Semitic word that would have been used frequently to describe the Romans gave me such a better understanding of how Satan evolved. In time, Satan became any human being, faith, or group that made itself an 'adversary' to traditional Jewish beliefs and eventually Christian beliefs.

Throughout the New Testament, anytime the word 'devil' is used, it is interchangeable with the word 'slanderer'. In the previous chapter on Mary Magdalene I was able to show that the Greek word for demon ('*daimon*') is not related to the concept of devils. In the New Testament many verses which make it sound as though the Devil is being discussed, may actually be using the word to refer to the many 'slanderers', 'testers', 'attackers', and 'adversaries' that early Christians faced prior to the legalization of their religion. Just as in the Old Testament, titles such as devil, satan, and adversary usually applied to flesh and blood people who were seen to be purposely persecuting or opposing Jews, and then (in the New Testament) the Christians.

As with Magdalene in the last chapter, it is time to ask just how Satan became the way we now know him. As Christians faced harsher persecutions, their ultimate 'adversary', 'slanderer', and 'tempter' became all things Roman. It was Roman authority that persecuted them, it was their Roman neighbors who 'slandered' them, and it was the decadence of Roman life with its glorying of violence, sex, and control that posed the greatest temptations to people trying to rid themselves of the vanities of the physical world. Often Gnostic writings affirm that the world around them seemed so wicked that there had to be a greater, unifying force behind the Roman machine, directing it in its wickedness and horrors. Eventually the terms of Devil and Satan evolved into its own mythology. Surely there was a greater Evil at work in Rome, pulling the strings behind the scenes. As believers came from all walks of life, elements of other beliefs came into Christianity, including the Zoroastrian concept of a literal evil deity who stood as God's opponent. Evil spirits and malefic beings abounded in Roman superstition, and theologians reasoned these evil entities must harken to their own master.

As the legend of a literal Satan took hold, his name began to be used with increasing frequency in relation to any religious group that the orthodox Church saw as being 'heretical'. Gnostics were portrayed to worship Satan (the adversary), for the orthodox refused to believe that anyone who did not heel to their views of God had to be in league with evil. Satan became a way to scare new converts out of their old 'pagan' ways. Even though the Church grew, many of its new believers refused to leave behind the spiritual beliefs and traditions they had always held and tried to worship as both pagan and Christian. Prior to the Church, Satan had never had a physical form, but soon Satan was being shown as a monster with horns and the lower body of a goat. Pagans both past and present would have realized that the Church had simply repurposed the image of the ancient god Pan.

The religion of Pan was a great rival for Christianity. While the early Church began to insist upon physical purity and control of sexuality and decadence, the worshippers of Pan insisted upon reveling in all earthly pleasures! Pan was a god who represented the wildness of nature and the unbridled passion of music. He was shown with horns and the lower body of a goat. The reason for this is that the goat was a symbol of male virility and power. While it's tempting to think Pan was nothing but the god of lust and good times, there was a deeper spirituality to this deity. Yes, Pan represented male sexuality, but he also represented the necessity of male fertility to the cycle of life. He was the god of the wild not because he was uncontrollable, but because he was part of the life force of the natural world along with the feminine. In his unbridled joy, he called those who celebrated him to take the time to see the beauty in the natural world and in their own bodies. Just as modern psychology has come to recognize that suppressing natural human emotions and drives leads to psychosis, Pan called his followers to let loose and get in touch with their most primal beings even if it was only for a night or a weekend. Little wonder that he was more popular than a religion that was becoming more and more frigid in its views on sex and the human body.

To combat this, the Church took an image they found the height of distaste and paired it with the concept of their ultimate Adversary. Satan even took on Pan's qualities. Before this, the *satan* was just an accuser and adversary, but after he takes on Pan's form Satan becomes a sort of *Lothario*, notorious for inciting lust in men and women and even enjoying sexual indulgence himself! Just as ancient men blamed Pan for their natural lusty ways, Satan became the ultimate excuse for men who refused to control their own sexual urges and either seduced or raped women. 'The Devil made me do it' became the ultimate excuse for any man who gave into his more violent and lascivious urges. As long as a man repented to the Church he could be pardoned with little more than a few prayers and some coins. Women who attempted the same excuse usually found themselves charged with witchcraft and tortured before being burnt or hanged. Not for the first time, Satan became man's best friend and woman's worst enemy.

More often than not the Church insisted that because women were the weaker sex, they were more prone to being used by Satan to tempt men and cause harm. The suppression and often violent abuse of women was seen as an effective method in fighting the 'Devil'.

Satan's backstory only kept getting more interesting the more I investigated it. Once Satan had all the lusty qualities of Pan, he was primed for taking on the burden of every sin the Church found unseemly. Suddenly they had a handy character on which to blame every ill of the world. Some converts began to ask why they should follow a God who allowed such horrible things to happen to people. In previous pagan beliefs, the deities were often a mix of good and bad, so people understood that life held a mix of positive and negative. Christianity was asking people to believe in a single God who was supposed to be the ultimate Good. But if God was good, then why were painful things happening in the world and especially to his own followers? Satan became the Church's handy answer for why evil still existed in the world. For Satan to take this role of the Evil One, he could not remain God's own henchman as he had been in the Book of Job. While reading through the Old Testament, church fathers took it upon themselves to see a corollary between separate stories.

The first was an obscure reference in Isaiah:

> "*How art thou fallen from heaven, O Lucifer, son of the morning! How art thou cut down to the ground, which didst weaken the nations! For thou hast said in thine heart, 'I will ascend into heaven, I will exact my throne above the stars of God: I will sit also upon the mount of the congregation, in the sides of the north. I will ascend above the heights of the clouds; I will be like the most High.' Yet thou shalt be brought down to hell, to the sides of the pit.*" Isaiah 14:13-15, KJV

In this narrative, church fathers felt that Lucifer must have been someone of great importance to God and this figure had dared to pride himself above God. Apparently they completely chose to ignore the fact that Jewish interpreters already knew who this text was talking about and it had nothing to do with the *satan*. If you read the very next verses (16-17), you'll discover that the text is talking about a human man:

> "*They that see thee shall narrowly look upon thee, and consider thee, saying: 'Is this the man that made the earth to tremble, that did shake kingdoms, that made the world as a wilderness, and destroyed the cities thereof; that opened not the house of his prisoners?*" Isaiah 14:16-17, KJV

Notice the wording: '*is this the man*'. There isn't a single reference to it describing a divine being, or a fallen angel, or any kind of entity. In the ancient world, the language of the heavens was well known to most peoples. The name 'Lucifer' means 'bearer of light' and the phrase 'son of the morning' referred to the Babylonian king who took the Jews into exile. The king saw himself as the ultimate bearer of light because he worshipped the 'morning star'.

In ancient times the 'morning star' was the planet Venus, and to the ancient Babylonians it represented their goddess Ishtar. To this day a look out at the sky in the twilight hours reveals the Morning (and Evening) star still shines bright in the heavens as the planet Venus. The entire verse is about the judgement Isaiah feels will come upon the mighty Babylonians for their slaughter and captivity of the Jewish people. Not a single thing to do with the *satan*. Yet Church doctrine insisted this 'Lucifer' must be the original name of Satan, and a detailed mythology began to build. Using no basis whatsoever in the very Bible they claimed to be the inerrant word of God, they invented their own belief that when God set out to create Adam that Lucifer had argued against the idea. He then outright rebelled against God when God commanded all the angels to bow down before Adam. When Lucifer refused, he was 'cast out' of heaven along with any angels who were loyal to him and this is the source of all demonic entities and the creation of Hell.

One would think that such an extremely crucial bit of information as this should be found right away in Genesis, the very book which is supposed to supply humanity with a recounting of their origins, but it is not. If the Jews were God's chosen people from the start, then why does this belief not exist in Judaism? The answer is that it never existed until the most rigid of church fathers like Justin Martyr, Tertullian, and Augustine needed it to exist. Satan became an easy response for answers they did not have.

Church fathers had another reason for linking the name 'Lucifer' with their doctrine of Satan. In Latin, the title 'Lucifer' means 'the light bearer'. The title of Light Bearer was a common one for any deity that was seen to give humanity

greater knowledge and wisdom. Deities like the Greek
Prometheus, Dionysus, the Persian Attis and Mithra, even the
Egyptian Horus (religions that all rivaled Christianity) were
called Light Bearers or *Lucifers*. Just as Pan became
incorporated into Satan, the identity of Lucifer was lumped
with him as well. Sadly, the principle of *lucifer* never had
anything to do with evil or harm. Technically, when Jesus says
in the Gospel of John that he is the way, the truth, and the
Light, he is calling himself a *lucifer*! Lucifer was always a title
meant to portray someone who was devoted to discovering
spiritual Light and then sharing it with the rest of humanity.
Once the Church declared that they were the only true source
of knowledge and salvation, all other sources were declared to
be Satanic. This is how Lucifer became synonymous with
Satan.

   With alarming frequency, any group that has sought the
Light of learning and knowledge outside of the Church has
been accused of the heresy of worshipping Lucifer. It is
dreadful to realize that this tactic is alive and well in our
modern day. I have heard fanatical Christians insist that the
Statue of Liberty that stands at the gates of New York City
should be melted down like so much trash because they feel
she represents a goddess, and because of the symbolism of her
crown and torch is that of a 'Lucifer'. This is technically true,
but only in that the Statue of Liberty does hold a torch of light
welcoming all those who seek refuge in the United States, not
because she somehow represents a devotion to Evil! Once
again, those who insist on believing something because of
blind religious faith instead of researching the history behind a
name will insist on a path of ignorant destruction.

   Organizations who have always sought the good of their
community and who include men of all faiths like the Masons
have been continuously accused of Satanism since the

inception of their brotherhoods back in the Middle Ages. The slander of this brotherhood of freethinkers has not stopped and only became worse in late 1800s when a notorious anti-Mason and anti-Catholic named Gabriel Jogand-Pages went under the name Leo Taxil and created a false document.

In this document, he wrote a forged account of Masonic leader Albert Pike supposedly teaching higher members that no one deserved greater honor than Lucifer and that the God of the Bible was a false god. Personally I find it amusing that there's a lot of truth in that statement, but ultimately it was never written by Pike. Taxil recanted the document and admitted he had made the whole thing up as a way to discredit Masons and embarrass the Catholic Church, but the damage was done. In an age where people's words were taken as gospel truth, Christians who already disliked the rituals and secrecy of Masonry grabbed on to any excuse they could to demonize the group and the lie persists to this day.

Lucifer was often used to accuse great scientists like Isaac Newton and Galileo of worshipping Satan so that the Church could find a reason to silence their discoveries. Over and over and over again Satan/Lucifer was used to bring charges against any man, woman, or organization the Church saw as threatening. Today we see modern 'mega-churches' bringing in massive sums of wealth from their parishioners, so imagine the kind of power the Church had back in a day where they held both religious and political power. For some time the wealthiest land owners in Europe were not kings, but the Church. Groups like the Masons had no choice but to meet in secret in order to avoid the persecuting eye of the Church. Masonic rituals are all allegories meant to bring the initiate to higher wisdom and truth, but ultimately the brotherhood provided safe places for any freethinker to present their thoughts, discoveries, or philosophies without fear.

Lucifer is a title which needs to be redeemed from the slander it has received from religion. In a way, anyone who pursues the Light of greater wisdom and seeks to share it with humanity is a Lucifer. Every medical doctor, scientist, philanthropist, humanitarian, and academic who has helped to make this world a better place would have been known as a *'lucifer'* in ancient times. Before the Church ruined the word it was always a title of honor. Every time I have witnessed someone imparting knowledge to someone else, I always harken back now to a word that should hold respect and wonder: Light Bearer (Lucifer). Technically, every woman named Lucy and man named Lucius share this same title of Lucifer. As I have tried so dearly to impart to the reader, knowing where our words originate is often the key to the Light (literally).

Perhaps the most ludicrous thing attributed to Satan is a doctrine that I still heard being preached during my time as a religious Christian, a belief called 'diabolical mimicry'. When I was a Christian, I didn't care about mythology. To me, mythology was nothing but the made-up stories of ignorant ancient people to explain their world. They were fiction, they were pointless, and they only served to show the darkness that ancient people were in who did not follow the Word of God as given to the Jews, or later rejected the Light of Christ after his death and resurrection. This is why it was a real surprise to me when my daughter suddenly took a passionate interest in mythology in her early teens.

I had witnessed many religious parents denying their children any access to information that wasn't Church approved, but I felt that my daughter deserved the freedom to explore and to learn about anything she wanted, so I never objected. I never expected that the subject of mythology would ignite a passion in her that would someday serve as a vital foundation for our work. I was never bothered by her interest because I had raised her to understand that myths were just stories, but the Word of God was Truth. I was never worried about her confusing the two because the Church already had an answer concerning why mythology even existed: Satan had invented it. This is the heart of the doctrine of 'diabolical mimicry'.

Looking back and realizing that I actually believed the doctrine of 'diabolical mimicry' makes me nauseous. Of all the more outlandish inventions of the early Church, this one defies all logic and relies on the total blindness of the faithful for acceptance. As the early Church was getting started, intelligent 'pagans' quickly noticed that Christians were embracing and spreading beliefs that many pagans already had. The story of a Son of God who was born of a virgin and a divine Father, who made wine from water, produced food from thin air, walked on water, and was sacrificed and rose from the dead after three days, was a story that was almost identical to that of far more ancient divine Sons like the Egyptian Horus, the Greek Dionysius, and the Persian Mithras.

Pagans did not care that Christians were spreading the message of what they saw as another incarnation of their beliefs. What they did care about was that Christians began to insist that **only** Jesus had ever done these things and that anyone who believed otherwise was the enemy.

A well known satirist and philosopher of the age named Celsus addressed this issue. Celsus' original works have been lost, but his arguments against Christianity were preserved by early church father Origen, who copied them so that he could debate against them in his own work titled *Against Celsus*:

*"Are those distinctive happenings unique to the Christians - and if so, how are they unique? Or are our beliefs to be accounted myths and theirs believed? What reasons do the Christians give for the distinctiveness of their beliefs? In truth **there is nothing at all unusual about what the Christians believe, except that they believe it to the exclusion of more comprehensive truths about God?**"* (emphasis added)

Christians could not give a solid answer for why pagans should believe that they carried the 'only truth', until early church fathers pegged the problem on Satan.
Justin Martyr, in his work *First Apology*, shot back an answer that pagans found ludicrous:

"Having heard it proclaimed through the prophets that the Christ was to come and that the ungodly among men were to be punished by fire, the wicked spirits put forward many to be called Sons of God, under the impression that they would be able to produce in men the idea that the things that were said with regard to Christ were merely marvelous tales, like the things that were said by the poets."

Basically orthodox Christian reasoning was this: Yes, there are many divine beings whose stories are almost identical to Christ, but only Christ's story is true. The rest of the stories are all lies that were spread by Satan and his demons in order to confuse the minds of humanity so that when the true story of Christ finally did happen, the pagans would not believe it.
Any time anyone dared to bring up the similarities between Christian teachings and the teachings of other faiths (such as Platonism, Mithraism, Zoroastrianism, or the Mystery Religions), Satan was always to blame for their very existence and this gave the Church a self-made reason for condemning

all other beliefs.

It is no coincidence that as the Roman Catholic Church's power grew, so did Satan's. As the Roman empire fell into discord and chaos, splitting between East and West, Satan seemed to lurk behind every corner. Satan was the source of the 'barbarians' who came from the north and pillaged Rome. Satan was behind every political coup and peasant revolt. Satan was the patron of anyone who dared to point out the pitfalls of Church doctrines. Any scientific discovery that challenged Church teaching was automatically the work of Satan. Women suffered more than anyone else under this constant terror and paranoia as the rhetoric of leaders like Tertullian and Augustine insisted that women and Satan had been in league with each other since Eve first disobeyed God. Satan became the source of all 'unnatural' urges, and while men continued to rape and created children out of wedlock with total immunity, women were reminded they had called the violence upon themselves by being the source through which Satan tempted virtuous men.

Satan is given his greatest power in the New Testament book of Revelation, and it is this particular book that brought together imagery of fallen angels. Once again we have a case of total misunderstandings and mistranslations. The most evangelical will insist that Revelation is a book about the future destiny of humanity, but people reading it at the height of persecution by the Roman Empire would have understood it differently. Our word 'revelation' comes from the Greek word *apocalypse*. *Apocalypse* in Greek simply means 'to be revealed' or 'to be unveiled'. The faithful have been told the book was written by the disciple of Jesus named John, but historians know this only means that *someone* named John is the credited author. John was as popular a name in the ancient world as it is in our modern time, so trying to pinpoint exactly who John was is next to impossible. Biblical scholars believe the book was written at least around AD 68 and the imagery it uses was common for a genre of literature of the day known as Apocalyptic writing.

Today Revelation is the only Apocalyptic literature that is well known, but in the days of the early Church there were numerous works such as the Apocalypse of Adam, the Apocalypse of Moses, and more. Apocalyptic writing all had one thing in common: they were written to console persecuted and exiled believers with the promise that all the wickedness in the world would be punished and God would bring a reign of everlasting peace.

Every generation since Revelation has insistently believed that it is living in the 'end times'. Every generation has predicted that the world would end in their time, and every generation has been **wrong** for over two thousand years. Biblical historians who know how to read Revelation are often left shaking their heads that anyone would still insist on believing that the book is relevant to modern situations.

Imagery such as a 'whore of Babylon' who sits on a dragon with seven heads was well known to early Christians as representing the cruelties of Rome. Rome was a city built on seven hills which Christians called the 'whore of Babylon' to compare it to the same way Babylon destroyed the Jewish Temple. The greatest evidence scholars have for this interpretation lies in a verse which Christian clergy have used for ages to identify Satan. Revelation 13 is a long description of a 'beast', but at the end it calls out to the reader to solve a riddle:

"Here is wisdom. Let him that hath understanding count the number of the beast: for it is the number of a man, and his number is six hundred threescore and six." Revelation 13:18, KJV

"This calls for wisdom. Let the person who has insight calculate the number of the beast, for it is the number of a man. That number is 666." Revelation 13:18, NIV

Ironically, while modern evangelicals identify this '666' with Satan and a figure they call the anti-Christ, for early Christians reading or hearing this message there was no mystery whatsoever concerning who this person was. The writer literally spells it out by saying: this is the number of a **man**. Today we have lost much of the ancient ways of divination and mysticism, but in the ancient world even of the Jews a practice existed called 'gematria'. Gematria is a form of numerology. In the Hebrew language, every letter represents not just a sound, but a number. Because of this, every Hebrew word and name carries a numerical value.

Scholars discovered that in the few ancient copies of Revelation that exist, there was a discrepancy in the number of the 'beast'. Some texts said the number was 666, some said the number was 616. When scholars began to play with certain names from the time period, they discovered that there were two correct ways to spell the name 'Cesar Nero' in Hebrew. Surely enough, one way amounted to the number 666, and the other amounted to 616. Both numbers were right, and both numbers confirmed the same historical man: the Roman Emperor Nero, who ruled between AD 54-68.

Truly Nero would have seemed like the great beast to early Christians, who found themselves violently persecuted under Nero's rule. Nero began his reign peacefully enough, but the man soon descended into decadence and madness, ignoring the problems of Rome as the city suffered earthquakes and a great fire. Instead of taking the reins of leadership, he began blaming minorities like the Christians. Even the assertion that the 'beast' suffered a mortal blow, yet managed to return to life mirrored a horrible rumor of the day that Nero would somehow return to life after having committed suicide in AD 68. This is akin to how many Iraqis refused to believe that Saddam Hussein and his wicked sons were truly dead even when Western media showed images of the executed Saddam. The fear Hussein had instilled in the Iraqis was so powerful that they could not believe he was truly dead and feared he might return to cause more terror. Nero's rule was a time of bloodshed, violence, disasters, and horror and truly early Christians would have believed it was all a sign of the 'end times' when God would finally purify the wicked world and avenge the righteous. They were wrong then, and any believer who insists in thinking Revelation foretells our modern future is wrong as well. Just as with so much of the rest of the Bible, people are seeing Satan where he simply does not exist.

Satan has been made to carry the weight of all evil in the world. It was easy for mankind to put this burden upon the figure, because doing so meant taking the burden off of themselves. Anytime a believer needed a reason to ostracize another human being, it became acceptable because the other person was in league with Satan. Anyone who disagreed with religious teachings had their arguments dismissed with the assertion that they were deceived by Satan. During the Inquisition tens of thousands of women and men were horrifically tortured, burned, hung, or drowned with the excuse that the Inquisitors were driving out Satan. Satan has always been the tool of the righteous to pardon their own wickedness against other human beings. Those who murder in the name of God never see themselves as being evil, instead they justify their own horrible cruelty by insisting that it is the other person who is Satanic.

In my own time, I still witnessed the pain of women who tried to expose men who had raped and attacked them, but always these men were forgiven by the congregation because they claimed 'Satan' had made them do it. Over and over and over again Satan bore the weight of the evil of human beings. Correction: Satan bore the weight of the evil of men, for all too often women were not afforded the luxury of blaming the devil. Instead women were seen to be in league with the Devil and suffered punishments that free men were pardoned from and clergy would never face. Satan has always miraculously shown up on the side of whatever group the religious authorities needed to do battle with. First it was the pagans of the early days, then Muslims of the Crusades, the scientists and freethinkers of the Enlightenment, and today evangelicals particularly place Satan on the side of Muslims, homosexuals, and atheists. Satan has become the excuse to dehumanize anyone who was different or wished to believe differently. When will it ever end?

I remember what Satan once meant to me. He was the greatest obstruction to God's will, and I was more than happy to see myself as a soldier in the fight for God. I was a crusader for Christ, a soldier of the Most High, a faithful warrior ready to do battle with all of Satan's forces of darkness. What I really was all along was a fool conscripted into a war that never existed. After coming to an understanding of the beliefs of the world, I have had to admit how ludicrously ignorant I was about my own beliefs. I realized that had anyone far more educated than I even tried to enlighten me about anything I would have met them with the unabashed knee-jerk reaction my religion had instilled in me: The world was wrong, it belonged to Satan who was the prince of lies, and only what was in the Bible held any Truth.

It didn't even matter if the other person had rock hard evidence; as completely stupid as it sounds, my ingrained response was always going to be the need to prove my loyalty to God by denying these people's 'lies' and 'deceptions'. I couldn't believe anyone who spoke against the Bible was telling the truth. In my eyes they were agents of the Devil trying to lead me down a path that would go straight to hell. Everything was a test. I never stopped to ask, why did my religion make Satan so powerful if God was in control of all things? I certainly never asked why my religion of Christianity, which came from Judaism, even believed in Satan when I found out that the Jews didn't. The Jews had their own answer for why there is evil in the world and it is plainly stated in Isaiah:

*"That they may know from the rising of the sun, and from the west, that there is none beside me. I am the Lord, and there is none else. I form the light, and create darkness. **I make peace and create evil. I the Lord do all these things**."* Isaiah 45:6-7, KJV (emphasis added).

In Judaism, God is responsible for all things, the good and the bad. Evil, for whatever reason, is under God's jurisdiction and no one else's, certainly not Satan. It is just another example of so, so many in which religious doctrine played 'pick and choose' with which Bible verses to apply and which to ignore, all the while indoctrinating believers to blindly follow every word out of Scripture (even when the average believer has no clue what all is actually written in the

Bible).

As I fought to come out of this mindset, I was constantly assaulted by my own mind. Was this all a test? Was God testing to see whether or not I would stay loyal to him and Jesus? Even to this day I can still feel my heart squeezing with the emotions that ran so deeply through my psyche. As if the pain I was putting myself through wasn't enough, I had to face the judgement of the people around me. I can honestly say that I have been on the giving end of believing other people were going to hell, and as I came out of my blindness I swiftly found myself on the receiving end of my former beliefs.

"You're going to hell. Do you even care that you're dragging your daughter with you?"

I remember my hand shaking as it held the telephone, my throat constricting, heart pounding as the words were delivered so flatly by a woman I had once called my good friend. She was a staunch Christian who prided herself on knowing the Bible inside and out and even had an interest in researching the Jewish roots of Christ. I had called her in the midst of my own crisis to share with her so many of the things I was learning about the Bible, especially how I could no longer believe that Christ had died for our sins when in that verse in John 4:22 he had said that the Jews already had salvation. I had made the mistake of confiding in her that I felt the Bible was full of manmade errors. Perhaps she mistook my silence for fear and believed she was getting through to me, because she added one last thing before hanging up the phone on me: "Whatever you do, don't tell anyone else this stuff. You know you're powerful and Satan will use you to bring a lot of people down if you let him. Just don't take anyone down with you."

As I hung up the phone, I wept bitterly. Not because I believed her or because her words had carried any ability to hurt me. In fact it was the opposite. I cried because I knew I had just been faced with what I had sounded like. I had just heard the same ugly ignorance with which I had lived my entire religious life for over fifty years. I felt an overwhelming sadness for her as I felt the bittersweet gratitude that by the grace of the Creator I had been delivered out of that mindset. I knew then what would await me as I kept going down this path. The same people who had once embraced me as being part of the 'body of Christ' would not thank me for showing the ignorance of Christianity. From here on out, I knew I would be labeled by their religious vernacular: sacrilegious, heretical, even Satanic. Others would see me the way I had once seen nonbelievers: deceived by Satan, a threat to be avoided and broken away from lest I lead them astray.

Late that night, more tears came. Tears of relief. In that moment I didn't care what opposition I might face. Only one word echoed in my mind and my heart: Free. I was truly free. I would never go back to what I used to be. Satan didn't have a hold of me because I finally knew who Satan was. The devil didn't have a hold on me because I knew who the devil was. No demons had a hold on me, because I knew who the demons were. I didn't find freedom because I lost my faith in God. I found freedom because I let go of my belief in Satan and all the manmade baggage that went with him.

What is the true identity of Satan? The more I learned, the more apparent it became that Satan evolved and grew with the religious need of humanity to deal with the constant upheavals and changes that came against Western religion. Satan grew right along with the Egos of the men who made the decision to become religious/political leaders and knew that Satan was a useful fear tactic to keep followers in line. It is no coincidence that the fear of Satan increased as the Church pushed the belief in hell, a concept that sprang right along with the habit of charging money for indulgences. These written documents guaranteed grieving families that their loved ones could be forgiven of their sins even after death because the church would intercede on their behalf. Fear is supposed to be an energy that can help humanity survive, but in the hands of dictators it became a more potent weapon than any other. It kept a clerical hierarchy in religious and economic power over an entire continent for nearly two thousand years, and it still brings masses of wealth and prestige to high ranking clergy who bend the ear of politicians, using their influence and clout to shape political policy in their favor (sneakily bypassing the mandates of separation of Church and State).

Ultimately, Satan represents the Ego of mankind. The Ego seeks fulfillment through acclaim, power, and the prestige of this world, just as Satan was created to lure humanity with promises of vanity, pleasure, wealth, and authority. This is where man himself has become the greatest obstacle and Adversary for humanity. It is said we are our own worst enemies, and this is the Satan within us. But this Satan which is our Ego is not our enemy. It was meant to be our teacher. We were meant to understand it, not banish it to the shadows. We were meant to be taught by it, not disgusted by it.

Evil in the world is only perpetuated when it is simply 'forgiven' instead of dealt with. Consider how the Ego becomes the 'adversary' when it goes into darkness. Thanks to religion the Ego has learned to get what it wants and blame it all on Satan. Whether it is rape, murder, pedophilia, sexual abuse, and violence, too often I saw men proclaim 'the Devil made me do it!' before repenting of their sins and 'miraculously' accepting Jesus Christ. The Church treated them as though they had a fresh slate, as if there were no more consequences to their actions. How much more powerful it would be if instead of miraculous forgiveness, we were taught to examine ourselves deeply, face the darkness of our own actions, and then reclaim our power by choosing to do everything in our power to make it right, to work to make ourselves better. When this mindset is taken, we are able to walk freely and come to the recognition of a power greater in this Universe than any religion holds or understands. It is a power filled with love, compassion, and understanding. This is the true purpose of the Light.

To prove my point, let me present a scenario which poses no difficulty at all to someone living in the compassionate reason of the Soul, but is a conundrum to the Ego of manmade religion. Anne Frank was a young teenager when she was taken from the attic in which she and her family hid for years from the Nazis. She ended her young life amidst the horrors of a concentration camp. She was Jewish, never accepting Christ into her life. She was also completely innocent, never having wronged anybody or committed any crimes against another living being. Adolph Hitler, the mastermind of the genocide of millions of people, was a confessed Christian. In the moments before his death, what if he thoroughly repented of his horrible crimes against humanity and sought God's forgiveness? By the doctrines of Christianity, Hitler is saved and may go to heaven, but Anne Frank was not and may end up in hell.

Any human being who has set aside the Ego of religion and hears the voice of their Soul knows that this idea is preposterous. It shouldn't matter how sincerely someone 'comes to God' if they have been one of the worst, most twisted individuals in the history of humanity. Even if there is such a thing as forgiveness, there must also be justice. There must be a balance.

We as human beings came into this world, our Soul accepted the human body and the Ego that came with it. With the Ego comes the Shadow or what religion deemed to call Satan. Until we learn how to balance the Ego, the Shadow, and the Light of our Soul, we will never find ourselves in peace and harmony with a Universe that has embraced us since the beginning of its own birth. When I let go of religion, I let go of Satan and a manmade 'God'.

I didn't lose my faith or my belief in the Creator.

I didn't lose my way.

I regained my Soul.

In regaining the Soul, I gained everything.

I had finally found my stolen Light.

22. Walking In the Light

There is no greater gift than to regain your Soul. There is no greater gift to the Soul than to give it back its Light. To know that the Ego has been joined with the Soul and its Light is what allows a human being to walk in harmony through this life. I will forever be grateful to have the knowledge that my Soul and my Ego have finally become one. I walk in the Light, I live in harmony with my life. I have been the recipient of this gift from the Universe because of releasing the tethers of manmade belief systems. Even if I tried to tell you how beautiful and wonderful life truly is with this Light, I would not be able to fully describe it to you. There is so much fear that without religion life will lose meaning and the world will tumble into chaos.

Really?

Religion has been established for thousands of years and it has not halted the spread of Evil. Hate, anger, rape, murder, abuse, and war are as prevalent now as they have always been. If religion truly worked, shouldn't we have seen some peace come to this world? Instead, religion has just become another way to divide human beings from each other.

I am here to say that it was only after I released my old beliefs that I found the true preciousness and wonder of this world and the next. I found reason and order within the chaos. I found purpose and answers that religion could not give me. Now when I hear the most horrific things happening in this world, I find comfort in my knowledge of why evil does exist. I no longer fear an imaginary Satan, and I refuse to fear the evil that is within human beings.

When I hear beautiful stories of humanity giving to one another, helping one another, even though they may have a language barrier, even in spite of being from different nations, beliefs, or races, my heart rejoices to know that the Soul is alive and well. Because of our technological advances, humanity can reach out to one another with compassion, love, and understanding more than ever before. This is not something that religion gave us. Our worldwide connections are the hard won efforts of the human mind inspired by the compassion of its heart and Soul. I know it is not my imagination to see that we are living in a world at a time when such great changes are coming in order to balance the feminine and the masculine. When I see men and women who are equally certain of their strength and their compassion, their intellect and their hearts, their need to lead and their need to nurture, I see the Soul coming into balance with the Light.

I am part of an older generation that still has a difficult time trying to understand our younger generations, but that is only due to the fact that these are individuals that refuse to enlighten themselves with the beauty of what has been given to us through the Light of our Soul. Too many of my generation still live in their Egos. They still hold on to their old ways and insist that their ways are better than the ways of the newer generations. In their judgement they feel certain that they are right. They pine for 'good old days' that, in truth, never really existed. All the evils of our time existed back in my day. Violence, murder, torture, rape, and abuse have happened in all generations, though perhaps my generation was just better at keeping it quiet. The 'don't ask, don't tell' mentality of the old days needs to end so that pain and suffering can be brought into the Light.
Without it, there is no healing for the Soul of women and men.

Too many walk with blinders and refuse to see the beauty that lies around them. Too many are bitter and some don't even want to be in this world anymore. I have heard this too many times from too many people, female and male alike. I wish that this was a mentality that had ended with my generation, but I see it perpetuated among the young and I weep. In forcing the younger generations to choose between blind faith and what their own reasoning tells them is true, our world has become more divided than ever and too many young Souls feel split, torn, and uncertain. They are adrift and have been fed the lie that the rejection of religion means the rejection of the Soul and its spirituality.

How desperately I want to impart to them that this is not true! Religion does not hold the reins of the Soul, and it is not the true source of the Light of spirituality. Our Egos will beckon for religion because it is manmade, but the Soul can only be quenched by what is unseen and felt. The true source of spirituality can only come from the realm of the unseen. We must come to remember what our most ancient ancestors knew long before the birth of the Bible or any other manmade text:

The Source lies within us, and in the wonders of the Universe all around us. The Light is readily available to those who dare to seek it. We can no longer be afraid to look outside of our own religious upbringings and embrace the incredible web of spirituality that exists in every corner of the world.

While so many people choose to stagnate and resent the changes that life brings, I have felt so blessed to be so accepting and open. Change is like the wind itself, at times gentle, at times with the forces of a tornado, yet I find myself always at the center of it all, experiencing the calmness simply because I let go.

It wasn't easy.

Not when you've been raised with such a mindset where everything around you comes from an unclean source, therefore you become part of that soiled mentality. In that mindset, no matter how good God is, you are always reminded that you are imperfect, sinful, and in need of salvation from something or someone other than yourself. Instead I now see the good and the bad. I cherish the lessons of both and use both to accept that I alone am responsible for who I choose to be in this world.

As the writing of this book comes to a close, an article was released in late 2014 by *USA Today* reporting that Pope Francis, legal and spiritual head of the Catholic Church, is 'agitating' conservative U.S. Catholics with his seeming liberalism. The Pope has begun a sort of revolution in the Catholic Church that is long overdue. On the issue of women in leadership he has shown a willing openness for discussion, when it comes to LGBT Catholics he has openly insisted that it is not his place to judge and he feels the churches must become welcoming to these brothers and sisters, and lastly on the issue of Satan he has dropped the old stance of seeing the world in moral black and white. For these 'drastic' changes, Archbishop Charles Chaput of Philadelphia has charged that the Pope is 'confusing' the faithful, adding snidely that 'confusion is of the devil'. Well, since the archbishop likely knows the truth that the devil is merely an 'adversary', I suppose Pope Francis is indeed an adversary to those who insist on keeping a status quo that has lined their pockets and kept their followers blind for over a thousand years. My heart truly goes out to this Pope simply because he is a man that has been put into a situation he never asked for. Pope Francis is trying to bring Light back to the Catholic Church, but he is surrounded by those who walk in their Ego and are filled with envy and fear. They know their livelihoods are at stake.

This is a man who has walked among the poor. He has seen the world as it truly is, how the majority of human beings are forced to live. Unlike so many of his fellow clergy, he has actually lived a life in imitation of Christ's teachings. I believe this Pope recognizes the injustices of the Church perhaps more than any other before him. He has access to religious writings and histories on an even greater scale than anything I have written here. He knows the truth. I believe he also believes in a Power that is greater than us all, but I sense he too has lost any faith in the god of man. Of course to ever say this would cause outright rebellion and charges of heresy. He is doing the best he can.

So many of the men he is surrounded by are filled with the image of god only according to how they insist in defining it. There is no room for justice or needed change when the majority in that ivory Vatican tower feel that their careers and sanctimonious Egos are at stake. It is fitting that even his own archbishops are grumbling that the workings of Satan are afoot, for the Catholic Church has not seen an adversary against its antiquated prejudice and ignorance like this Pope in far too long a time. Because they resist even the most commonsense change, it will be interesting to see if this 'divided house' will be able to keep standing, as Jesus warned.

There is a new beginning on the horizon, and it will bring forth an Enlightenment like has never been seen before. Perhaps that is because we have never had to so much to lose before. More and more human beings are seeing the hypocrisy in religious systems that are full of men and women back biting and plotting one over the other. I will say it a hundred times over that what has created this Universe has brought us into this world to be a true rainbow of diversity. We are meant to be a garden, full of beauty, color, shapes, sizes, and species, but as we become more connected it is as though the weeds become stronger, seeking to choke out the beauty of everyone else so they can hoard the powers and resources of this world for themselves.

Will there ever come a time when humanity will be able to stand together in harmony? A time where the color of the skin of a human being will only be looked upon as being a beautiful gift to that individual. Where the texture of the hair will only lend itself to wondrous beauty. Where personal beliefs are set aside for the greater good and a compassionate respect is the gift given by all to one another. I know that as the world grows smaller and humanity has the ability to travel around this world and become friends without borders that religious leaders and politicians will not be able to hold back the tides of time. They will not be able to restrain the awakening of all human Souls. For this reason, the violence may increase by religious fanatics, but they are ultimately fighting a losing battle.

I have always considered myself someone who is very grounded. But it wasn't until I decided to step out of my faith in my religious beliefs that I truly became aware of the world around me. Even as I write, I feel a sense of freedom; a sense of wonderment.

It's as if I am seeing the world for the first time.

I understand it.

I look forward to waking up every day of my life, stepping outside and looking at the true beauty of this planet we live on. I look upwards to the Universe at nighttime and see that beautiful moon and I understand what it meant to our most ancient ancestors. A chill will run up and down my spine, realizing that it's the very same moon that has been there for 4.527 billion years! It is the same moon that watched her sister Earth develop, the same moon that has controlled the tides since before there was life, the same moon that the dinosaurs slept under, the same moon that lit the night for the first human beings, and the same moon that has seen all of recorded history unfold.

I think this, and I become saddened to remember that at one time when I looked upon it I thought it was a paltry 6,000 years old. I took this as absolute truth from people who had no background whatsoever to even comprehend the true age or scientific wonder of the Moon. I accepted this because certain sects of a religion believed it was true only because the Bible said it was true and for no other evidence or proof beyond that. In a court of law that evidence would not only be thrown out, it would be laughed at! Yet I once believed this and it is painful to know that others still do too. More painful still to know that they will throw away the scientific work of hundreds of years just to smugly assert that Satan has fooled humanity. How much power can you honestly believe your God has when the answer to every little thing that contradicts your belief comes back to Satan?

Ignorance is not bliss, and it never will be. I have discovered that the truth will only be granted when you truly seek the answers to life for yourself. Every day as I come across other human beings for the first time, I greet them with a smile. Some will return that smile and others will turn their heads and ignore it. To me, all that matters is understanding that I made the first gesture. In doing so, I gave something at that very moment. I gave a sincere greeting from one human being to another. I acknowledged them in that moment for whoever they were, wherever they came from, whatever their own personal lives, because they are a member of the family of humanity. Without religion, humanity no longer has divisions in my eyes.

Make no mistake that religion is powerful. For all the harm its division has caused, there has been goodness too. I promised back in the first chapter of this book that I would address why some people who have near death experiences see Christ. For these people, they return to life with an even greater faith than ever before. At least this is how I used to see it. At the time of writing this work, there has been a slew of books and even movies based upon true stories about men, women, and even children, who experienced death and in their vision of the afterlife saw Christ and God. Back when I was a devout Christian there was no greater proof of my faith than stories like these.

When I experienced death, I saw none of this. In researching I found I was not the only one. So why do people's experiences differ? Despite the claims from some of these people that they were 'not religious', a quick look into their early lives reveals that all of these people grew up in Christian homes. They may not have been religious, but they were exposed to the teachings of the Church and Christianity early on. Knowing this, it shouldn't be a surprise that they experience a Christianized Other Side. Because they have not fully crossed over, I believe the mind still holds onto whatever preconceptions they held about the Other Side. Humanity since before the dawn of religion has acknowledged the existence of spiritual beings that care for us and guide us. In these instances, I believe the Other Side takes on whatever form is most suitable to help these people. The evidence for this is that we do not see people from other faiths having visions of 'Christ' when they die! Honestly, I would have been tempted to hang onto my faith if I had been able to find even one instance of a little Hindu child saying they had seen Jesus Christ in heaven when they died, but I didn't. There aren't any accounts of a Japanese person, born and raised in their own native Shinto-Buddhist faith, having a near death experience and seeing Christ. Even if a person insists they were previously an atheist, they still end up seeing something they perceive to be Christian because it is the culture they grew up with. It is as if that Other Side is so kind, that when we find ourselves in-between life and death, they will use whatever they must to bring us the peace and love we need in that moment.

So why didn't that happen for me? When I first went through my near death experience, I honestly didn't have words to even describe what had happened. Now, after many years of study of religion and metaphysics, I better understand what I witnessed. For me, there was no 'heaven', but there was the unlimited joy of the Universe itself. Sounds resonated, vibrating through my Soul with essences of pure love and joy. Colors that do not even exist for us with our human eyes swirled and collided in a dance of birth and rebirth. Filaments of energy wove through every living piece of creation, from the atoms to the galaxies, connecting us all to each other and to a vast Universe. In those moments, what I found was that our little concept of 'God' is far too small, and the mythological war god of the Bible Yahweh was too minuscule to even exist.

There is Something greater.

Its Power weaves through the Cosmos to unite us all in the balance of Masculine and Feminine energies. Our Souls are a divine energy given to us at the moment we are born and they tie us to the energy of the Universe even while we exist in these limited human bodies. When we limit our idea of the divine to the decaying pages of a manmade text, we have blinded ourselves to the Light that infuses the whole of the Universe. Religion had robbed me of the Light that was in my

Soul and only through this experience would I dare to break away to find it once more. I believe They allowed me to see this because They knew I was ready for the change. They knew I would spread the word. As They had said that night in the hospital, I would teach.

When the day is full of life and the sun is out, I enjoy watching the birds going about their business. The different colors of so many species captivates me. When I see a fox running across the field with her kits following, I am in awe at their skills of survival. I wonder to myself: How many of her young will grow to maturity? As I watch the people walking by with their dogs, so preoccupied while their dog busily sniffs the grass or a post, the male cocks his leg as if to say 'this is mine'. The dog does so because others had done the same before him. It brings home the reality that it isn't just humans who mark their territory and say: 'this belongs to me'. It is a consciousness that exists among all of us whether human or animal.

On that same day as the clouds move in, I watch some of the most incredible designs being painted by the formation of the atmosphere. I have witnessed the sun still partially out, even as the rain comes down on one side, yet never fully extending its watery reach all the way across the street. The rain drops sparkle as they hit the sunlight, the meeting of a storm and sunshine, and I stand there in awe.

Can there be any greater beauty than the freedom you feel when you are no longer threatened with an ideology that there is a god watching every move you make? You live your whole life sincerely believing that your thoughts need to be pure, that your actions need to be guarded, because you need to walk a straight and narrow path. That is not my life anymore. I accept my thoughts now, whether good or bad. I am free to think, to question, and to even feel anger towards the powers that for so long had been deemed righteous by the religious establishment. Freedom is a beautiful word, but it's an even more wondrous feeling.

Even though I am a person that has tried to live a life filled with fairness and understanding, I am only human. With being human comes a wealth of imperfections. These imperfections are not the result of being 'broken'. They do not need to be healed by a divine source. Instead they are realities that I respect, acknowledge, and honor by working to make myself a better human being in this world. I have found it interesting that I have learned to accept everyone just the way they are, but I have rarely been accepted just the way I am. The ones who have accepted me are few and far between. Mostly I have found judgement, and yet I have not judged them. This is not an easy path because I do understand where they come from. I understand why they think the way they do and why they feel the way they do. I have even found judgement in the world of the nonreligious because I insist on still teaching about the Soul and the reality of the spiritual forces for Light in our Universe. I have never professed to have all the answers, but I have willingly taught others the lessons I have learned from my own spiritual journey. Because of this, I have gained a kind of reputation among the many people I have encountered and spoken with. Some have told me they feel that I'm an 'empath' because I am able to show a complete understanding of the emotional traumas of everyone I have met. Some have said I have psychic abilities because even since before my near death experiences I often had verifiable experiences that could not be explained. Some wished to call me a healer, because so often they found solace and peace for the first time in their lives after hearing my teachings. Some told me that they felt I had a direct line to the Other Side and have called me a mystic. Truth be told, I take stock in none of these titles. The only title that matters to me is that I am a human being and I have a responsibility to this world to help in whatever way I can.

Every single day of my life I wake up and there isn't a time that I do not say 'thank you' to Them, that I do not take the time to praise Them, that I do not spend countless hours in meditation with Them. In my studies I found that a mystic is an ordinary human being who becomes so in touch with their Soul that they find it easy to connect with the spiritual realm. Some people call this realm the 'Other Side'. Because of this love for spirituality, the mystic has devoted much of their life to serious study and they understand the mysteries of both religion and spirituality in order to seek the Light. They are often judged, misunderstood, and rejected by their religious communities, yet find that what they have to teach is embraced by human beings eager to find their Light and restore their Souls. So if I must have any kind of title put upon me, this one at least makes sense. In truth, I will go to my grave insisting that the only title that I will ever want bestowed upon me is that I was a compassionate, loving Human Being.

I have had so many come to me through the years. They want to learn. They want to achieve what I have achieved. My dream is to someday see a school where anyone who wants to learn from the great body of knowledge that I have drawn from can come and do so freely. This time will come when it is right. I know I am here to teach, but I can only teach people who want to know. As many of you know, teachers are valued, but many are not respected. No matter what area of study they choose to teach, many are worn out and tired from the choice of the career that they have decided to make a living from. For me, I did not choose to teach, nor did I choose to want to go down this path. I was quite content (or at least I thought I was) keeping my blinders on, minding my own business, and only when someone needed to talk about Jesus was I ready to drop everything to speak about religion. My true desire was to travel throughout Europe. I became interested in artwork, painting and drawing, and that's what I thought I would do. I expected my daughter would eventually go off to a university of her choosing because the years I had homeschooled her had prepared her for the rigorous demands of academic life. Now that has all changed.

Fate intervened that day on the mountain when everything I had planned my life around changed. A severe head injury, learning to talk again, trying to regain my once photographic memory, allowing the brain to heal, and after all those struggles coming to the point of adrenal failure that nearly killed me had certainly never entered my plans. Fate decided otherwise, and because of it, my life has become something so much greater.

Years ago, I had the pleasure of speaking with a popular local rabbi; deeply immersed in the study of Kabbalah, he also considered himself a mystic. Hearing my story, he told me that the universe had knocked me onto the course I had always been born for. He said I would build a bridge for humanity, a bridge for others to walk upon and unite. As my spirituality grew and fate kept bringing people from all walks of life and beliefs onto my path, I had the deep honor of conversing with shamans (the holy men and women of Native American, as well as Tibetan, and Mongolian religious traditions). When they heard my story and of my death experience, they acknowledged that I had undergone the painful death and rebirth experience that marked one who is called out to speak on behalf of the spirits as well as humanity. They asked about my dreams.

I told them that once I let go of religion, I had dreamt one night that I was soaring high above the earth and I saw myself not just with the wings of a great eagle, but as a golden eagle. As I swooped down to earth, my form shifted, and I walked upon the sand with the power and form of a black jaguar. I was told that in their native villages I would have been known as Wise One, One Who Knows, Shaman, they told me I was a Walker Between Worlds. I had been gifted to see the Truth of this world represented by the eagle of the Sun, and I could see the Truth that lay beyond sight in the spirit world represented by the jaguar of the Moon.

I do not share these experiences to build myself up, or use them to insist that everything I write is any kind of ultimate truth. I am not a self-proclaimed anything. Those who know me know that in all my years, I have never sought wealth or acclaim from my experiences. I am just trying to share with you the doors that have opened, the visions that have been given to me, but most of all, the richness and beauty that is available to the Soul when we open ourselves to the whole diversity of belief that exists in this world. The love and acceptance that humanity craves can only come from all walks of life, from all nationalities, from all beliefs - never just one belief.

The time has come for humanity to walk hand in hand with each other, to say to all those that proclaim that their way is the only way that enough is enough. I am here to teach each individual to find their Light again so that their Soul can be released to teach the Ego how to live in a world that has become so black and white. It is about finding that rainbow that exists in all of us. When we are done shedding our tears of pain and sorrow, it is then that tears will come filled with joy. Through them we can see the rainbow of a promise of better things to come.

This is who I am, a visionary who believes without a shadow of a doubt that peace, love, and understanding can be possible. If a person wants to believe in their religion, they can do so, but it must be done with the understanding of how their religion came to be, why it became what it is, who were the people behind it, and what their motives were. As I discovered in Christianity, the motives were not always from a Creator that was filled with love for its own creation, but from a god that was created by man. Religion has been created by man and the god of religion will always resemble the divided nature of human men because it is an image they created, therefore in worshipping this god they are ultimately worshipping themselves and their own agendas. I refuse to ever accept the religion I grew up in, or the god of the Bible.

Yahweh is known to be the god of war. Historians have known this because he is among the many mythological gods that have been part of human religious belief for many thousands of years. This is no coincidence, it is simply the pattern that has existed since mankind chose to believe in something that only he could attain through his actions of war, hatred, and domination. Why do I always use 'he'? You might ask, haven't women chosen this just as much as men? The answer to that is a simple: No. A look at any of the monotheistic religions reveals that never have women been given a say in these beliefs. Every bit of ritual, dogma, and line of sacred text that was chosen, carried out, or written by men was done so with the total exclusion of female opinion or input. And yet we do not call religion a dictatorship even though an all-male clergy has chosen the course of religious history for thousands of years while denying any voice for the half of humanity that is female. Change must come.

In the first chapter of this book I told the reader about one of the first dreams that came to me after my near death experience. I remember so vividly even now how it felt to see myself with stacks of books on either side of me. One side were titles I recognized like the Bible, Tanakh, and Koran. The side of books I could not name were the religious texts of the East: the Hindu Vedas and Upanishads, the Buddhist Dhammapada, and even the writings of Chinese masters about the Tao. As I held the Bible and opened it, I panicked to see every line on every page blacked out. In the light of the last decade, I understand what the Other Side was telling me through this dream. It was showing the path I would walk, how it would begin with fear as I had to face the reality that the Bible would no longer be the source of my faith. But why did I see an old man who resembled the evangelist Billy Graham comfort me with the words: 'Don't worry, it's happened to me before'?

In doing a little research, I discovered that there was a time early in Rev. Graham's ministry where he taught that he believed people would be allowed to go to heaven even if they didn't accept Christ. As long as they were good people, he felt they were living lives 'like Christ' which would merit heaven in God's eyes. Like me, Reverend Graham had also puzzled on the question of how a loving God could condemn good people to hell just because they belonged to a different faith. I wish so deeply that Rev. Graham had held onto this instinct that came from the Light of his soul, but alas, he was quickly censured by other leaders in his denomination to the point that he recanted. From that point on, he towed his religious party's line on the inerrancy of the Bible and that only Christians could attain heaven. Imagine the kind of peace he could have brought to this world had he stuck with the message of his Soul and taught respect for other beliefs instead of the division of only one.

I believe that there is a greater Power than any of us will ever come to understand. Do I have faith in that? I do, but it will never again be blind faith. What faith I have is now informed hand in hand by the intuition of my Soul and the wondrous truths that continue to be discovered about our miraculous Universe. Some people might wonder why I didn't end up following another religion like Buddhism or Hinduism, since they favor enlightenment over judgement. While I deeply respect and have studied both of these religions, I have seen just as many pitfalls in their doctrines as any other. This is not to say that they do not hold wonderful advice and lessons for enlightenment, just as I still feel the teachings of Jesus do even though I am no longer a Christian.

Buddhism is a religion that is older than Christianity by at least 400 years, and so many of the Buddha's teachings are so similar to Christ's that many scholars think Jesus may have either heard them or been aware of them. As I have mentioned before, the Roman Empire was a big place and people from all religious backgrounds traveled back and forth. For the Buddhists, a core aspect of their belief is that the world is full of suffering and that the only way to find peace for yourself and the world is to overcome the illusion of physical reality. In Buddhist thought, the mind is the first source of separation and suffering. It teaches that the mind has to be mastered, emotions brought to balance, and there must come a spiritual detachment in order to become one with the universe.

Ultimately it is our Egos that create the painful, imperfect world around us. The soul in Buddhism is often seen not as any kind of personal guide, but as the spark of life that is eternal and when we die simply goes on to spark a new life. Personally, I do not agree with this view, but that does not mean that I cannot learn from it and accept it. The greatest beauty of Buddhism is that is seeks to end suffering and teach people how to find peace for themselves and the world. But just as so many religious paths begin with the highest of ideals, a look at the history of Asia shows that Buddhist ideals have not stopped their believers from partaking in the atrocities of war and religiously fueled battles. Here is a religion of peace, yet the nations it became so deeply ingrained in have not found peace and are as divided and torn as any other. Perhaps it is because believing the world around us is an illusion can cause as much harm as good, for if suffering is an illusion, then it gives far too many people the impression that we should not care to change the situation for anyone but ourselves. This is not what the Buddha taught, but it has certainly been the actions of far too many in nations who claim to follow his teachings. Like Christianity, Buddhism has gone through its divisions and has multiple different sects, but ultimately I respect Buddhists as people who choose to try to live a life of peace and enlightenment.

Perhaps nowhere did knowledge open a greater door for understanding other faiths than when I explored Hinduism. Not only is Hinduism the oldest organized religion, it is the only one that does not give glory to a single founder the way that Judaism does with Abraham, Christianity does with Jesus, Islam with Mohammed, or Buddhism with the Buddha. Though it may confuse the other religions, Hinduism does worship hundreds of different gods and goddesses, but at its core Hindus recognize that all deities are simply masks worn by the One, the Ultimate Truth and Reality called Brahma. Hinduism is a single word for what is really hundreds, if not thousands, of different religious sects all over the Indian subcontinent and trying to pin down one aspect of their faith is like trying to grab a single water droplet from the ocean. To its greatest credit, Hinduism is a religion that embraces all paths and honors all beliefs, insisting that every religious path a person takes is an equal truth. Every path to god and enlightenment is seen as valid.

Only one thing has always stunned and disappointed me about Hinduism. For all the goddesses that Hinduism honors, India has become a nation where human women are subjected to violence, abuse, rape, and inequality. Also, it has been unable to evolve past a caste system that allows those in authority to remain so because the lower castes are convinced they have been born into a situation that they cannot rise out of. Still, with the exception of defending itself against Muslim invaders, Hinduism has managed to exist peacefully in the world for thousands of years.

The three monotheistic religions have been constantly at war or causing war since their inception. In my mind this makes sense because they all share a belief in the same God and a house divided cannot stand. One interesting question I was once asked was, if the god of the Bible is a god of war, and Jesus was supposed to be his son, then why was Jesus a teacher of peace? I answer that because the god that is worshipped by these three faiths is a mythological god like any other, the stories of Christ's birth are also mythological and they bear resemblance to many, many ancient stories. Does this mean I feel Jesus' story is irrelevant? No. I do believe that there was a human man who inspired a spiritual awakening, but the details of his life and mission became sewn together with spiritual truths and myths from other traditions. It kept evolving into the religion we know today. Perhaps the most poignant reason that both Judaism and Christianity took hold is because they did elevate the sanctity of life. As Christianity entered 'pagan' lands, it did away with both the ritual sacrifice of animals and humans. I believe that the reason Jesus' story remains so impactful today is simple: whether real or imaginary, the story of a man who was so willing to die for what he believed will always speak to us.

Jesus saw that there was no longer a need for the senseless mass slaughter of so many living creatures at the Temple with the excuse of 'pleasing God' when really it only fed the bellies of priests and kept up a thriving priestly economy. He saw the writing on the wall for his own people and knew that they needed to find a path back to God that was filled with spiritual simplicity instead of needless ritual. By dying for his message, Jesus did sacrifice himself for the sake of others. There is something so incredible in the reality of one human who is willing to lay down their life for another, to sacrifice everything not for the riches of the world, but for what is beyond this world.

I still love the story of Jesus, not because he sacrificed himself and died on the cross in order to 'free' us from our 'sins'. Instead I see in his story a parallel between him and any person who has shown the dedication and courage to fight for what they believe is right even if it means death. What that story tells me is that every woman and man in this world who has willing gone off to war so that others have the freedom to believe whatever they want in life are the true heroes and 'Christ' figures. At the expense of their own life, these male and female soldiers sacrifice themselves to keep others safe. They leave their blood on foreign soil selflessly and they are greater representations of the daughters and sons of the

Creator than any myth. To those still walking with blinders this may seem like a mockery, but for those that understand the true heart of Jesus' words, they understand that no greater gift can any man give than to give of his life for another. This is the ultimate sacrifice and it is what our men and women have done through generations, not just in this country but all countries. Wherever there has been war, men and women of all faiths have given of themselves and sacrificed for the good of others.

Jesus' story is not one of divine intervention, not of glorifying himself, but of the lesson that we must all learn if we wish to walk in the Light and bring that Light to others. Whether Jesus was a real man or simply a mythological figure, by the decisions he made he represents what is good in all of us when we seek to live not for ourselves but for a higher purpose. He represents the Light that is in all of us. He represents the Way of that we must walk in order to find a path that will lead us to the acceptance of the freedom that was given to each and every one of us. He represents the Truth we will find when we release our old preconceptions.

Understanding that there is a greater Power in this Universe, we must all come to an agreement that whatever that power is, we will respect it. We do that by respecting this planet that gives so freely so that we may live and thrive. We respect it by being good stewards to it. We respect it by respecting one another, for we all must live together.

Do I believe in heaven?

Not the way it is taught by the Church.

Do I believe in hell?

No.

What I do believe is that the soul is indeed immortal and that when we die we embark on a greater Journey than anyone can imagine. I also believe that our loved ones are never far from us, and that the barrier that religion has created by making people think their loved ones are separated in some faraway afterlife is not true.

I want to teach humanity not to be afraid.

I want to show them what I have seen and what I have learned.

What I have shared in this book was simply a beginning to the things that I discovered about my Soul and the spiritual world around us. I can at least say that energies that belong in different worlds do stay in touch with us. Whether a person wants to call these energies angels, spirits, guides, or totems makes no difference. To many this may even sound like I'm talking about aliens from other planets, and I will admit that I do agree to a certain point that there has to be life in other worlds beyond our own. Life is not just ours, it is not some special privilege given to this world alone.

The whole Universe has a life of its own.

We are part of the 'DNA' of this whole wondrous Universe because every bit of us, down to the tiniest atom was born from the cosmic energies that made everything else from stars to galaxies to interstellar wonders!

I have seen some of the more religious try to portray scientists as people who are trying to prove that there is no God. Overwhelmingly scientists are just human beings pursuing the mysteries of this world out of curiosity with no religious agenda whatsoever. Through their hard work and research, they are trying to understand the Source behind everything that functions around us. I admit that even at my most religious, I recognized the hypocrisy of people who criticized science yet had no issue with going to a hospital the moment anything went wrong medically. Truly science and medicine are one. Because of science, those who study to become surgeons, doctors, and nurses grow in their understanding of the workings and repair of the human body with every year that passes.

The legacy of their work extends far back into the ancient past long before religion to the shamans of the world. The only difference is that the shaman sought to heal both the body and the Soul. As science found itself completely alienated by religion, it came to focus solely on the mechanics of the body. Only recently are medicine and the holistic approaches of 'natural healing' (shamanism) finally coming together, but for so many it is too late. Healing is more than just being stitched up and reset, it is incorporating our Souls so that we may feel whole.

Those who have shown the wisdom of seeking out both the benefits of modern medicine and the healing holism of the ancient ways have learned to use what the Universe freely gives to all who seek. Sometimes healing is not enough, and in these times those who have come to understand their Souls have left this world at peace with the knowledge it was their time to go. Instead of fear, they accept their journey without procrastinating by using the drugs of man to prolong a time of suffering. There is something so beautiful about finally accepting the peace that comes with the Journey. I know those who must say their goodbyes to their loved ones feel left behind and they will find this hard to understand. It is said that grief is the price of love and no one can understand it until they have gone through it, but I wish humanity could understand that our loved ones are never gone. Because of my own personal experiences, I have told many that I look forward to my Journey back home someday.

I say this with all the love I can send to you, the reader. This world is beautiful when it is filled with life, love, and joy, but the place that we Journey to is even greater. It is far beyond anything the Ego can ever comprehend. I have witnessed many of those that have said goodbye to their loved ones before their Journey. When I have looked into their eyes I have seen the Soul depart and what was left behind was the consent of the Ego thanking me for being there. Afterwards there has been such a change in the room, and through the tears and the sobbing I have seen an incredible radiant light. As the Ego in the form of the human body lays there motionless, the true essence of life, the Soul has departed in peace and beauty on the Journey it was always meant to take. I am only sorry that their loved ones have not been taught how to see through the mirrors of the Soul that is part of their Light.

I have learned and opened myself to an awful lot over my many years. I can honestly say that I have lived a very full life. I have witnessed miracles and I have been blessed to hold the hands of those that go on their Journey, only wishing that I could go with them. But it's not been my time. As my friends like to tell me: "Heaven doesn't want you yet, and Hell's afraid you'd take over!"

To which another wise lady responded, "Yeah, we can just see you going right up to Satan himself, giving him a big hug and telling him: 'There, there, you're not really evil, you've just been doing humanity a service by weeding out all the rotten people, so don't be so hard on yourself!'"

That has certainly been one of the funniest and truest things anyone has ever said about me!

Life has been tumultuous, but I believe that this is part of the human experience. We all must go through our own initiation that we have to try to decipher. Some are not strong enough to do so, and others, well, they are blessed to just be able to survive. What makes this world livable is that there are people who care enough to help. There are people in this world who have come to positions of great wealth and influence and use this blessing to impact our world in major ways. It is the Oprah Winfreys, Angelina Jolies, Ellen Degeneres, and Bill and Melinda Gates of the world who in spite of their wealth fight to bring attention to the plight of humanity. Why I single out these individuals is that they are examples of human beings who help because it is the right thing to do and they do it with no religious agenda whatsoever!

These are the souls that have come into this world to show what is possible when you become a human being who cares about progress and humanity. They have put a face and an image to the genders that they represent, but in reality it is their Souls that has made them put their heart into their wealth.

Oprah Winfrey has shown that she is a mother to the world. So many have called upon her and she has responded as a mother caring for her children. She has brought great change and Light into the lives of many for generations to come. This is why she was put on this earth, to Light the path for so many others that would need her and to do so without any pretense of religion. The Other Side knew that this Soul would do it with all the love that exists within her human body.

Angelina Jolie has adopted the children of the world and brought together her own rainbow of peace. She became the true representation of a mother to the world long before she had her own biologically. She has shown that this was possible while still being true to her own independent spirit. In living this truth she found another Soul with whom to fulfill this mission. Through her life and actions, she has tried to teach the balance of acceptance. She and her husband made a commitment to this world that has been furthered by their incredible love for each other. I know in my heart that they are an example of a promise made between two Souls that was kept beyond the veil of this world. They made a very public commitment not to marry until they saw equality being shown to the gay community and in doing so elevated the plight of marriage equality. They took a stand and showed the world that as a young couple they possessed the ability to teach with dignity and honor. They showed that a family is what you make, not what is given to you.

Ellen Degeneres is an incredible human being that I count among this short list of examples because she was born into this world with the form of a female and its feminine aspect, but through it all she has taught the world the beauty of the masculine that also exists within all of us. She has withstood the pain and rejection that has come with her existence in this world. Yet she never gave up, she never gave in, she kept fighting to be able to voice her mind and heart, and she battled for the right to show the world that love is genderless and unbiased. Again, here is a Soul that was willing to come into this world to help enlighten and show us the beauty that lies beyond the sight of man. What you see is not what is there. She is a beacon of Light, much more beautiful than the eyes can see. She gives of herself tirelessly and lives her life by the phrase she uses: 'Be Kind to one another." I could not agree with her more.

Bill Gates is a man that has matured and grown in leaps and bounds in his later years and has shown the world that in spite of his wealth he is a beacon of Light and hope filled with a desire to make a difference in this world. He has been blessed and he has been giving that blessing back to the world tenfold. He knows that the vessel that he is part of can only hold so much and it is only right that he takes much of that energy to leave this world better than when he came into it. He and his wife Melinda have given tirelessly to humanity and they have committed their resources to continuing to do so long after they have shed their human bodies.

Then there are the millions who never make headlines. Individuals that give and are constantly doing whatever they can to make things right for others that have had the misfortune of being born with so little. These are all individuals who have one thing in common: they have done good in the world with no religious agenda. They work for the Light not because of an agenda of faith or belief, but because they are human beings who have come into this world with a Light for humanity. I feel that these are people who have been chosen to give us all hope. When everything is finally uncovered, and everything that man has created is destroyed, there is only one thing that is left and that is the energy that helps us all to become compassionate to one another, to understand one another, and to live with one another. That energy is an essence that comes from the Feminine and the Masculine aspects that have been part of this Universe and is known to all of us as Love

My daughter has always said to me: "Mom, you wear your heart on your sleeve. People have already hurt you, why do you keep on letting them? Don't put your heart in the open, Mom, don't let them know how you feel."
I will share with all of you what I told my daughter. I have worn my heart on my sleeve because it is too painful to carry it inside my chest. When I carry it on my sleeve, it has the freedom to exist, to beat with the rhythm of the Universe. I

feel like I'm more alive and yes, there are those who out of curiosity will say or do things that can cause its delicate existence to feel pain and sorrow. I would rather deal with that, than to put it back in its little cage where it knows nothing else but the rhythm of my body and my Ego. My heart was never meant to be part of my Ego. My heart was meant to experience the Soul.

I now walk in the Light that has been shared by others throughout time. The women of history, like Hypatia, and the women of our own time have opened doors and were willing to sacrifice it all. Their names were often cast into the wind, but now because of them, I make a promise that woman's name will no longer be forgotten to time. Women should never have to hide their achievements under the mysterious title of 'anonymous' ever again. No man should ever feel ashamed that he has the strength to embrace the Feminine, and no woman should ever be made to feel less for acknowledging that the Light of life was a gift placed within her hands.

I am walking in the Light that has given me peace, understanding, and love.

No one can hurt me anymore, at least not without my permission.

I am free. Free in thought, in mind, in body, and in Soul. I wish the same for all.

May the Light that delivered your Soul into the care of the human Ego be able to walk in this world with harmony. I see a bridge being built by humanity that will lead the generations into a world filled with Love, Peace, and Light. I believe it will happen.

That world already exists on the Other Side, and I know it is possible here on earth if we follow the Light of our own Souls.

Afterword: Living Spiritually Without Religion

(Celebrating the True Holidays)

I said at the beginning of this book that this was a book about faith. If after all you have read you have been able to walk away with elements of your religious belief intact, I respect that. At least with this information at your side, you can now acknowledge that no religion or faith has the right or ability to claim a path of 'absolute Truth', let alone a monopoly on salvation. If anyone still believes that after all they have read in this book, I can only say that they are in total denial and nothing will ever be able to persuade them otherwise. Some will say that I have no faith in God, but to that I say that my faith is very much intact when it comes to a Creator of this Universe. What I have lost faith in is in the God of man. With every ounce of conviction I can now say that the god portrayed in the Bible is not my God. That god is simply too small.

My great hope was never that this book would abolish a person's faith, only that it would enlighten every individual to understand how their beliefs have been used and corrupted by the politics and agendas of very fallible human beings. For myself, the quest for truth was so absolute that I made the choice to release all of my long held religious beliefs. I do not see myself as belonging to any religious persuasion. I am not a Christian, nor a Jew, Muslim, Buddhist, Hindu, Pagan, or any other label humanity has come up with to try and stuff spirituality into a neatly identifiable box.

I am a human being.

I am a very spiritual human being.

I promised in the beginning of this book that losing religion does not mean having to lose faith and spirituality. To be honest, my faith and spirituality only grew when my Soul found its Light.

It was a journey of many, many years.

So where does my spirituality now lie? How do I celebrate and mark life without the trappings of religious celebrations? What literal and physical things have I found to feed and encourage my Soul?

Religion is intimately tied with community, and leaving its boundaries can result in excommunication from friends and family. Ironic that one of religion's greatest strengths is ultimately one of its greatest weapons. I have seen too many families broken apart and too many people ostracized. There is no 'love of God' in a community which shuns those who dare to question, or commits emotional blackmail by withholding love from an individual until they come back into the fold. Too many people hide behind defending 'God's will' when really they are simply controlling that individual. A religion or belief that cannot withstand its own members questioning and refuses to evolve with the needs of humanity will never survive without resorting to mental control, constant conditioning, and emotional blackmail to keep its members in line, but I digress…

When you have been used to the structure of religion, it's hard to imagine life without it. Personally, I loved holidays. Christmas meant the world to me and without a belief in Christ I wondered how I could possibly celebrate the birth of someone I still admired but no longer saw as my religious 'savior'. On top of that, where could I now go to find a sense of community and celebration? In the early time of my journey, I could not imagine that I would find a deeper sense of spiritual connection and celebration than I had ever known before. But now I can honestly say that I no longer feel at a loss when it comes to the holidays.

There is a spiritual connection we as humans have that transcends all other beliefs and bonds. No matter what your background, race, ethnicity, age, or gender, every single person on this planet depends upon the living earth around them. Our planet existed long before human beings became who they are and it will likely survive long past us. Scientific research is just now proving what ancient cultures knew for hundreds of thousands of years: our planet is alive. Every living being on this planet owes its life and existence to the Earth. The more science explores how every part of the planet is interconnected, the more it has begun to acknowledge that the Earth is its own life form. No matter how much manmade religions have tried to cut ties with nature, ultimately 'Mother Nature' continues to outlive them all.

The fact that even people who are not spiritual or religious still refer to our world as 'Mother Earth' and 'Mother Nature' shows that deep down we all recognize that without a healthy, nurturing Earth, we would have nothing. For aeons many ancient cultures insisted that the Earth has her own consciousness (her own Soul), and some biologists and scientists are starting to agree. Long before the rise of Western religion, humanity celebrated the Earth. They took painstaking calculations of the stars and connected it to the seasons of their Mother Earth. They built magnificent 'calendars' on the land to mark the seasons. For them, time was not some straight line from a moment of creation to an ultimate apocalyptic end. Instead, time was made by the Earth itself, and the earth's time is cyclical. Things grow in the Spring. They mature through the Summer. The fruit of all the work done in spring and summer are harvested in Autumn. Ultimately, everything comes to a place of peace and rest in the Winter. Then the cycle begins again. It was a sacred cycle and the ancients recognized it applied to all life. Perhaps for this reason more than any other so many ancient societies believed in reincarnation. They saw life always repeating the cycle of birth, growth, death, only to be reborn again, so they likely believed that their souls did the same... but that is a subject for another book.

Far too many 'modern' people look back to ancient times and assume their ancestors were just 'dumb cavemen'. In reality ancient people going back even into the Ice Age were brave explorers and survivors who quickly learned to map the stars. Great stone structures all throughout the world attest that ancient women and men understood astronomy, time, and mathematics long before the written word. One of the things they established was that the Earth had its own 'markers', fixed moments on the calendar that symbolically represented where Mother Nature was in her cycles. Today we know these times as the equinoxes and solstices. These vital dates were times of great celebration for ancient human beings and for cultures that still hold a reverence for the earth they remain guiding times of celebration and thanksgiving. They are times to be shared by human beings regardless of their differences. They are also dates still celebrated by most everyone in the West without even knowing it!

I will begin with my favorite holiday: Christmas. A careful reading of the New Testament shows that no date is ever given for Christ's birth. Scholarly examination has led Biblical researchers to believe that since the text references shepherds in the fields, that Jesus would have been born in the spring. So why do we have Christmas on December 25? Because the entire ancient world was already celebrating the 'Birth of the Light' on that day as the Winter Solstice! The winter solstice is a pivotal moment in the earth's cycle. It is the moment when daylight is shortest and the hours of darkness are at their longest. The winter solstice is the turning point where the Light begins to return bit by bit until eventually the hours of daylight lengthen. Cultures from the Native Americans to the Celts, the Romans to the Persians, all acknowledged and celebrated this day. They knew and understood that when the Winter Solstice arrived that it was connecting them to the end of their hard labor, whether it was farming, construction, or hunting. They knew that their part of the world was ready to rest and they themselves needed to rest. But along with that, they also understood that it was more important than ever to come together and fill their homes with light because darkness came too early.

For them, they came up with mythic stories to explain this momentous symbolism, and often those stories took the form of the birth of a 'divine child' that represented the Sun (the Light). So beloved and important was this celebration that the early Church simply could not get rid of it and winter solstice celebrations were absorbed into Christianity. Jesus Christ became the new model for all the mythic stories that had come before. All of our beloved Christmas traditions such as gift giving, lights, and decorated evergreen trees all existed for ages before the birth of Jesus. Even that most beloved figure of Santa Claus has his origins in wise, compassionate mythic figures from long ago. How I reveled in Christmas as I never had before when I learned all these things! I can't begin to describe how amused I become when I see these religious campaigns every holiday season saying things like 'Remember the reason for the season' or 'Put the 'Christ' back in Christmas!'. The truth is there is a 'christ' in Christmas, but only because the Greek word '*christos*' means the 'Light'. It never had anything to do with the Bible, but it does have everything to do with acknowledging our gratitude as human beings that we live on an earth where we are promised that no matter how dark it gets, the Light will always return.

As time progresses, winter is a time of rest and quiet as the earth replenishes. Just as modern human beings start to get antsy for the winter to end, the Light keeps growing and we are promised Renewal just as the ancients were. On the Western calendar, we look to Easter. Christianity claims this time as being the moment they celebrate Jesus' death and resurrection, but again we are dealing with the absorption of much, much more ancient celebrations. Just as the day has lengthened, there comes a time in the earth's cycle that inevitably marks the return of life. Days lengthen, things warm, and the plants begin to show budding life. Even animals sense this change in the air and begin to come together to ensure the conception of new life. It is the Spring Equinox. The equinoxes mark the moments in time when the hours of daylight and sunlight are equal, while the solstices mark the greatest changes in sunlight. For ancient cultures and those which are still earth based spiritually, the spring equinox is the culmination of life. Light won against darkness during the winter solstice, but now it is back in full with great promise and the reassurance that life will not just survive, but thrive.

I always cringe when I hear people criticize the holidays, especially Easter. I hear things like how the Easter bunny and those little chicks and eggs are just inventions of the candy and greeting card companies and I am left saddened at their ignorance. Granted, perhaps the ancients did not have access the myriad of chocolates, toys, and sweets that we now do, but the spring equinox was indeed a time filled with the symbols of bunnies, eggs, and babies! In Europe, rabbits were a symbol of fertility (for obvious reasons) as were eggs. The painting of eggs goes back far into antiquity and was done to celebrate a goddess of the earth known as Eostara. Yes, we get the holiday name of Easter from a goddess, not from anywhere in the Bible. All the symbols of this beautiful time are meant to celebrate the resurrection of all life: trees, flowers, animals, livestock, and even human beings. To be honest, I had always been lukewarm about celebrating Easter, but once I knew the true spiritual significance, I have painted eggs, bunnies, and flowers galore in my home! Nothing is more beautiful to me than celebrating the promised rebirth of the Soul as I celebrate the return of Mother Nature's life around me.

My life is more full of celebration and special times of the year than it ever was before. All of our 'modern' holidays are in fact the remnants of ancient celebrations meant to show honor and gratitude to the Earth and to each other. As a woman of Celtic background, I discovered that not only were the four seasons celebrated, but they were divided further into a kind of sacred 'wheel' of the year. Beginning with the winter solstice (known as Yule in Europe), the Light returns, and around February 2 they believed spring truly began with the first stirrings of life before coming to full bloom on the spring equinox (Easter).

Many older readers might remember that May Day celebrations were once quite common. This is because May 1 was once seen to be the true start of summer and a time to celebrate the full culmination of life. To this day May 1 is a special day in Europe to buy flowers for the women in your life and it all hearkens back to the awareness that all life depends upon the Feminine for nurturing. May Day is a day to revel in physical love and show gratitude to the women who bore and raised you. For groups who still celebrate May Day, the tradition of a May pole remains a beautiful leftover from ancient Germanic and Scandinavian traditions. The dance of children weaving multi-color ribbons around the pole were meant to insure good health and vitality upon the new generation as they honored their Mother Earth.

The summer solstice was often a time for celebration, but also work as the lengthening Light allowed time to accomplish more in the fields, but it was also a time to acknowledge that from that moment onwards the Light would begin to dwindle. Most cultures have lost the significance of August 2, but in ancient Europe this time was known as Lughnassah (or Lammas) and was the first of the three great Harvest celebrations. It ushered in the very start of the seasons that would reap the rewards for all the hard work done in the spring and summer.

We all know the autumn equinox, and in the ancient world it was this date that was most like the American Thanksgiving. It was the mid-point of autumn for ancient Europeans and was the time to start winding down their activity. Celebrations were held with meat, drink, and bonfires as the nights turned colder. Feasting became more common at this time. As long as the harvest had been plentiful, ancient men and women had much to celebrate and might find they had enough excess to have parties and celebrations. Often if there had been a boom in livestock, this was the time to slaughter animals that were aging or that they would not be able to feed over the winter, resulting in more meat to be shared with the community.

This was their season of Gratitude. They were grateful to the earth which had provided, to the animals which were sacrificed so they might live, and with this atmosphere of reflection upon life and death, they began to remember the loved ones no longer with them...

I have to confess, when I was a Christian I never celebrated Halloween. While many Christians have no issues with this holiday, I fell into the more extreme category and believed that it was evil. It was a time when children were encouraged by Satan, and all those poor fools enjoying themselves had no idea they were playing into the hands of demons. It was, after all, a 'pagan' holiday. Well, at least the Church got that part right! Hopefully the reader will remember that the word 'pagan' does not deserve the fear and horrible energy it has been given. Pagan began as a French word that meant 'country dweller'. Technically anyone who still lives or works on a farm out in the country could still be called a pagan! Pagan simply became the title given to anything that existed before Christianity and did not come under the umbrella of the Bible (even Muslims and Buddhists were called pagans at one point or another by the church). When I came out of my religious conditioning and studied the holidays, I ended up embracing Halloween to the point that it is now almost equal to Christmas in my holiday esteem.

While it's true that Halloween has become very commercialized, the truth is that all holidays are. I respect people who want to be 'purists' and get rid of what they see to be too much commercial trappings, but I personally revel in it. Our economies are far too intimately woven into our modern holiday season and knowing that every bit I contribute to it only helps men and women have more opportunities to have jobs and take care of their own families is a win-win in my eyes. Does this mean everyone should go bankrupt celebrating? Of course not. As always, everyone must find their own balance and what they are comfortable with. When it comes to Halloween, I discovered that the name comes from 'All Hallow's Eve', with the word hallow meaning 'sacred'. What was so sacred about this day that is now known for cheap thrills and candy?

It seems no coincidence that the Latin-Indian cultures of Central America celebrate The Day of the Dead at the same time that the West celebrates Halloween. The Mexican Day of the Dead is a beautiful time that exemplifies the true meaning of this time of the year in the earth's cycle. The dead are not feared, but celebrated. All of the bright colors, costumes, candy, and feasts are geared towards a remembrance and reverence for loved ones who have passed away and the ancestors of our bloodline. It turns out that this same energy existed in Celtic Europe long before Christ. For the ancient Celts, the time was known as Samhain (pronounced Sow-een).

It was a three day period in which it was believed the veils between the world of the living and the world of the dead (spirits) became thinner and it was possible for our loved ones on the Other Side to communicate more clearly with us. Fear did not come into the picture until much later. Feasts were held to celebrate life, honor the dead, and even invite the ancestors to dine with them. Merriment, dance, bonfires, feasting, drinking, and song were all part of this holy time. For this reason my home is now 'Halloween house' for the entire neighborhood. I do not buy into the sad energy of horror and gore that so many have abused this sacred time with. Instead, my home is adorned with harvest lights and decorations meant to invite and delight both young and old. My door is open and in the true spirit there is warmth, feasting, and laughter for both the living and the spirit. I cannot tell you the joy my family now has on Halloween and how many lives have been changed as I educate about how this time of year is meant to bring us closer to our loved ones who have gone on their Journey to the Other Side.

Everything I have recounted here is easy to research and find. I encourage you that if you wish to come into a closer connection with your own Soul, connect to the spirituality that infuses our physical world. This is not about becoming a 'pagan' or any other kind of label that is put upon people who choose to express their soul outside of mainstream religion. If you choose to follow an alternative path, all I can say is that every Soul will find its Light wherever it needs to. As for community, the truth is that more people than ever around the world are declaring themselves 'spiritual' without religion. We are not as alone as we once thought we were. Thanks to the internet it is so much easier to find people and groups who share our spiritual openness and awareness regardless of where they come from or what they have been. Just as you open your Soul, open your mind and begin to ask questions and investigate. You will find more compatriots than you know.

As with anything, always remember that extremism and cult mentalities exist in all religions, faiths, and beliefs. The moment anyone of any belief begins to show signs of control, emotional blackmail, tries to break you away from friends and family, claims absolute truth, or any other issues that sends a red flag up in your mind is the time to say goodbye and seek a new path. I will say this always: You have the answers deep within you. If you can trust and believe in yourself, then you will know that the Soul and the Ego were meant to walk together as friends and allies. The Soul brings knowledge from what is beyond this world, but the Ego brings the knowledge of how it has survived in this world. Bring these two to balance and learn from them and therein lies your salvation.

I am here to spark the Light within you and I sincerely hope this book has helped that happen. After that, you must trust yourself, for you were given the gift and the answers are all within you. The world is awakening and it is discovering that the Soul was never meant to be enclosed in the small walls of religious belief. There is so much Light in this world. Connect to that which unites us as human beings, discover your own connection to our Mother Earth, and reclaim your connection to the wondrous Universe around you. Whether your journey has just begun or is already well underway, may you walk it in Light, Peace, and Love.

Acknowledgements

Saying 'thank you' to my husband and daughter will never be enough! Our daughter has been my rock and foundation. Through our journey she has stood by my side and reminded me of who I am. She held my hands and walked with me through the darkest periods of my life. She encouraged me to not give up and insisted I believe in my calling as a mystic. More than anyone else, she opened the door for me to not be afraid of my gifts, reminding me over and over again that the Other Side will always trust me to do the right thing and so I must trust in myself. A gifted writer in her own right, I know she will be given the same gift. You cannot sacrifice your time and give so much of yourself without the laws of reciprocity giving back tenfold. My husband calls us sisters and he's right. I have been given a daughter, a sister, and a friend.

To my husband who has been there for both of us, I say with the deepest gratitude and all my love: Thank you for your unwavering support. This book, this opportunity, and our lives, would never have been possible without you.

A deep thanks goes to the few women that I have been blessed to call friends. Throughout the years they have provided more encouragement than they know and in being entrusted with their thoughts, questions, and experiences, contributed to this work in ways they cannot imagine. To say I love each and every one of them goes without saying. In each of them I see the Light manifesting itself in this world for the better. They are gifts to this world.

To my sister by heart, Kathy, without whom the journey

of my daughter and I would have ended before it ever began…
you saved our lives and in doing so have impacted every
person whose life I have touched. Words will never be
enough. And for Anita, her cousin, who makes my heart sing
with her joy. I love my Kentucky ladies!

For Kathie R., who has known us the longest and shares
our passion for the written word. Beautiful and strong, you're
a force to be reckoned with and I am proud to be your friend,
my Viking sister. And for Nancy, her cousin. The two of you
are as radiant as Kansas sunflowers.

For Corrine W., who came into my life when I needed it
most and made a hard transition infinitely easier. I am so
grateful that it was you who welcomed me into my newly
discovered family. Thank you for being my Campbell sister.
You do the name proud. I will greatly enjoy watching your
own bright star rise.

For Diane E., who walks softly in this world and inspires
everyone with her compassion and understanding. She is truly
a sister that everyone would want to spend time with. And for
Anna, beautiful as her mother in body and soul, whose future
shines brightly. May you always walk in your own Light.

For Maureen B., my friend and the best professor I ever
had. Without you, we would have suffered far longer than
necessary on our academic paths. You bolstered my
confidence and changed our course for the better. Because of
you, my first response to everything is: "How do we know?"
I love you so much, my Irish sister!

For Vida S., her husband, and her boys. With your
friendship you opened a new door of understanding for me
and my daughter. You welcomed us into your home and
showed us the true beauty of the Iranian people.
You are a true Persian princess and our sister. I hope your
family will always be blessed with the same kindness and

generosity that you have shown. And for your mother, Fatima, for showing me the beauty of a Muslim woman who carries her faith in the true spirit of peace that the Prophet intended.

For Carol C., who knows the struggles of writing and the weight of counseling more than most. Thank you, my Scandinavian sister, for the laughs, your encouragement, and your honesty.

For Betsy O., who came to my door reaching out for my help, and instead helped me to see the true beauty that lies within all women. Unknowingly, you held a mirror that reminded me of my own artist's soul. May you always bring beauty into the world and walk confidently in your gifts, my Scottish sister.

For Sherry C., who witnessed the glory and the agony of this entire process from beginning to end, and her son Matthew, two of the best souls I know.

For Marilyn S., who inadvertently began to open my mind so many years ago by introducing me to the Quakers. Because of them I learned that it was possible to follow a Christian path that truly held no judgement and valued peace and openness above all.

For Linda R., thank you for opening up and letting me into your world. It reminded me how important the message I carry is and I'm grateful for the introduction to your amazing son who I know is with you always.

For Belinda M., a genuinely beautiful, petite little ball of fire. Thank you for sharing that wonderful smile!

For Connie G., thank you for opening your home to me and my husband, we hope to visit again soon.

For Sandy J., our meeting was brief, but I walked away knowing I'd met a true spiritual goddess.

For Juanita, Angie B., and her son Brady, thank you for your friendship and may you be blessed with success in all your endeavors.

Lastly but never least, for Beth N., Debbie, Pat F., Shannon, Sue, Eve, Melissa, Rhonda, Cindy, Kari, Kati S., Katie W., Sheila (our Iranian princess), Lori (our French princess), Linda B., Linda J., 'Queen' Elizabeth, and with great love to three generations of awesome women: Frances, Barbara, and Alex - thank you for allowing me to meet your Katie.

Finally, for our godfather, Hank A., for asking every single time he saw me without fail: "When am I going to be able to buy a book?"

Now, Hank. Now you can buy the book.

References and Recommended Resources

This book could never have been written without the tireless work and dedication of numerous academics, scholars, mystics, writers, and seekers of the Light. We are truly blessed to live at a time when knowledge is at our fingertips in the form of books, articles, videos, and internet resources! This list contains the resources that shaped my understanding of religion, history, and spirituality as portrayed in this book. I present it to you not just so you can check on my sources, but so that you may find the inspiration to read some of these invaluable works as well. The information is readily available for any who wish to find it.

All quoted Bible verses used from the King James Version and the New International Version can be looked up via the online database www.biblehub.com.
Hebrew and Greek word translations were taken from:
Strong, James. *The New Strong's Exhaustive Concordance of the Bible*. Thomas Nelson Publishers. Nashville, TN. 1995.

Chapter 3 The Forbidden Truth

Armstrong, Karen. *A History of God*. Gramercy Books. New York, New York. 1993.

A Historical Atlas of the Jewish People: From the Time of the Patriarchs to the Present. Gen. Ed. Eli Barnavi. Schocken Books. New York, New York. 1992

Tertullian. *De Cultu Feminarum (On Female Fashion, Book 1).*

Luther, Martin. *Works 12.94.*

Calvin, John. *Commentary on Genesis Volume 1.*

Chapter 5 Eve

Baring, Anne and Jules Cashford. *The Myth of the Goddess: Evolution of an Image.* Penguin Books. New York, NY. 1993

Greenberg, Gary. *101 Myths of the Bible: How Ancient Scribes Invented Biblical History.* Sourcebooks Inc. Naperville, IL. 2000.

Meyers, Carol. *Rediscovering Eve: Ancient Israelite Women in Context.* Oxford University Press. Oxford, UK. 2013.

Norris, Pamela. *Eve, A Biography.* New York University Press. New York, NY. 1998

Pagels, Elaine. *Adam, Eve, and the Serpent.* Vintage Books. New York, NY. 1988.

Pakkala, Juha. "The Monotheism of the Deuteronomistic History." *SJOT: Scandinavian Journal of the Old Testament* 21.2 (2007): 159-178.

"Queen Victoria". History Channel. Available here: www.history.co.uk/biographies/queen-victoria

Stewart, Anne W. "Eve and Her Interpreters." *Women's Bible Commentary, 20th Anniversary Edition.* Ed. Carol Newsom, Sharon Ringe, Jaqueline Lapsley. Westminster John Knox Press. Louisville, KY. 2012.

Tyldesley, Joyce. *Daughters of Isis: Women of Ancient Egypt.* Penguin Books. New York, NY. 1995

Chapter 6 The Serpent

Baring, Anne and Jules Cashford. *The Myth of the Goddess: Evolution of an Image.* Penguin Books. New York, NY. 1993

Bloom, Harold. *Jesus and Yahweh: The Names Divine.* Riverhead Books. New York, NY. 2005

Day, John. *Yahweh and the Gods and Goddesses of Canaan.* Sheffield Academic Press. London, UK. 2002.

Holland, Glenn S. "Mesopotamia: Inanna the Goddess" Religion in the Ancient Mediterranean World. The Teaching Company. DVD. 2005

Pagels, Elaine. *Adam, Eve, and the Serpent.* Vintage Books. New York, NY. 1988.

Stone, Merlin. *When God Was A Woman.* Harcourt Inc. New York, NY. 1976

Witt, R.E. *Isis in the Ancient World.* John Hopkins University Press. Baltimore, MD. 1971.

Wolkstein, Diane and Samuel N. Kramer. *Inanna, Queen of Heaven and Earth: Her Stories and Hymns From Sumer.* Harper and Row. New York, NY. 1983.

Chapter 7 Lilith

Banned From the Bible 2. Writ. Marcy Marzuki. Prod. Geofrey Madeja and Marcy Marzuki. DVD. History Channel. 2008.

Bloom, Harold. *Jesus and Yahweh: The Names Divine.* Riverhead Books. New York, NY. 2005

"Haggadah: Jewish Legend from Midrash, Pseudopigraphia and Early Kabbalah" *The Other Bible.* Ed. Willis Barnstone. Harper San Francisco. New York, NY. 2005.

Lesses, Rebecca. "Lilith" *Jewish Women: A Comprehensive Historical Encyclopedia.* 20 March 2009. Jewish Women's Archive. Available at: http://jwa.org/encyclopedia/article/lilith
        Sjoo, Monica and Barbara Mor. *The Great Cosmic Mother.* Harper San Francisco. New York, NY. 1991.

Chapter 8 Asherah

Bird, Phyllis. *Missing Persons and Mistaken Identities: Women and Gender in Ancient Israel.* Augsberg Fortress. Minneapolis, MN. 1997.
        Byrne, Ryan. "Lie Back and Think of Judah: The Reproductive Politics of Pillar Figurines." *Near Eastern Archaeology* 67.3 (2004): 137-151.
        Day, John. "Asherah in the Hebrew Bible and Northwest Semitic Literature." *Journal of Biblical Literature* 105.3 (1986): 385-408.
        Dever, William G. *Did God Have A Wife?: Archaeology and Folk Religion in Ancient Israel.* Wm. B. Eerdmans Publishing Co. Grand Rapids, MI. 2005.
        Patai, Raphael. *The Hebrew Goddess.* Wayne State University Press. Detroit, MI. 1990.
        Smith, Mark S. *The Early History of God: Yahweh and Other Deities in Ancient Israel.* Harper San Francisco. New York, NY. 1990.

Ibid. "God Male and Female in the Old Testament: Yahweh and His Asherah." *Theological Studies* 48.2 (1987): 333-340.
        Stone, Merlin. *When God Was A Woman.* Harcourt Inc. New York, NY. 1976.

Wiggins, Steve. "Of Asherahs and Trees: Some Methodological Questions." *Journal of Ancient Near Eastern Religions* 1.1 (2002): 158-187.

Chapter 9 Stolen Identity

Harrington, Hannah K. "Leviticus." *Women's Bible Commentary, 20th Anniversary Edition.* Ed. Carol Newsom, Sharon Ringe, Jaqueline Lapsley. Westminster John Knox Press. Louisville, KY. 2012.
Ilan, Tal. *Jewish Women in Greco-Roman Palestine.* Hendrickson Publishers. Peabody, MA. 1996.
Riddle, John M. *Eve's Herbs: A History of Contraception and Abortion in the West.* Harvard University Press. Cambridge, MA. 1997.
"Sex." The Bible Rules. Prod. Brian Meer and Mike Stiller. Left Right, LLC for H2 Network (A and E Networks). 23 March 2014.
"Sex and the Scriptures." Bible Secrets Revealed. Writ. Kevin Burns, Kaylan Eggert, and Savas Georgalis. Dir. Mari Johnson. Prometheus Entertainment for History Channel (A and E Networks). 23 January 2014.

Chapter 11 Leviticus and the Origins of Hate

The Dead Sea Scroll Bible. Martin Abegg Jr., Peter Flint, and Eugene Ulrich, gen. Ed. Harper San Francisco. New York, NY. 1999.
Kirsch, Jonathan. *The Harlot By the Side of the Road.* Ballantine Books. New York, NY. 1997.

Helminiak, Daniel A. *What the Bible Really Says About Homosexuality*. Alamo Square Press. Tajique, NM. 2000.

Horner, Tom. *Jonathan Loved David: Homosexuality in Biblical Times*. Westminster Press. Philadelphia, PA. 1978.

Rothbaum, Rabbi Michael. "The Problem of Homophobia in Leviticus." The Huffington Post. 10 July 2013. Available at: www.huffingtonpost.com/rabbi-michael-rothbaum/the-problem-of-homophobia-in-Leviticus_b_3563972.html

"Sex and the Scriptures." Bible Secrets Revealed. Writ. Kevin Burns, Kaylan Eggert, and Savas Georgalis. Dir. Mari Johnson. Prometheus Entertainment for History Channel (A and E Networks). 23 January 2014.

Chapter 12 A Sexually Diverse Ancient World

Rupp, Leila J. *Sapphistries: A Global History of Love Between Women*. New York University Press. New York, NY. 2011

Cohn-Sherbok, Dan. "Greece: Home of Hellenistic Civilization." *Atlas of the World's Religions, 2nd Ed.* Ed. Ninian Smart and Frederick Denny. Oxford University Press. Oxford, UK. 2007.

"Sex and the Scriptures." Bible Secrets Revealed. Writ. Kevin Burns, Kaylan Eggert, and Savas Georgalis. Dir. Mari Johnson. Prometheus Entertainment for History Channel (A and E Networks). 23 January 2014.

Sjoo, Monica and Barbara Mor. *The Great Cosmic Mother*. Harper San Francisco. New York, NY. 1991.

Chapter 13 Sodom and Gomorrah: Seeing What Isn't There

Bailey, D. Sherwin. *Homosexuality and the Western Tradition.* Longmans, Green and Co. London, UK. 1955.

Furnish, Victor Paul. "The Bible and Homosexuality: Reading the Texts in Context." *Homosexuality in the Church: Both Sides of the Debate.* Ed. J.S. Siker. Westminster John Knox Press. Louisville, KY. 1994

Helminiak, Daniel A. *What the Bible Really Says About Homosexuality.* Alamo Square Press. Tajique, NM. 2000.

"Sex and the Scriptures." Bible Secrets Revealed. Writ. Kevin Burns, Kaylan Eggert, and Savas Georgalis. Dir. Mari Johnson. Prometheus Entertainment for History Channel (A and E Networks). 23 January 2014.

Toensing, Holly Joan. "Women of Sodom and Gomorrah: Collateral Damage in the War Against Homosexuality?" *Journal of Feminist Studies in Religion* (Indiana University Press) 21.2 (2005): 61-74.

Chapter 14 Jesus' Silence Speaks the Truth

"Bet Hillel and Bet Shammai." The Jewish Encyclopedia Online. 2011. Available at: www.jewishencyclopedia.com/ articles/3190-bet-hillel-and-bet-shammai

Kolatch, Alfred J. *The Second Jewish Book of Why.* Jonathan David Publishers INC. Middle Village, NY. 1985.

Wein, Berel. "Hillel and Shammai." Jewish History.Org. Available at: www.jewishhistory.org/hillel-and-shammai

Chapter 15 Homosexuality and Paul

Boswell, John. *Christianity, Social Tolerance, and Homosexuality*. University of Chicago Press. Chicago, IL. 1980.

Brooten, Bernadette J. *Love Between Women: Early Christian Responses to Female Homoeroticism*. University of Chicago Press. Chicago, IL. 1998.

Countryman, L. William. *Dirt, Greed, and Sex: Sexual Ethics in the New Testament and their Implications for Today*. Fortress Press. Philadelphia, PA. 1988.

Ehrman, Bart D. *Forgery and Counterforgery: The Use of Literary Deceit in Early Christian Polemics*. Oxford University Press. Oxford, UK. 2013.

Helminiak, Daniel A. *What the Bible Really Says About Homosexuality*. Alamo Square Press. Tajique, NM. 2000.

Scroggs, Robin. *Homosexuality in the New Testament: Contextual Background for Contemporary Debate*. Fortress Press. Philadelphia, PA. 1983.

Chapter 17 From Old Misogyny to New

Ilan, Tal. *Jewish Women in Greco-Roman Palestine*. Hendrickson Publishers. Peabody, MA. 1996.

Lee, Eunny P. "Ruth." *Women's Bible Commentary, 20th Anniversary Edition*. Ed. Carol Newsom, Sharon Ringe, Jaqueline Lapsley. Westminster John Knox Press. Louisville, KY. 2012.

Lefkowitz, Mary R. and Maureen B. Fant. *Women's Life in Greece and Rome: A Source Book In Translation, 2nd ed*. John Hopkins University Press. Baltimore, MD. 1992.

Pomeroy, Sarah B. *Goddesses, Whores, Wives, and Slaves: Women in Classical Antiquity. Schocken Books. New York, NY. 1995.*

"Sex and the Scriptures." <u>Bible Secrets Revealed</u>. Writ. Kevin Burns, Kaylan Eggert, and Savas Georgalis. Dir. Mari Johnson. Prometheus Entertainment for History Channel (A and E Networks). 23 January 2014.

Chapter 18 A Christian Revolution?

Cohen, Shaye I.D. "Legitimization Under Constantine." <u>Frontline, PBS</u>. 1998. Available at: http://www.pbs.org/wgbh/pages/frontline/shows/religion/why/legitimization.html

Derrett, J. Duncan M. "The Buddhist Dimension of John." *Numen: International Review for the History of Religions* 51.2 (2004): 182-210.

Ehrman, Bart D. *Forged: Writing in the Name of God, Why the Bible's Authors Are Not Who We Think They Are.* Harper One. New York, NY. 2011.

Ibid. "Is Paul the Real Founder of Christianity?" *The Greatest Controversies of Early Christian History.* The Teaching Company. DVD. 2013

"Did the Disciples Write the Gospels?" Ibid.

Freeman, Charles. *A.D. 381: Heretics, Pagans, and the Dawn of the Monotheistic State.* Overlook Press. New York, NY. 2008.

Ibid. *The Closing of the Western Mind: The Rise of Faith and the Fall of Reason.* Vintage. New York, NY. 2005.

Harl, Kenneth W. "Religious Conflict in the Roman World" <u>The Fall of the Pagans and the Origins of Medieval Christianity</u>. The Teaching Company. DVD. 2011

"The Conversion of Constantine." Ibid.

Lemche, Niels Peter. "How Christianity Won the World." *Scandinavian Journal of the Old Testament* 23.1 (2009): 103-121.

"Lost In Translation." Bible Secrets Revealed. Writ. Kevin Burns. Dir. Mari Johnson. Prometheus Entertainment for History Channel (A and E Networks). 11 November 2013.

Morse, Donald R. "Mithraism and Christianity: How Are They Related?" *Journal of Religion and Psychical Research* 22.1 (1999): 33-43.

Nabarz, Payam. *The Mysteries of Mithras: The Pagan Belief that Shaped the Christian World.* Inner Traditions. Rochester, VT. 2005.

Pomeroy, Sarah B. *Goddesses, Whores, Wives, and Slaves: Women in Classical Antiquity.* Schocken Books. New York, NY. 1995.

Price, Robert M. *The Amazing Colossal Apostle: The Search for the Historical Paul.* Signature Books. Salt Lake City, UT. 2012.

Thomas, Yan. "The Division of the Sexes in Roman Law." *A History of Women in the West: From Ancient Goddesses to Christian Saints.* Gen. Ed. Geoges Duby and Michelle Perrot. Harvard University Press. Cambridge, MA. 2002.

Wills, Gary. *What Paul Meant.* Penguin Books. New York, NY. 2006.

Chapter 19 Eve and Mary: The Sinner and the Redeemed

Apuleius. *The Golden Ass or Metamorphoses.* Translated by E.J. Kenney. Penguin Classics. New York, New York. 1998.

Baring, Anne and Jules Cashford. *The Myth of the Goddess: Evolution of an Image.* Penguin Books. New York, NY. 1993

Beattie, Tina. "Mary, Eve, and the Church." *Maria: A Journal of Marian Studies* 1.2 (2001): 5-20.

Butler, Hazel. "The Cult of Isis and Early Christianity." *Hohonu: A Journal of Academic Writing* (University of Hawaii, Hilo) 5.1 (2007): 72-77. Available here: www.hilo.hawaii.edu/academics/hohonu/Volume_5.php

Ehrman, Bart D. "Was Jesus' Mother A Virgin?" The Greatest Controversies of Early Christian History. The Teaching Company. DVD. 2013.

Holland, Glenn S. "Rome: Saviors and Divine Men." Religion in the Ancient Mediterranean World. The Teaching Company. DVD. 2005.

Kraemer, Ross Shepard. *Her Share of the Blessings: Women's Religions Among Pagans, Jews, and Christians in the Greco-Roman World.* Oxford University Press. Oxford, UK. 1992.

Norris, Pamela. *Eve, A Biography.* New York University Press. New York, NY. 1998

"Sex and the Scriptures." Bible Secrets Revealed. Writ. Kevin Burns, Kaylan Eggert, and Savas Georgalis. Dir. Mari Johnson. Prometheus Entertainment for History Channel (A and E Networks). 23 January 2014.

Ward, Tim. *Savage Breast: One Man's Search for the Goddess.* O Books. Winchester, UK. 2006.

Warner, Marina. *Alone of All Her Sex: The Myth and the Cult of the Virgin Mary.* Vintage. New York, NY.1976.

Wolkstein, Diane and Samuel N. Kramer. *Inanna, Queen of Heaven and Earth: Her Stories and Hymns From Sumer.* Harper and Row. New York, NY. 1983.

Wood, Alice E. "Mary's Role as Co-Redemptrix in the Drama of the Trinity." *Maria: A Journal of Marian Studies* 2.2 (2002): 42-79.

Chapter 20 Magdalene: Saint or Harlot?

Deakin, Michael A. B. *Hypatia of Alexandria: Mathematician and Martyr.* Prometheus Books. New York, NY. 2007.

Ehrman, Bart D. *Forged: Writing in the Name of God, Why the Bible's Authors Are Not Who We Think They Are.* Harper One. New York, NY. 2011.

Ibid. *Lost Christianities: The Battle for Scripture and the Faiths We Never Knew.* Oxford University Press. Oxford, UK. 2003.

Ibid. "How Close Were Jesus and Mary Magdalene?" The Greatest Controversies of Early Christian History. The Teaching Company. DVD. 2013.

"Was Jesus Married?" Ibid.

Freke, Timothy and Peter Gandy. *The Jesus Mysteries: Was the Original Jesus a Pagan God?* Three Rivers Press. New York, NY. 1999.

"The Forbidden Scriptures." <u>Bible Secrets Revealed</u>. Writ. Kevin Burns and Kaylan Eggert. Dir. Mari Johnson. Prometheus Entertainment for History Channel (A and E Networks). 27 November 2013.

Harl, Kenneth W. "Platonism and Stoicism." <u>The Fall of the Pagans and the Origins of Medieval Christianity.</u> The Teaching Company. DVD. 2011.

Lash, John Lamb. *Not In His Image: Gnostic Vision, Sacred Ecology, and the Future of Belief.* Chelsea Green. White River Junction, VT. 2006.

Leloup, Jean-Yves. *The Gospel of Mary Magdalene*. Inner Traditions. Rochester, VT. 2002.

Moore, Edward. "Gnosticism." The Internet Encyclopedia of Philsophy (University of Tennessee). *The Nag Hammadi Scriptures: The International Edition*. Ed. Marvin Meyer. Harper One. New York, NY. 2008.

Pagels, Elaine. *The Gnostic Gospels*. Random House. New York, NY. 1979.

Picknett, Lynn. *Mary Magdalene: Christianity's Hidden Goddess*. Carroll and Graf Publishers. New York, NY. 2004.

Wilson, Brittany E. "Mary Magdalene and Her Interpreters." *Women's Bible Commentary, 20th Anniversary Edition*. Ed. Carol Newsom, Sharon Ringe, Jaqueline Lapsley. Westminster John Knox Press. Louisville, KY. 2012.

Chapter 21 Satan, the Devil, and God: A Human Trinity

Awwad, Johnny. "Satan in Biblical Imagination." *Theological Review* 26.2 (2005): 111-126.

Bernstein, Alan E. *The Formation of Hell: Death and Retribution in the Ancient and Early Christian Worlds*. UCL Press Limited. London, UK. 2003.

Boyce, Mary. Textual Sources for the Study of Zoroastrianism. University of Chicago Press. Chicago, IL. 1984.

Chosky, Jamsheed K. "Hagiography and Monotheism in History: Doctrinal Encounters Between Zoroastrianism, Judaism, and Christianity." *Islam and Christian-Muslim Relations* 14.4 (2003): 407-421.

Ehrman, Bart D. Misquoting Jesus: The Story Behind Who Changed the Bible and Why. Harper San Francisco. New York, NY. 2005

Ibid. "Is the Book of Revelation About Our Future?" The Greatest Controversies of Early Christian History. The Teaching Company. DVD. 2013.

Forsyth, Neil. *The Old Enemy: Satan and the Combat Myth*. Princeton University Press. Princeton, NJ. 1987.

Freeman, Charles. *The Closing of the Western Mind: The Rise of Faith and the Fall of Reason*. Vintage. New York, NY. 2005.

Harl, Kenneth W. "Turning Point: Theodosius I." The Fall of the Pagans and the Origins of Medieval Christianity. The Teaching Company. 2011

"Justinian and the Demise of Paganism."Ibid.

Holland, Glenn S. "The Jesus Movement in the Greco-Roman World." Religion in the Ancient Mediterranean World. The Teaching Company. DVD. 2005

"The Death and Rebirth of the Old Gods." Ibid.

Kyrtatas, Dimitris J. "The Origins of Christian Hell." *Numen: International Review for the History of Religions*. 56.2 (2009): 282-297.

Martin, Dale Basil. "When Did Angels Become Demons?" *Journal of Biblical Literature* 129.4 (2010): 657-677.

Maxwell, P.G. Maxwell. *Satan: A Biography*. Amberley Publishing. Gloucestshire, UK. 2009.

McCall, Andrew. *The Medieval Underworld*. Dorset Press. New York, NY. 1979.

O'Loughlin, Thomas. "Zoroastrianism and its Offshoots." *Atlas of the World's Religions, 2nd ed*. Ed. Ninian Smart and Frederick W. Denny. Oxford University Press. Oxford, UK. 2007.

Pagels, Elaine. *The Origin of Satan*. Vintage. New York, NY. 1995.

Ibid. *Revelations: Visions, Prophecy, and Politics in the*

Book of Revelations. Viking. New York. 2012.

Picknett, Lynn. The Secret History of Lucifer. Constable and Robinson. London, UK. 2005

Russell, Jeffrey Burton. *The Devil: Perceptions of Evil from Antiquity to Primitive Christianity*. Cornell University Press. Ithaca, NY. 1977.

Ibid. *Satan: The Early Christian Tradition*. Cornell University Press. Ithaca, NY. 1981.

"Statue of Liberty." Brad Meltzer's Decoded. Prod. Gary Aurback, Gail Berman, Lloyd Braun, Tina Gazzerro, and Brad Meltzer. Go Go Lucky Entertainment, INC and BermanBraun for History Channel (A and E Networks). 16 December 2010.

Stausberg, Michael. "Hell in Zoroastrian History." *Numen: International Review for the History of Religions* 56.2 (2009): 217-253.

Ibid. "On the State and Prospects of the Study of Zoroastrianism." *Numen: International Review for the History of Religions* 55.5 (2008): 561-600.

Stewart, Anne W. "Job's Wife and Her Interpreters." *Women's Bible Commentary, 20th Anniversary Edition*. Ed. Carol Newsom, Sharon Ringe, Jaqueline Lapsley. Westminster John Knox Press. Louisville, KY. 2012.

Tan, Carolyn Eng Looi. "Humanity's Devil." *Evangelical Review of Theology* 34.2 (2010): 136-154.

Wernick, Robert. "Who the Devil is the Devil?" *Smithsonian Magazine* 30.7 (1999): 112-119.

Chapter 22 Walking in the Light

Hampson, Rick. "Pope Francis Agitates Conservative U.S. Catholics." USA Today. 2 November 2014. Available at: www.usatoday.com/story/news/nation/2014/11/01/pope-francis-catholics-americans-culture/18263293/

About the Author

C.C. Campbell has committed decades of personal research into religiously relevant topics such as history, politics, and gender studies. She has always shared her message of light and knowledge with anyone brought into her path, and now does so worldwide via the podcast *What Lies Beyond,* a show dedicated to helping humanity explore the realms of spirituality, religion, science, and the paranormal.

When not writing, lecturing, or recording, Campbell enjoys spending time with her family in the beautiful wilds of Colorado, the Pacific Northwest, and the highlands and islands of Scotland.

You can hear her at www.cwhatliesbeyond.com and learn more about her at her author's site www.cccampbell.org

Notes

Made in the USA
Charleston, SC
18 April 2016